# Catholic Borderlands

# Catholic Borderlands

## Mapping Catholicism onto
## American Empire, 1905–1935

ANNE M. MARTÍNEZ

University of Nebraska Press
Lincoln & London

© 2014 by the Board of Regents of the University of Nebraska

Publication of this volume was assisted by a grant from the Office of the Vice President for Research at the University of Texas at Austin.

The illustrations in this volume are courtesy of Loyola University Chicago Archives and Special Collections.

Library of Congress Cataloging-in-Publication Data
Martínez, Anne M., 1966–
Catholic borderlands: mapping Catholicism onto American empire, 1905–1935 / Anne M. Martínez.
pages   cm
Includes bibliographical references and index.
ISBN 978-0-8032-4877-9 (cloth: alk. paper)
ISBN 978-0-8032-7409-9 (epub)
ISBN 978-0-8032-7410-5 (mobi)
ISBN 978-0-8032-7408-2 (pdf)
1. Catholic Church Extension Society of the United States of America—History. 2. Catholic Church—United States—History—20th century. 3. Catholic Church—Missions—United States. 4. Kelley, Francis Clement, 1870–1948. 5. Catholic Church—Mexico. I. Title.
BV2190.M37 2014
282'.709041—dc23
2014019188

Set in Adobe Garamond Pro by L. Auten.

For my first teachers,
Mom and Pop,
and my favorite students,
Hadley, James, John, Marianna, Christina, and Michael

# Contents

# Illustrations

# Preface

As a senior in high school I visited the University of Michigan, where I had been admitted and where my brother, David, was a graduate student in the School of Music. While David was busy one morning, I had a lengthy conversation with Zaragosa Vargas, who was finishing his PhD in American culture at Michigan. I still remember Zaragosa saying to me, "You can do for Chicago what I'm doing for Detroit." At the time, I had absolutely no idea what he meant and was too polite (or too dense) to ask him to clarify.

A year later, after an inauspicious start as an astronomy major at Michigan, I registered for a class in Chicano history, taught by John R. Chávez. In that course I learned that my family's arrival in Chicago in the 1910s was part of a much broader story of migration north after the Mexican Revolution; that their "return" to Mexico in 1930 was part of a mass repatriation of Mexicans; and that their subsequent "return" to Chicago in 1944 was driven by shifts in the economy during World War II. I came to understand what Zaragosa had said to me a year earlier, and with him as my first mentor I began my journey to unwrap this era in Mexican American history. I invested years of blood, sweat, and tears into the establishment of the Latino studies program at Michigan and learned from the experiences and guidance of Zaragosa, John, Frances Aparicio, Hector Delgado, Neil F. Foley, Margarita de la Vega Hurtado, Raúl Villa, and Enid Zimmerman.

After doing a few other things, I started graduate school intending to write a social history of Mexican Chicago in the 1910s and 1920s. I recalled vivid stories my great-uncle Librado Rivera told, often in

Spanish, later repeated to us in English. Librado was born in 1903 and left for the United States thirteen years later. He was old enough to remember the Revolution, as well as the journey north, which his sister, Ramona—my beloved Abuela—four years younger, did not recall in great detail. I was fascinated by the strength and determination of this generation and wanted to tell their story.

My first research trip to Chicago after I started graduate school included a visit to Louise Año Nuevo Kerr, whose well-worn (and autographed!) dissertation on Mexican Chicago still sits on my bookshelf. Louise suggested I start at the diocesan archives, since she had not been able to access church records for her study. Days later, at the Archdiocese of Chicago's Joseph Cardinal Bernardin Archives and Records Center, I perused the reading room bookshelves while waiting for my requested documents to be delivered. The provocatively title *Blood-Drenched Altars* demanded to be pulled from the shelf. In those few minutes flipping through the pages, as I awaited parish annual reports, Francis Clement Kelley captured my imagination and never let go.

My fascination with *Blood-Drenched Altars* intersected with my earlier interests to produce *Catholic Borderlands*, which provides an even broader context for my family history. This is an institutional, intellectual, cultural, and diplomatic history of U.S. Catholic interest and involvement in Mexico, led in this era by Francis Kelley.

My immersion in this project has led me to place Catholicism at the center of my scholarly work, a development I had not anticipated, but it seems more than overdue in Mexican American studies. I look forward to returning to a social and cultural history of Mexicans in Catholic Chicago in my future work.

# Acknowledgments

This book began as a doctoral dissertation in American studies at the University of Minnesota under the guidance of Catherine Ceniza Choy, David W. Noble, Jean O'Brien, Dave Roediger, and Zaragosa Vargas. My dissertation research and writing were funded by the Louisville Institute, the Erasmus Institute at the University of Notre Dame, and the Department of American Studies, the Graduate School, and the Race, Ethnicity, and Migration Seminar at the University of Minnesota. I am grateful for research support from the Center for the Study of Race, Politics and Culture at the University of Chicago, Latina/Latino Studies and the Department of History at the University of Illinois, Urbana-Champaign, and the College of Liberal Arts, the Department of History, the Institute for Historical Studies, the Center for Mexican American Studies, the C. B. Smith, Sr. Centennial Chair in U.S.-Mexico Relations, and the Walter Prescott Webb Chair in American History at the University of Texas at Austin.

I received guidance and support from countless mentors and friends at my fellowship and other stopovers before landing at the University of Texas at Austin. At the University of Michigan, Frances Aparicio, John R. Chávez, Mark Chesler, Neil F. Foley, Peggie Hollingsworth, Conrad Kottak, Charles D. Moody, Sr., Maxwell Owusu, Raúl Villa, and Zaragosa Vargas inspired my path into the academy, for which I long ago forgave them. In my work life before graduate school, Carol J. Guardo provided valuable direction, and she continues to be my sounding board for all things professional. I received immeasurable support from Nancy "Rusty" Barceló, Edén

Torres, and Dionicio Nodín Valdés while in the Twin Cities. At the University of Notre Dame, Kathleen Sprows Cummings, Suellen Hoy, Paul Kollman, Timothy Matovina, John McGreevy, and Jerry Poyo made me feel welcome in a foreign land. In my short stay at the University of Illinois, Urbana-Champaign, Jenny Barrett, Jim Barrett, Antoinette Burton, Barrington Edwards, Eileen Diaz McConnell, Kristin Hoganson, Alejandro Lugo, Martina Miranda-Lugo, Isabel Molina Guzman, Kathy Oberdeck, Cynthia Radding, and my Latina/o students provided great support and good cheer. I was fortunate to be a postdoctoral fellow at the Center for the Study of Race, Politics, and Culture at the University of Chicago. I cannot thank Cathy Cohen enough for the opportunity and for mentoring me during my time there. I am grateful to have spent time with Emilio Kourí, Mae Ngai, and long-lost fellow traveler Tracye Matthews while there.

My work on this project was interrupted by five years of health crises. My team at Sports Performance International (SPI), especially Ariel Quintana, got me through months of rehab following a broken ankle. Dr. Lynne Knowles and company at Texas Oncology saw me through two major abdominal surgeries in eighteen months as well as the unfathomable complications that accompany such bodily trauma. Dr. Sherry Neyman, Dr. Robert Northway, Dr. Angela Shih, Dr. Ted Spears, and Ariel Quintana reassembled me in the aftermath of the surgeries and the many challenges they presented. I am especially grateful to Dr. Spears and Ariel for—three years after the first surgery—finding the source of the pain and figuring out how to make it go away without prescribing more narcotics; and to Dr. Northway for providing the stunning visual evidence of the unidentified anomalies in my body, which I found incredibly convincing and oddly comforting. My glimpses of life with limited mobility, cancer, and chronic pain scarred my outlook for some time. As it turns out, it takes the body, the mind, the heart, the soul, the bank account, and the career a long time to recover from being gutted like a fish (twice). I continue to be in awe of fellow survivors Phil Cole, Phil Giles, Michelle Klarich, the irrepressible Elisa Linda

Facio, and the late Sheila Becker Gailius; they have shown me fine examples for living with grace in the face of cancer. I only wish I had been remotely graceful in my own journey.

I am profoundly grateful to an assortment of caretakers who looked after me in the many months when I was unable to care for myself. Elsa Barboza, Matt Basso, Erika Bsumek, Jorge Cañizares Esguerra, Carolyn Eastman, Gaye Theresa Johnson, Brian Klopotek, Teresa Martínez, Angela M. Smith, and my parents all did the kind of labor you would only do for someone you love. I am so fortunate to have them in my life. There is undoubtedly a special place in heaven for those who took care of Coco, my special needs dog, when I was incapacitated, especially Kristin Cheasty Miller, Penne Restad, and Brenda Sendejo.

So many of my colleagues at the University of Texas supported me with an array of kind words and deeds, including Kimberly Alidio, Susan Boettcher, Judy Coffin, David Crew, Yoav Di-Capua, Richard Flores, Neil Foley, the ever-startled George Forgie, Frank Guridy, Heather Hindman, Tony Hopkins, Madeline Hsu, Jackie Jones, David Leal, Marilyn Lehman, Brian Levack, Tatjana Lichtenstein, José Limón, John Mckiernan González, Tracie Matysik, Leonard Moore, Stephennie Mulder, Joan Neuberger, Rob Oppenheim, Deborah Paredez, Domino Pérez, Maggie Rivas Rodríguez, Jim Sidbury, Michael Stoff, Martin Summers, Tom Tweed, Ann Twinam, Angela Valenzuela, Andy Villalon, and Charters Wynn. Virginia Garrard Burnett, Michal Glaser, and Mighty Howard Miller shaped my world in indescribable ways about which I am contractually obligated never to speak. Dorothea Adams, Laura Flack, Richard Flores, and Dona Kurtz negotiated bureaucracies for me and treated me as a valued member of the university community. I am also indebted to a number of graduate students. Brenda Beza, Leah Deane, Cheasty Miller, Cristina Salinas, Heather Teague, Therese Tran, Mandy Young-Kutz, and especially Amanda E. Gray, did all manner of tasks for me with good cheer, great loyalty, and absolute professionalism.

My heartfelt thanks to my dear, dear friends who have weathered this turbulence with me, especially Bernadette Anderson Martin, Frances Aparicio, Elsa Barboza, Nancy "Rusty" Barceló, Matt Basso, John Beilein, Tom Benoît, David Blevins, Stephanie Blevins, Bryan Bradbury, Rachel Anne Bradbury, the perpetually levitating Norma Elia Cantú, Antonia Castañeda, Jason Chang, Cathy Choy, Martha Cotera, Theresa Delgadillo, Eileen Diaz McConnell, Jill Doerfler, Kirsten Elliott, Chris Ernst, Elisa Facio, Lilia Fernández, Rubén Flores, Matt García, Kirsten Gardner, Adrian Sparty Gaskins, Kathryn Gilje, Rhonda Gonzales, Anita Gonzalez, Kate Griffin, Carol Guardo, Matthew Guterl, Dan Hannon, Kim Heikkila, Tim Hershner, Jennifer Hill Hershner, Brady Hoke, Suellen Hoy, Aida Hurtado, Gaye Johnson, Brian Klopotek, Zaneta Kosiba-Vargas, Scott Laderman, Sandi Latcha, Amy Lonetree, Kyle Longley, Alejandro Lugo, Tracye Matthews, Michigan-hater John Martin, Malachy McCarthy, Martina Miranda-Lugo, Isabel Molina Guzman, Elvia Niebla, David Noble, Gail Koch Noble, Karleen Pendleton-Jiménez, Steve Rosswurm, Jason Ruiz, the spectacular Vicki Ruiz, Felicity Amaya Schaeffer, Brenda Sendejo, the late Jimmy Shendo, Ellen Skerrett, Angela Smith, Heidi Stark, Jill Torres, Zaragosa Vargas, Matt Wood, and Diane Ybarra Pok. In times when hope was fleeting and the future seemed out of reach, I found out who my friends really were. I continue to be awed by how many of you there are. Thank you, again, for every hug, phone call, note, flower, and meal delivered to my door in those long, dark days of the winter of my soul. It still means the world to me, and this book could not have happened without your support.

My time at the University of Texas has been enriched by my affiliation with the Center for Mexican American Studies (CMAS). José Limón cheered me on from the moment we met. I thank Jason Casellas, Cary Córdova, Pat García, John Morán Gonzáles, Gloria González López, David Leal, John Mckiernan González, Martha Menchaca, Deborah Paredez, Domino Pérez, Maggie Rivas Rodríguez, Luis Urrieta, Angela Valenzuela, and my CMAS students for their solidarity and ongoing support.

Erika Bsumek, Ginny Burnett, Jorge Cañizares Esguerra, Rubén

Flores, Felipe Hinojosa, Gaye Johnson, Julio Moreno, Felicity Schaeffer, and Jim Sidbury read the entire manuscript at various times and provided vital feedback and inspiration. Hannah Ballard, Justin Doran, Lizeth Elizondo, Greg Gonzales, Adrian Masters, Albert Palacios, and Darcy Rendón, students in my "Religion in the Borderlands" graduate seminar, shared in a productive discussion of the manuscript. I appreciate their enthusiasm for the project. Amy Lonetree, Joan Neuberger, Felicity Schaeffer, Jim Sidbury, and Tom Tweed read portions of the manuscript near the end and thoughtfully guided my revisions.

Ater the trauma, the drama, and the Vicodin, once I really had my legs under me, I fell in love with this project all over again. This amazing gift, along with some profoundly generous souls, sustained me in the final months. I am so grateful to my guardian angels: Erika Bsumek was the consummate senior colleague. I have no words to describe her kindness and loyalty. Jorge Cañizares Esguerra went to the ends of the earth on my behalf—ironically fitting given that I was once an astronomy major and he is a historian of science. David Leal dispensed appropriate measures of exasperation, calm, and levity to keep the chaos at bay. Tom Tweed was my trusted guide, constant supporter, and ardent cheerleader in uncertain times. Hell's angel, Jim Sidbury, brightened many a dark day with his relentless effervescence. He demonstrated his limitless devotion to our friendship with his willingness to say novenas as needed—and were they needed! I am indebted to each of these kindred spirits for their investment in me, and in this book. I would be remiss if I did not also thank Pieter Kroon and Troy Winward at SPI for getting me to the finish line.

Matthew Bokovoy, senior acquisitions editor for University of Nebraska Press, embraced the manuscript from the start. As a borderlands historian, he offered insightful queries and suggestions that strengthened the project greatly. He always had an encouraging word and a helpful source to recommend. The anonymous reviewers likewise understood the value of this book and were exceedingly generous in offering their expertise to improve the manuscript.

I have benefited from the guidance and support of numerous archivists and librarians, including Adán Benavides, Susan Brosnan, the late Michael Grace, Margo Gutiérrez, Malachy McCarthy, Lorraine Olley, Julie Satzik, Mark Schrauth, and Kathy Young. My thanks to Archbishop Emeritus Eusebius Beltran and the late Rev. John Steichen for allowing me to commune with the ghost of Francis Kelley at the Pastoral Center in Oklahoma City. I feel a special kinship with Anna Kielian and the seminarians of the Feehan Memorial Library at Mundelein Seminary, who made me feel welcome in my home away from home for a number of years.

I cannot thank my family enough for always supporting me, even when they had no idea what I was doing, or were not allowed to ask. My parents instilled in me the idea that education is transformative, which has shaped my life. Concepción Martínez kept Abuela and Uncle Librado alive through their stories, which ignited my desire to study this moment in Mexican and U.S. histories. My family in Mexico hosted many visits and looked after my every need while I trolled the archives: Curt Hartleben opened his home to me, Mina and Claus Hartleben treated me like their own daughter, and Francisco Martínez made sure I was always appropriately looked after and inappropriately entertained. Bryan Bradbury, Tim Hershner, Andy Martínez, David Martínez, Mike Martínez, and Teresa Martínez have treated me as their favorite sister, for which I am eternally grateful. Mike, Christina, Mari, John, James, and Hadley have reminded me, so often, of the world beyond this book, and have made me proud over and over again. May this book remind them of the importance of doing something you love in life.

# Introduction

## *Excavating the Borderlands*

In 1922, Rev. Francis Clement Kelley wrote *The Story of Extension*, detailing the history of the Catholic Church Extension Society of the United States of America, which he founded in 1905 and had led since. Kelley spent two chapters recounting what he called "the most interesting event in the Society's life": the Extension Society's involvement in "the Mexican situation." Starting in 1913, Mexican Catholic leaders fled the anticlerical waves of the Mexican Revolution to wait out the violence and upheaval of civil war in the United States. In 1914, four exiled Mexican archbishops made their way north to seek the support of Archbishop James Quigley of Chicago, and ultimately they befriended Kelley. "How they loved Mexico!" Kelley wrote. "At first I used to hope that the United States would intervene and take over the unhappy country to save her from herself," he noted, echoing calls of business and banking leaders. But, he continued, the religious migrants "took pains to try to correct my erroneous views." Still, Kelley admitted, he remained "but half-converted." Indeed, by 1922 Kelley had spent the better part of a decade working to get the U.S. government to intervene in large and small ways in Mexico. His relationship with the exiled archbishops was so close that they adopted him as one of their own. "I am now an Honorary Canon of three of their Cathedrals," Kelley wrote. He was sure, however, that "nine-tenths of the pleasure in the appointments went to the givers of the honors." He concluded, "I am half a Mexican now and proud of it." Canadian by birth, Kelley did not quite become Mexican, but his commitment to Mexico created what I call a Catholic borderlands, a trans-imperial, transhistorical space built on the Spanish Catholic past but enhanced by a U.S. Catholic presence in the early twentieth century. *Catholic Borderlands* draws on Mexico's historic Catholicity, the shifting place of U.S. Catholics in the United States, and the expanding role of the United States on the global stage to reveal a Catholic project committed to countering U.S. Protestant activity within the American empire, and building a U.S. Catholic ethos in the process.[1]

This book illustrates the ways U.S. Catholics participated in American expansion across the continent and around the world in the early twentieth century. Kelley was not alone in extending American empire to Mexico. U.S. government officials, often at the behest of U.S. Catholics, intervened in Mexican affairs during and after the Mexican Revolution. Kelley's work as president of the Extension Society and as representative of the Mexican Catholic hierarchy in the United States crossed many geographic, political, racial, and social boundaries. In the first volumes of *Extension Magazine*, Kelley began constructing a narrative that drew on the Spanish history of the southern and western United States. This discourse reminded the magazine's readers that Catholics were not the recent immigrants they were cast as in the East. Rather, they had inherited this continent from their Spanish Catholic forefathers who had established colonial missions dotting the West and South before Anglo-American Protestants landed at Plymouth Rock. The home missioner, I suggest, framed the ragged edges of the nation for audiences east of the Mississippi River, especially in urban areas, in the early twentieth century. This identification with the American national landscape was not just a message of uplift for a developing American Catholic identity. It was a call to action: U.S. Catholics had a responsibility to sustain the faithful in these historically Catholic lands within the expanding sphere of U.S. influence. U.S. Catholics created a space for themselves in the American empire and participated in that empire in order to sustain a long-standing trans-imperial Catholicism in the borderlands of empire. Catholic borderlands disrupted the

White Anglo-Saxon Protestant narratives of a progressive, Protestant future by creating a space within the empire for an American Catholic future—one that was built on the Spanish Catholic past yet American to its core.

The Spanish borderlands of the eighteenth and nineteenth centuries and the U.S.-Mexico borderlands of the twentieth century share not only a largely common geographic space but also a similar role within the Spanish and U.S. empires: they were the ragged edges of the imperial landscape, where historical and contemporary circumstances created phenomena that were often unfamiliar to those in the hearts of the empires. In these spaces, at the intersection of the Iberian Century and the American Century, Catholicism played an important role that has been largely overlooked by historians of the twentieth-century United States. Yet the forces that played out in these borderlands captured the tensions and contradictions that drove competition between the Spanish and British empires in the sixteenth through eighteenth centuries, the Spanish and U.S. empires in the nineteenth century, and, ultimately, Mexico and the United States in the early twentieth century. This book embraces the entangled histories of the Spanish empire and the burgeoning U.S. empire, viewed through a Catholic lens, to link the Spanish borderlands to the U.S.-Mexico borderlands in the transimperial Catholic borderlands. I define "Catholic borderlands" as former Spanish territories that had to find their respective places within a growing U.S. sphere of political, economic, and cultural influence in the first three decades of the twentieth century. American Catholics had a special, prior claim on these territories, and that claim justified their aggressive stand against Protestant poachers in the form of proselytizers, public school teachers, and government agencies. Mexico did not become a political province of the United States, but Kelley treated it as something of a cultural province, one that could and should be shaped by its more "advanced" and "civilized" northern neighbor. In this regard, Kelley was in league with a group of U.S. politicians, oilmen, and financiers who also saw Mexico as open for both business and influence.

## Writing a Borderlands History

*Catholic Borderlands* exists at the geographic and temporal interstices of Herbert Eugene Bolton's Greater America and Américo Paredes's Greater Mexico. "Modern historiography is inextricably linked with the modern nation," Thomas Bender writes, "silencing stories both smaller and larger than the nation."[2] *Catholic Borderlands* considers Catholic history as both a smaller U.S. history and one that is larger than the nation. Twentieth century U.S. Catholicism must be understood in all its layered complexity. Catholicism was rooted in the Vatican, but when Spain dominated Europe and the New World, the Spanish empire had its own powerful version of the faith that landed on these shores. Subsequent European migration to New England and eventually the United States brought other models of the universal church to the Western Hemisphere, along with the Catholicism crossing north from Mexico in the bodies of migrants in the nineteenth and twentieth centuries. Most importantly for the purposes of this project are the Catholic currents moving *from* the predominantly Protestant United States *to* Catholic Mexico, the Philippine Islands, and Puerto Rico, as parts of the broadly conceived American empire, in the actions of U.S. government and religious bodies, in the early twentieth century.

*Catholic Borderlands* seeks to understand related discourses that transcended the border, and even expanded beyond the North American continent, in the spirit of Bolton's Greater America. Bolton suggested that the nations of the Western Hemisphere had more in common with each other than with the rest of the world. Each "local story will have clearer meaning when studied in the light of the others; . . . much of what has been written of each national history is but a thread of a larger strand."[3] Mexican and U.S. national narratives are in fact intertwined through much of the twentieth century; if nothing else, each country defined itself in contrast to the other. I resist a comparative approach, however, that might inadvertently reinforce the boundedness of Mexico and the United States. I strive to accomplish what Bolton suggests by inserting religion into tried-and-true narratives of the Mexican Revolution, U.S.-Mexican relations, and U.S. empire-building in the rising American Century. This is a U.S. history, but one that does not stop at the nation's edges—it also considers the ways Mexico shaped the United States. *Catholic Borderlands* considers how Mexico's religious crisis shaped interactions not only between the United States and Mexico but also within the United States, "to shed light on neglected aspects of American history," as advocated by a growing group of historians in the twenty-first century.[4]

New possibilities emerge when we conceive of empire and Catholicism in Greater America rather than just the United States. New epistemologies are revealed when we are not limited by the nationalist discourses, canons, or historiographies of the United States or Mexico. *Catholic Borderlands* seeks "to break the hold the nation has on the historiographical imagination," offering a perspective on American empire that has been ignored: how Catholics participated in the U.S. expansionist narrative. Bringing Catholicism to bear on U.S. empire and nationalism sharpens our understanding of the complex forces at work in the urban Northeast and Midwest and can reveal how these regions related to the South, the West, and U.S. territories further afield.[5]

It is not enough to expand beyond the United States to tell this story. Greater Mexico provides a second lens through which to understand the enmeshed United States and Mexico. Paredes defined "Greater Mexico" as "the areas inhabited by people of Mexican culture—not only within the present limits of the Republic of Mexico but in the United States as well—in a cultural rather than a political sense." It is in that cultural sense that Kelley embraced Greater Mexico, as a Catholic body that transcended political boundaries, and drew on the deep Catholic cultural roots of the continent.[6]

As an early and prolific border scholar, Paredes had an immeasurable influence on subsequent novelists, historians, literary critics, and folklorists. His writing defied the U.S.-Mexico border as early as the 1940s—long before it became popular to do so in academic discourses. Likely first used by Bolton, but surely popularized by Gloria Anzaldúa's 1987 book, *Borderlands/La Frontera: The New Mestiza*, the "borderlands" discourse expanded significantly beyond the U.S.-Mexico border to consider endless identities and spaces that were neither/nor or both. Much of this scholarship is too focused on cultural mixing at the expense of power relations. The best work in this area reinserts power and difference into the equation. Alejandro Lugo, for example, theorizes border inspection to reinvoke power in the "exchanges" that happen to border crossers. "Inspection stations," he suggests, "inspect, monitor, and survey what goes in and out in the name of class, race and nation." These inspections are not just about citizenship; they are also about ethnicity, gender, skin tone, and class.[7] In the early twentieth century, religion was also part of the border inspection ritual. The severity of border inspections varied according to who was crossing, where, when, and in which direction. Likewise, the density of the border changed with time, place, subject, directional movement, language, and religion.

Catholics crossing the border were inspected severely at times. Mexican clergy were forced out of Mexico as religious repression raged from 1913 to 1917. When they attempted to return to Mexico in those tense years, they faced stringent border inspections. If they were able to return, it was often by sneaking back under cover of darkness or in disguise. Mexican migrants heading north faced Protestant missionary societies in U.S. border towns and cities trying to "pervert" Catholics away from the Mother Church.[8] During the Cristero Rebellion (1926–29), Mexicans crossed the border to attend mass in El Paso when Catholic services were not allowed in Mexico. Mexican officials warned them to avoid anti-government priests in exile. In contrast, Protestant missionaries freely passed border inspections heading south, where they were welcomed by anticlerical administrations seeking to prove they embraced religious liberty. Catholicism proved difficult to contain for both nations, but inspections of Catholics occurred in their many crossings of the border.

*Catholic Borderlands* works to free our understanding of the border from the either/or strictures that have largely contained it, to consider the ways both nations and peoples negotiated empire and religion, in particular, and to recognize that empire, religion, and nation were constantly changing categories. Francis Kelley skillfully wove together the Spanish Catholic past and the U.S. Catholic present to create this space in which Catholic mission work brought together the best of both of these worlds. Kelley was far from the highest-ranking cleric in the United States, but through *Extension Magazine* and the rising Archdiocese of Chicago he gained a prominent voice, especially with regard to Mexico. At his insistence, U.S. government officials and other American Catholic leadership and laypeople joined him in interventions in Mexico.[9]

*Catholic Borderlands* addresses the cultures of global empire, looking at the commitments of U.S. Catholics abroad as well as their shifting role at home, in recognition that political, geographic, and metaphorical borders are constantly in flux. Religion, especially Catholicism, is rarely central to historical or American studies scholarship of the early twentieth century, particularly in U.S. relations with other nations. *Catholic Borderlands* pushes the geographic limitations of the borderlands as they have been widely used: the Louisiana Purchase, the Mexican War, and the annexation of territories after the Spanish-American War show that expansion-minded U.S. officials were committed to collecting former Spanish territories. Hence, the give-and-take between British and Spanish ideas, cultures, languages, and religions framed the acquisition and subsequent domination of these territories. Recognizing these earlier land acquisitions as evidence of a U.S. empire broadens our understanding of the borderlands and the long-standing Catholic presence in North America. Although not all of Mexico was acquired in 1848 or post-Revolution, as some Americans had hoped, Mexico was increasingly at the mercy of its powerful neighbor economically, politically, and, as this book shows, religiously, in this era.[10]

The U.S. presence in Latin America in the early twentieth century was formidable but hardly predictable. It is not enough to identify the Colossus of the North as the force intervening, at will, in twentieth-century Latin America, empowered by the Monroe Doctrine (1823) and the Roosevelt Corollary (1904). *Catholic Borderlands* takes a more nuanced approach to understanding the U.S. presence in Mexico and considers the ways U.S. society was influenced by these interactions. The United States used the liberal commitment to religious liberty to intervene—formally and informally—in Mexico, thus securing U.S. economic interests there but not necessarily U.S. Catholic religious interests. The latter were not always aligned with the desires of U.S. government officials.

My interest in Greater America and Greater Mexico is complicated by my desire to splice the story of interaction between the United States and Mexico within the larger Spanish and Roman Catholic empires. The discourse of Catholic borderlands provides an intellectual framework for understanding a U.S. Catholic approach to Mexicans and Mexico. It is not a recuperative space; nor is it a redemptive space for Mexicans or Mexican Americans. Rather, it is the way Francis Kelley viewed American Catholicism: as a component of American empire, but one designed to undermine the Protestantization of the United States and its formal and informal territories.

### Religion, Temporality, and Empire

*Catholic Borderlands* reinserts Spain's presence in both the United States and Mexico, through the Catholic Church. The American understanding of the Spanish past is shaped by ideas of colonial Spain in the U.S. historical imagination. Richard Kagan coined the term "Prescott's paradigm" to describe "the juxtaposition of Spanish decadence and American progress," ideas that dominated U.S. studies of Spain throughout the nineteenth century and into the twentieth. William Hickling Prescott (1796–1859) and his contemporaries advocated the Black Legend, based on details described by Bartlomé de las Casas in his 1552 *Brevísima relación de la destrucción de las Indias* and widely promoted by Dutch and English Protestant writers from the sixteenth century onward. The Black Legend cast the Spanish as exceptionally cruel and intolerant in their interactions with indigenous peoples in the New World. Spain was characterized as outside of the European Protestant mainstream in both its interactions within Europe and in the Americas. In 1898 Spain was cast as the antithesis to the United States: where the United States stood for progress, prosperity, and liberty, Spain was characterized by absolutism, clericalism and bigotry. Kagan notes, "America was the future—republican, enterprising, rational; while Spain—monarchical, indolent, fanatic—represented the past." Mexico, the most glorious of Spain's offspring, inherited the "grave Spanish temperament and the strictures of the Catholic Church" in the nationalist historiography.[11] Spain, and therefore Mexico, was inherently antimodern. Prescott's paradigm haunted U.S. interaction with Mexico during their mid-nineteenth-century war and was certainly reinforced by the Spanish-American War in 1898. Despite efforts like Bolton's to paint a White Legend of Spanish friars on the frontier civilizing Mexicans and Indians, rather than exterminating them, the historiographical habit of seeing Spain—and the fruit of its conquest, Mexico—in a villainous light persisted.[12] This, of course, erased early American interactions with indigenous populations, which more often led to elimination or forced migration than integration. American exceptionalism was confirmed by interactions with Spain and Mexico. As destined as the United States was to prosper, Spain and Mexico were destined to fail. Mexico's inheritance from Spain, in this respect, affirmed the link between geopolitics and chronopolitics: Mexico's independence from Spain did nothing to free it from the Black Legend, and Mexico was cemented into a permanent past in reference to the United States.[13]

Kelley converted the backward Spanish past into the heroic Spanish past by emphasizing the civilizing work the Spanish friars had done in the expanding American empire. Spanish exceptionalism was working in opposing directions: *hispanismo* glorified the Spanish presence around the world, but particularly in the New World, while Prescott's paradigm denigrated Spain, emphasizing its decline, brought about by clericalism and backwardness.[14] The Spanish influence, both real and perceived, continued to be part of the story. Reconstructing the Spanish past cemented Kelley's loyalty to the United States; this was a critical aspect of empire, remaking the Catholic contributions to the United States. Kelley subverted the association of the civilizing of the West with a White Anglo-Saxon Protestant future. He remade the American West, offering the same progressive future, but with a Catholic flair rather than a Protestant one.

In the early-twentieth-century Southwest there were efforts to revive a particular Spanish past. Anglos in southern California who had not inherited the Spanish colonial landscape produced a Spanish golden age that passed to them with reference to neither the Mexican national era nor their Mexican contemporaries. The San Diego World's Fair (1915–16), for example, was designed to build on the Spanish architectural legacy in California. The blend, Matthew F. Bokovoy writes, "of regionalism and nationalism during the Progressive Era gave egalitarian substance to the modern Spanish heritage." This imagined democratic future never materialized, and the Spanish "representation" managed to erase the Mexican and Indian bodies still part of the California landscape. Mexicans were whitewashed out of even the architectural history of southern California, in a mourning, one might say, of what one has destroyed. Richard Kagan has shown that this Spanish revival was not limited to California, or even the Southwest. Artists, writers, and architects across the nation found a refuge from rapid industrialization in the picturesque visions of an imagined Spanish past in both the New and Old Worlds.[15]

Although many of these architectural and artistic visions embraced the California missions and the heroics of Spanish friars, they rarely embraced Catholicism itself.[16] Kelley produced a strictly Catholic inheritance for *Extension Magazine* readers, one in which the American West, including the landscape and its Mexican and Indian peoples, was the Catholic part of the American empire. This narrative was explicitly designed to raise funds for U.S. Catholic missions, creating a uniquely twentieth-century mission for urban American Catholics. Their place in the American empire was dependent on their financial support for Kelley's Catholic borderlands vision, which was committed to saving Mexicans, Indians, and the very landscape of the Catholic past in the American present and future territories.

Spanish domination of the global stage from the sixteenth century through the eighteenth is largely erased in U.S. historiography. Christopher Schmidt-Nowara and John Nieto-Phillips urge historians to reintroduce Spanish domination into discussions of empire and postcolonialism in Latin America. The same must be said of the Spanish borderlands, as Bolton called the present-day southwestern United States, though his concern was limited to the colonial era. The separation of U.S. and Mexican historiographies resists a trans-imperial and transhistorical study of the U.S.-Mexico borderlands, which seeks to understand the ways Catholicism was sustained and reimagined, regardless of changing imperial possession. Kelley played on the Catholic heritage as a sustaining feature of the landscape, which may have been disrupted in 1845–48, but could—indeed must—be repaired by the work of Catholic missionaries, with the financial support of U.S. Catholics through the Extension Society. The sacrifices of the Spanish friars could not be wasted, and, more significantly, the Southwest could be woven into the fabric of American empire through the recovery and maintenance of this long-Catholic space.[17]

## A Spiritual Cartography of American Empire

Frances Kelley contested the sacred geography of "America" by invoking the earlier Catholic claim to the same space. The nation-defining West of Frederick Jackson Turner's "Frontier Thesis," in fact, had a prior Euro-American history, a Catholic history. *Catholic Borderlands* maps Catholics onto the hemisphere, the continent, and the American landscape as a permanent feature. This triumphalist Americanism, as Thomas Tweed terms it, not only countered the dominant narrative of the U.S. West; it also supported the U.S. Catholic narrative formulated in the context of Pope Leo XIII's apostolic letter condemning the embrace of modernist forms of Catholicism perceived to be rampant in the United States. U.S. bishops and priests, led by Cardinal James Gibbons, staked a claim for the Catholic origins of democracy, tied in part to Maryland's colonial separation of church and state. Kelley strengthened the Catholic prior claim on America by invoking the Spanish Catholic forefathers in broad swaths of U.S. continental and island territories that once belonged to Spain. The rewriting of the conquest of the West shifted U.S. Catholics into a new position in relation to their neighbors in the East. Kelley was cognizant of the "legacy of conquest" and reimagined that legacy: Catholics not only originated the civilizing of the West but also continued to sustain that influence in the early twentieth century. Catholics had a prior claim to the continent, rebuking attacks by Protestants on their very Americanness.[18]

Catholics are not well represented in U.S. history, and they are even less visible in American foreign relations. John Fairbank noted in his 1968 American Historical Association presidential address, "The missionary in foreign parts seems to be the invisible man of American history." Fairbank envisioned the work and writing of Protestant foreign missionaries as a means for historians to understand the assigned foreign territory as well as the home nation.[19] Walter LaFeber's classic, *The New Empire: An Interpretation of American Expansion, 1860–1898*, included a short section on "Josiah Strong and the Missionary Frontier." LaFeber likened Strong, a Congregationalist pastor, to Frederick Jackson Turner, "for Strong stressed the necessity of finding a new world frontier to replace the internal frontier which Turner so eloquently described."[20] Strong was virulently anti-Catholic and was best known for *Our Country: Its Possible Future and Its Present Crisis*, in which he identified Romanism as one of the main perils endangering the nation. This threat was perhaps most striking in California, Strong warned, where Catholics outnumbered Protestants four to one.[21] These California Catholics were Mexican, too, making their threat to the nation that much more ominous. Strong, like Turner, was mapping a future for the United States, and for Strong, Catholics endangered that future. For LaFeber and many other historians, the Catholic foreign missionary is even more absent in American history than the Catholic home missioner. Kelley, through *Extension Magazine*, redefined the nation by explicitly linking Catholics in the Northeast with those in the Southwest and abroad, building an American Catholic ethos that was part of the very fabric of America's developing empire.[22]

Kelley contributed to defining the Catholic Church's racial and national location in a country that neither accepted nor wholeheartedly rejected the religion as its own. Given Catholicism's tenuous existence in the United States up to this point, such positioning could not be escaped. The Extension Society also took a stance—evolving and ambiguous as it was—in global racial politics. The vexing issues of race, empire, and Catholicism in the United States were woven together in uneven and sometimes contradictory ways. Nowhere are those contradictions more apparent than in the U.S. Catholic Church's attention to and involvement in Mexico in the aftermath of the Mexican Revolution.

Global, religious, and racial issues came together in complex ways as the United States expanded overseas. The supposed closing of the frontier, the growth of industry, and the Spanish-American War—when Spain surrendered its last colonial outposts to the United States—were foundational in the establishment of the United States' role as a global power. The jewel in the Spanish crown, Mexico, had already passed from Spain (through independence) to the United States in 1848, when Mexico lost half of its remaining territory through the Treaty of Guadalupe Hidalgo. Kelley's re-visioning of the church's role in contemporary politics provides a window into an emerging and expansive worldview. Kelley's commitment to Catholicism and to all Catholics effectively enlarged the scope of what we understand as imperial action, leading him to seek to bring all of Mexico into the United States' sphere of religious influence. This imperial decision was made possible by a broader gaze which included all territories that had been part of the Spanish empire and in the twentieth century found themselves formally or informally within the gravitational pull of the United States.

Early work in U.S. Catholic history emphasized devotionalism among Catholic immigrants as a cultural manifestation of home communities and Old World practices of Catholicism in the United States. From the mid-eighteenth century to 1920, the U.S. Catholic

Church is characterized in the literature as the immigrant church. This era began with the influx of Irish immigrants fleeing the potato famine. In the early twentieth century, immigrants from Italy, Poland, and, after 1910, Mexico filled the pews of the immigrant church. In this era, U.S. Catholic historiography emphasizes national parishes in burgeoning northeastern and midwestern cities, paying limited attention to rural Catholics. Lost in this dominant narrative is the role these rising Catholics played in the Anglo-Protestant project of taming the land and uplifting its people from coast to coast. American Catholics, under the leadership of Kelley and the Extension Society, adopted that same project as their own mission. The society funded missioners working with immigrants across the United States, especially targeting those at risk from Protestant proselytizers. Kelley expanded the immigrant church, however, with his attention to the anticlericalism in Mexico, taking the U.S. mission society's agenda to the home country of recent immigrants. Kelley's project subverted the modernist timeline that linked Catholicism with the past and Protestantism with the future. His mapping of the Spanish past into these Catholic borderlands affirmed a Catholic future for the United States and its territories.[23]

U.S. Catholic history, especially intellectual history, largely maps on to Irish American history.[24] Kelley, a Canadian of Irish descent, may seem, at first blush, an odd figure around whom to fashion a Mexican American history. Yet this is a cultural history that charts the diplomatic, social, and intellectual interactions of this era and demonstrates the way the U.S. Catholic Church ultimately reified its status as an American institution through Kelley's maneuverings at home and abroad, particularly in Mexico. This early-twentieth-century cultural and intellectual history reveals a quintessentially American embrace of Manifest Destiny through an unlikely actor: the Catholic Church. Kelley used *Extension Magazine*, which in 1910 had a larger circulation than *National Geographic* and *Atlantic Monthly* combined, to preach a Catholic history of the United States that embraced the Spanish Catholic past in the Southwest. *Extension Magazine* was designed to raise funds for the Extension Society, a key mechanism in maintaining the Catholic populations in both the West and East. Eastern Catholics reveled in the chance to chart the American future in the West. They also affirmed their own Catholic identity through their boosterism. Kelley justified his maneuverings in and around Mexico as part of this same Catholic birthright. He repeatedly invoked this history through *Extension Magazine* and his own writing prior to, during, and after the Mexican Revolution.[25]

American Catholics were coming into their own in the early twentieth century, especially in urban areas in the Northeast and Midwest. Generations of Catholics were largely assimilated and rising in the local political hierarchies in many cities, and they participated in the labor movement regionally and nationally. Along with *Extension Magazine*, Kelley worked through organizations like the Knights of Columbus to reach Catholics across the country. He took that a step further by immersing American Catholics into a broader narrative of faith and conversion that embraced the U.S. imperialist project and its subjects, actual and potential, in Mexico, especially. The U.S. possession of these territories gave the Catholic home mission society access to these areas, but Kelley constantly reminded his readers that these lands and their people were Catholic first. It was not only the Extension Society's right to be there; it was its duty to hold off the American Protestant missionaries, American public school teachers, and others trying to separate the people from their natural faith, Catholicism.

Whether or not the Extension Society succeeded in this mission of holding back the Protestant tide, it succeeded in getting U.S. Catholics to buy in to the urgent pleas to save Catholicism in the borderlands of the American empire through their donations. One might argue that there was little consequence for the recipients of this missionary work: they were "civilized" by the Protestants or the Catholics, and in either case, their prior state was considered unacceptable. But for white Catholics this imagined community with deep ties to the American landscape was an important part of sealing their own identities as 100 percent Americans in this nativist era. This project changed U.S. Catholics more than it did the

Mexican and other subjects of their missionary work. Kelley was American when it gave him opportunities, yet he used those opportunities to contest the Protestant-informed assumptions behind conventional visions of American assimilation. Although Mexico was not formally a possession of the United States, institutions like the Catholic Church sought to foster the deep connections that existed between present-day American Catholics and former Spanish territories through a shared religious heritage. These connections affirmed the U.S. Catholic providence over the national landscape. Catholics were no longer foreigners; they had inherited this land from their Catholic forefathers, the Spanish.

As early as 1914, Kelley and the U.S. government joined forces to intervene and save the Catholic Church in Mexico. The involvement of U.S. Catholic organizations and of Ambassador Dwight Morrow in the resolution of the Cristero Rebellion (1926–29) is well documented.[26] *Catholic Borderlands* forces us to be attentive to the prior decade and a half during which Kelley and the Extension Society claimed a space not only for Catholics in Mexico but for Catholics in the United States as well. Kelley led a transformation of American Catholics from outsiders to true Americans not only in language and loyalty but also in spirit, complete with an American civilizing mission. Saving the Catholic Church in Mexico was an important part of making the U.S. Catholic Church truly American. It bolstered Catholic self-confidence; embracing religious liberty in Mexico was the ultimate declaration of support for democracy and other American ideals. To be sure, many Americans still saw Catholics as foreigners, but Catholics themselves embraced a U.S. Catholic identity and came to see themselves as consummate Americans. They did this, in part, through their engagement and evolving relationship with Mexico and Mexican Catholicism. U.S. Catholics claimed their position as contributors to American empire by seeking to forge an American Catholic ethos, within, of course, what they continued to see as a universal church.

Scholarly attention to Latina/o religious practices and theologies has increased in the last thirty years, often emphasizing Mexican folk practices in contrast to institutionalized practices of Catholicism in the United States, or the growing evangelical Latina/o population.[27] In the last decade and a half, religious histories of the United States have pushed beyond the boundaries of the nation to attempt to understand American religion in broader international contexts.[28] I historicize the Mexican Catholic experience and examine religion in a broader social and political context that considers migration, racialization, and nation-building at home and abroad. This approach allows us to understand Catholicism as a component of nation-building in Mexico, a factor in national discourses in the twentieth-century United States, and an element of American empire-building.[29]

South of the border, the situation of the Catholic Church had also undergone major changes in the previous century. In the aftermath of the war with the United States, after Mexico lost half of its territory, Mexican liberals clamored for change. In 1855, Benito Juárez ousted Antonio López de Santa Anna and pushed for reforms limiting the power and privilege of the Catholic Church and the military. Church properties other than those used for religious purposes were confiscated, cemeteries were nationalized, and marriage became a civil institution. Land-reform programs were designed to reduce inequality but were largely unsuccessful. After Juárez suspended debt payments to France, Spain, and Britain, France invaded and occupied Mexico from 1862 to 1867. Conservatives hoped they had a leader in Maximilian, but his agenda was neither conservative enough nor liberal enough to sustain a loyal following in Mexico. Juárez and the liberals had U.S. support, but while the United States was engaged in its own civil war and reconstruction, European powers were able to intervene in Mexico. When Juárez regained the presidency in 1867, he set about rebuilding the economy and establishing a public education system to replace the church-run schools that dominated the nation. After Juárez's death in 1872, his successor, Sebastián Lerdo de Tejada, returned to the Constitution of 1857 to strengthen the reforms. Lerdo emphasized clear separation of church and state and removed religious references from court and state functions; religious liberty was guaranteed with the hope of loosening the hold of the Catholic Church on the nation.[30]

Porfirio Díaz first took office in 1876, and other than one term he served continuously until he was ousted in 1911. Díaz affirmed the democratic goals of Mexico's mid- to late-nineteenth-century reform era, but he was more committed to progress and order than to liberty. The financial and social stability provided by Díaz's leadership buoyed foreign investment, particularly from the United States. However, that came at a price, as U.S. firms acquired land and access to natural and national resources. Additionally, without changing the Constitution of 1857, Díaz relaxed regulations on the church and the military, allowing both to regain significant power and resources. This concentration of power in the administration, foreigners, and the church concerned intellectuals, labor leaders, and others and led to the Mexican Revolution.

A fuller understanding of U.S. imperialism depends not only on a broader definition of empire but also on the recognition that the cultural, social, and religious residue of centuries of the Spanish presence remains after the political transfer of territories. The United States was a rising imperial power in the first three decades of the twentieth century, and it continued to model its empire as the antithesis of the Spanish empire. One goal in this relational study is to avoid the temporal trap that places Mexico in the traditional, parochial past, in comparison to the modern, cosmopolitan U.S. present and future. I am attentive to "the excavation and connection of alternative histories and their different temporalities that cannot be contained by the progressive narrative of Western developmentalism," as Lowe and Lloyd suggest.[31] Mexico's late-nineteenth- and early-twentieth-century struggles with modernization are well documented. The presumption from both inside and outside the nation that progress and modernization would come from the United States, however, has weighed heavily on both nations and relations between them.[32]

Catholicism remained a powerful social, cultural, and political force in Mexico. A number of fine examinations of the Mexican Revolution focus on regional uprisings of the Mexican peasantry or the heroics of revolutionary leaders. However, these works do not analyze the role of the United States in revolutionary Mexico. Studies of U.S. involvement in Mexico emphasize oil and banking issues with little regard for the culture or politics of revolutionary Mexico. As noted earlier, there is a significant body of scholarship on U.S. and Catholic involvement in the Cristero Rebellion, but the stage had been set for this activity a decade earlier. In fact, the tension between anticlericalism and anti-Catholicism in Mexico, between Catholic Mexico and the Protestant-dominated United States, and between U.S. Catholics and their government made religion critical to interactions within and between these two nations.[33]

### Foreign Relations and the Borderlands of Empires

The cases of the United States and Mexico in this era contradict our understanding of the United States as a Protestant and inherently anti-Catholic nation. U.S. officials could not ignore the concerns of U.S. Catholics, who had created a place for themselves in the political and social terrain of major cities like Philadelphia, Boston, Chicago, New York, and Baltimore. Kelley bridged the rural/urban divide by creating a project for urban Catholics to invest in the rural South and West, Mexico, and other former Spanish territories, not only to sustain and expand the faith but also as a consummately American project. Catholic borderlands would not have been possible without the U.S. surge to global power in the early twentieth century.

U.S. involvement in the "religion question" in Mexico persisted through 1929. Kelley's own commitment to this reached its apex in 1935 with the publication of *Blood-Drenched Altars*.[34] The entanglements that linked Mexico to the United States extend far beyond diplomatic relations. In part this is a diplomatic history, but relations between nations are not limited to the actions of the nation-states. Social relations happen between organizations and individuals as well as between governments, formally and informally.[35] Rarely have religious organizations—especially Catholic ones—been studied as elements of U.S. foreign relations.[36] *Catholic Borderlands* charts a space where politics, culture, and the economy interacted, with results that defy our previous understanding of this era.

Mexico's role in the twentieth-century U.S. imagination was shaped by the mid-nineteenth-century war between the two nations. For Catholics in the United States, foreign relations and foreign wars raised concerns on the home front. Prejudice against Catholic Mexico was rampant in the U.S. press. Historian Gene Brack writes of the Mexican-American War (1846–48), "Mexicans were as scornful of American Protestantism as Americans were of Mexican Catholicism. But American Protestantism nurtured also the 'work ethic,' which exaggerated the supercilious attitudes of Americans toward Mexico and her people." These tensions shaped U.S. relations with not just Mexico but the Americas as a whole. The Black Legend of Spanish impotence was driven by Prescott and other historians as well as by popular literature of the era.[37]

There was prejudice against Catholic Mexico at this time, as well as overt discrimination and violence against Catholics in the United States. The *Philadelphia Ledger* reported on "Native American" violence toward "Irish and Papists" in Kensington, Pennsylvania, in 1844: "Numerous attempts were made to burn various Catholic Churches in the city. Threats were made against the priests, who on this account wore no clerical dress and remained in hiding or left the city."[38] Accusations that American Catholics supported the pope rather than the president were common and acquired heightened importance during the course of the war. Studies have found that high percentages of Catholics, encouraged and supported by U.S. Catholic leadership and clergy, fought in the Mexican-American War. Still, Catholics were positioned as foreigners who had to prove their Americanness by serving in the war.[39]

On both sides of the border, public opinion was split on the war. Mexican views on involvement in the war varied, but the sentiment toward the United States was uniform: "Whether liberal, conservative, Marxist, traditionalist or revisionists, Mexican writers share a common view of the United States as the aggressor." Anti-American sentiment had become popular in Mexican newspapers a decade earlier, during the period of Texas independence, when the term "Colossus of the North" was coined. From the appointment of diplomats to the open desire for expansion, the United States seemed determined to become a thorn in Mexico's side.[40]

Public debate in the United States was focused not on Mexico but rather on regional tension within the country, with New Englanders suspicious of a southern conspiracy to expand slavery, and southerners and westerners anxious for expansion. Even popular literature featured scenes of U.S. empire- and nation-building. Uniformly, however, public opinion depicted Mexico as weak—a legacy of its Spanish heritage—and its people as racially inferior to people in the United States. Of course, by the time the war was over, many of Mexico's people had become the spoils of the United States. And by the time the war was "won," many Americans who had opposed it gave in to the patriotic and paternalistic fervor that followed. When the war was over, Mexican people, as well as land, became the spoils of the United States. Notions of race and citizenship in the United States were shattered by the sudden acquisition of thousands of non-white landholding peoples.[41]

With three hundred years of Anglo-Spanish rivalry preceding the war, perhaps the United States and Mexico, the offspring of these rivals, were destined to clash. As the United States came to covet former Spanish territories, religion was guaranteed to be a factor. The war with Mexico (1846–48) was not just about religion and U.S.-Mexican relations. It was a defining moment in the formation of the United States and its identity as an imperial power. The war also was critical in framing U.S. relations with Europe. Walt Whitman wrote, countering European attacks on President James Polk and the expansionist United States, "Let the Old World wag on under its cumbrous load of form and conservatism, we are of a newer and fresher race and land." Whitman separated the U.S. war with Mexico, which ultimately resulted in expansion across the continent, from colonialism or imperialism as practiced by European powers.[42]

U.S. expansion into northern Mexico was clearly imperialist, and it set the stage for economic imperialisms that followed in 1898. "While it is important to understand the specificities of the imperialisms of 1848 and 1898," Shelley Streeby writes, "to reserve the term 'imperialism' for the 1890s is to reproduce that tenuous and certainly ideological distinction and to marginalize a much longer history of U.S. imperialism in the Americas."[43] This U.S. imperialism was connected to Anglo imperialism in a racial and cultural framework that extended white, northern European superiority to the Anglo-American population over the decadent, Spanish empire and its former colonies. Inherent in this competition between Spanish and British imperial families was the legacy of Catholic-Protestant conflict.

Yet another nexus of religion and imperialism in U.S. foreign relations occurred during and after the Spanish-American War. Kelley used the Catholic past of the Philippine Islands to connect the Spanish and American empires through Catholicism. This Catholic borderlands in the Philippine Islands, like in the one the American Southwest, was built on the imperial foundation laid by the Spanish and reengaged by U.S. Catholics as part of the American empire.

An important part of the imperial project was defining the geopolitical and racial boundaries of the empire. Historians have tended to focus on inter-imperial competition, but inter-imperial connections—shared ideas and practices—have not received the same kind of attention. Paul Kramer shows how the Anglo and U.S. empires in the late nineteenth and early twentieth centuries fed each other in racial, linguistic, and national terms. "Having begun as a British defense of the superiority of the Anglican Church and having early confronted Catholic 'others,'" he writes, "Anglo-Saxonism was closely allied to Protestantism and was often said to share its values." Protestantism was an important legacy of the Anglo-Saxon empire and was readily exported to the Philippines in the form of Protestant missionaries, U.S. schoolteachers, and government structures. But the isolation of Catholicism from American empire has rendered invisible the mission work of Catholics like Kelley and the Extension Society. The United States exported Protestantism to former Spanish territories in an attempt to civilize these dark, mysterious others, but Kelley and American Catholics did extensive fund-raising at home and evangelizing abroad to protect Filipino Catholics from the secular and proselytizing forces from the United States.[44]

When the Mexican Revolution erupted, U.S. public opinion was again divided—this time along religious lines. Catholics had become a more accepted part of U.S. society and culture, but there was still much suspicion and condescension toward neighboring "Catholic" Mexico. President Woodrow Wilson embodied that enmity toward the Roman Catholic Church with his writing on "the social problem" in France, which cast the church as holding the nation back.[45] Wilson's first term as president was dominated by relations with Mexico in the thick of the Mexican Revolution. Much of the scholarship on Wilson acknowledges moral underpinnings for his foreign-policy decisions, but recent work has tied his approach more definitively to Presbyterian covenant theology. Wilson rejected the dollar diplomacy of President William Howard Taft in favor of an international moral leadership. He also embraced the spiritual connection between nations of the New World and thus believed that Mexico could be saved by the right leadership.[46] Wilson and Kelley did not see eye to eye on Mexico, but Wilson recognized Kelley's prominence as a Catholic spokesman and tried to appease Kelley by attending to religious liberty in Mexico.

Mexico's proximity, the presence of Mexican nationals in the U.S. nation space, and the fortuitous appointment by the Mexican Catholic hierarchy of Kelley as their spokesman in the United States all allowed Kelley to take a much bigger role in saving Catholicism in Mexico than he was able to do elsewhere. This extension of Catholic borderlands to Mexico, which was not a U.S. territory, demonstrates that Kelley's trans-imperial vision transcended the political limits of his imperial home, the United States. Kelley took his work a step further with Mexico, empowered by the faith placed in him by the Mexican Catholic hierarchy.

Kelley's work was not "resistance" as we tend to think about it within empire. Rather, it represents a well-placed, if far from dominant, voice from within the empire that tried to influence events by constructing a narrative to explain what was happening at the edges of the empire. He simultaneously benefited from being an invisible, unacknowledged part of the imperial body while seeking to under-mine—or at least complicate—its cultural conquests. Kelley's ultimate contribution to Catholic borderlands was his epic *Blood-Drenched Altars*, which was selected as the Catholic Book Club's book of the month in April 1935. Through the National Catholic Welfare Con-ference, copies were distributed to legislators in Washington, DC, broadening Kelley's audience beyond the Catholic faithful.

Kelley's history of Mexico was striking for his embrace of *mestizaje*, or racial mixing, in Mexico. Mixed-race people posed special challenges to imperial institutions. "The idea of race," Robert Young writes, "shows itself to be profoundly dialectical: it only works when defined against potential intermixture, which also threatens to undo its calculation altogether."[47] The threat Young identifies to racial purity is the same threat that Mexico and Mexicans posed to the racial order and separation of the United States. Yet, Kelley cited that very mixing as evidence of the success of the Spanish colonial project. This swipe at the Mexican Revolution for attempting to oust the church, an important vestige of civilization in Mexico, was also a swipe at the United States, in the midst of the eugenic, anti-immigrant, and anti-Catholic sentiment of the 1920s and 1930s. Kelley's mission was made possible by his social location in the United States, but he con-tinued to chip away at the American empire from within. In *Blood-Drenched Altars*, Kelley reasserted the Catholic claim on Mexico and documented the epic struggle between good and evil that had taken place there. He drew on contemporary racialized movements in the United States and Mexico to reintroduce the broad Spanish borderland into a twentieth-century historical narrative as a Cath-olic borderlands. Kelley rewrote Mexican history to allow the U.S. Catholic Church to finish the project the Spanish Catholic Church started: civilizing the Mexican savage. He countered the dominant narratives of American empire, which eschewed racial others in favor of a racially and religiously white Anglo-Saxon Protestant whole, by asserting that racial mixture did not, in itself, mark one as uncivilized.

## Catholic Borderlands

Catholic borderlands are spaces that over the course of time, through geopolitical shifts, layer a Catholic past with a Catholic present, challenging universalist ideas about Catholicism as well as the spatial and temporal boundaries of empires. In this case, Catholic borderlands were spaces at the edges of the growing U.S. empire in the early twentieth century that had Spanish, and therefore Catholic, pasts. These spaces were also at the boundaries of the Spanish empire, where the church was often more present in the lives of the inhabitants than were other colonial institutions. In these Catholic borderlands, I argue, we find a means for U.S. Catholics to link themselves with the North American continent in ways that made Catholicism a natural, permanent marker in the U.S. past. This recasting of American history also cemented a place for Catholics in the American empire, regardless of the activities of nativist, anti-Catholic, and racialist elements of society. In this narrative, Mexicans in both the United States and Mexico were subjects to be saved—saved not only from a presumed pagan past but, more importantly, in this era, from the meddling proselytizer who was trying to separate the faithful from the Catholic Church. Kelley disrupted the Protestant progressive narrative of the era and replaced it with a Catholic discourse with deep historical roots *and* a modern American future.

Kelley constructed a narrative to rescue the Spanish past through *Extension Magazine.* Chapter 1 traces this narrative in the Catholic borderlands of the continental United States. Through his magazine, the fund-raising arm of the Extension Society, Kelley laid the foundation for a triumphalist Americanism: an inherently Catholic and thoroughly American narrative of belonging and responsibility for his readers. U.S. Catholics responded by funding Kelley's vision throughout the U.S. South, West, and Southwest. Catholic borderlands did not exist in the heart of the empire—the Northeast—but it could be sold to Catholics there. Catholic borderlands were made possible, in part, by the sparsely populated or distantly controlled territories on the fringes of the Spanish and U.S. empires. It was here where the Spanish friars exerted more of their influence and where American Catholics, under the leadership of Kelley and the Extension Society, sought to make their mark. The U.S. project of Americanization and Protestant uplift was converted to a Catholic one, as part of the same U.S. imperial project, but also rooted in a Spanish Catholic past. Kelley and his funders were convinced that blacks, American Indians, and Mexicans could remain, or become, Catholic and still be modern American subjects.

In the first decades of the twentieth century, Catholic borderlands could also be understood to exist in the recently acquired U.S. territories of Puerto Rico and the Philippine Islands. As I show in chapter 2, "The Devil Is Having a Great Time" was Kelley's call to American Catholics to save the church in Puerto Rico, the cradle of the faith in the New World, as well as the Philippines, the anchor of the church in the Pacific. As newly acquired U.S. territories, the populations of these islands were threatened by U.S. forces in the form of U.S. government officials, public school teachers, and Protestant proselytizers. After the Mexican Revolution, as anticlericalism raged in the 1910s, Kelley turned his attention to Mexico. Although it was not formally under U.S. control, Mexico was within the U.S. economic and cultural sphere of influence. This was enough for Kelley to stake his claim to a broader Catholic project on the North American continent—one that could not be contained by the border between Mexico and the United States.

Catholic borderlands were affirmed by the attention of U.S. government officials to Catholic concern in the aftermath of the Mexican Revolution. Chapter 3 shows how U.S. Catholic lay and clerical leadership revealed their disregard for the political boundary between the United States and Mexico by forcing their government to attend to religious repression in Mexico. At the same time, Mexican Catholics recognized the porosity of the political border and also approached the U.S. government seeking support for their religious cause in Mexico. Despite the anti-Catholic past and present of the United States, chapter 3 shows, Catholic activity ensured that the religion question in Mexico received attention in the United States. Catholics in both countries were crucial in shaping policy and relations between the two nations, furthering Catholic borderlands as a transnational space that included both the United States and Mexico. This chapter attends to the cultural implications of the diplomatic and economic commitments of the United States in Mexico during and after the Revolution. This is not to replace an economic examination with a cultural one. The entanglements of economics, politics, and religion, however, seem to render the religious component invisible in the scholarship on this era.

*Catholic Borderlands* is a history that travels the same sorts of currents that migrants, capital, religion, and other forces traversed. Chapter 4 considers Kelley's interactions outside of and in contrast to the state—those that subverted, provoked, or wrested control from the state. Intervention has been understood as strictly a political or military strategy. In fact, it was a cultural one as well. Kelley's mission saw few boundaries; he dabbled in the economic and political affairs of Mexico and the Versailles talks in 1919, as extensions of home mission concerns. Catholic borderlands offered Kelley the opportunity to intervene in the Catholic affairs of not only Mexico but Germany and other countries whose missionary investments were in danger after World War I.

Kelley's star was certainly tied to the Archdiocese of Chicago. The city rose to international status in the early twentieth century, as shown by its selection to host the International Eucharistic Congress in 1926. The planning committee, which included Kelley, who was then the bishop of Oklahoma, focused significant attention on the religious repression in Mexico in the months leading up to the congress, making Chicago the center of the Catholic borderlands. The U.S. Catholic hierarchy disregarded the political boundary between the two countries in asserting its desires for a Catholic future in Mexico. As a result, President Plutarco Elías Calles placed government officials throughout Chicago to monitor the actions of Mexican Catholic leadership during the June celebration. Chapter 5 suggests that U.S. Catholic activism contributed to the enactment of the Calles Laws in July, which placed severe limits on the Mexican Catholic Church, leading to the Cristero Rebellion (1926–29).

Kelley's resistance to the eugenic status quo of the United States and the mestizo nationalist rhetoric of Mexico produced *Blood-Drenched Altars*, a pro-mestizo, pro-Catholic history of Mexico. Whereas the Spanish colonial project included *castas*, emphasizing racial purity and distinction, Kelley's modern take embraced *mestizaje* as a civilizing force in Mesoamerica. Chapter 6, "Preaching *Mestizaje*," shows that in contrast to the eugenic and segregationist United States, the social order in the Catholic borderlands embraced racial mixing. This was a theoretical proposition—a radical one—but one that drew on both the Spanish and U.S. empires to create a uniquely Catholic position in the early twentieth century.

For both the United States and Mexico, the years from 1910 to 1929 marked a transformation in the role of the Catholic Church. In the United States, Catholics were at last finding their place. They were numerous enough in many cities to nurture strong local and national leadership to give voice to Catholic concerns. In Mexico, revolutionary discourses spoke of decentering the Catholic Church in the 1910s, or destroying it in the 1920s. In spite of this, the Catholic Church in Mexico remained a dominant cultural force through the 1910s and 1920s and, many would argue, remains so today.

Catholic borderlands reshaped the relationships between the United States and Mexico and between U.S. Catholics and American empire. Religion was more significant in U.S.-Mexican relations during the Mexican Revolution than has previously been acknowledged. Mexico and the United States both sought the separation of church and state, and neither wanted the United States involved in Mexican internal affairs. In the end, however, Mexico recognized that its political, social, and economic future depended upon returning the church to Mexican daily life, and therefore it allowed the United States to intervene in the religion question in 1929. This imperial oversight was driven in part by the push, over the previous two decades, by American Catholics to retain the Catholicity of former Spanish territories.

*Catholic Borderlands* demonstrates that religion and nation worked in unexpected ways for Catholics. For U.S. Catholics, the early twentieth century represented a rise in power and numbers that gave many a sense of pride in their religious identity. This confidence led some Catholic organizations to doggedly pursue the issue of religious liberty in Mexico, a practice that increased their moral authority locally and nationally. American Catholics found a space for themselves within the American empire by embracing their faith and insisting that its democratic and historical precedence be acknowledged. *Catholic Borderlands* understands the border as porous but also multidimensional. Catholic borderlands were not redemptive spaces; they were not spaces of retreat or protection for Mexicans, Mexican Americans, mestizos, or others. Rather, they were spaces where multiple imperial projects—the Spanish empire, American empire, and a twentieth-century U.S. Catholic empire—redefined the geopolitical landscape of U.S. territorial, social, cultural, and political reach. Multiple populations, characterized by multiple identities, took advantage of opportunities on both sides of the border—opportunities provided by the trans-imperial and transhistorical Catholic borderlands.

# I

## An American Catholic Borderlands

*The Spanish Past in the United States*

In 1907, Richard Aumerle published a short fictional piece in *Extension Magazine.* "Juanita" told the story of John Barr, an Irishman tramping the Southwest for fifty years, who traveled with a young Mexican girl, Juanita. "Where or by what queer ways Juanita had come to be his, does not appear. It would have required an extravagant stretch of imagination to have fancied any relationship between them," Aumerle wrote. And yet, from the time Juanita was two or three years old till she was eighteen, she accompanied Barr on his travels. Juanita was portrayed as shy, wild, and impulsive, while Barr was moody and unsociable. When Father Corbin came to town, Barr suggested the priest make his way back to whence he came.[1]

Barr was "the old West, dying fast," and Corbin was determined that Barr ought not die without knowing the faith. Barr rebuffed the priest on multiple occasions, but he got the message that he was the past and the Catholic town being established down the hill was the future. He also understood that the time had come for him to "free" Juanita. When he broached this topic with her, she was angry and realized that Father Corbin was the influence pushing for change. Juanita was determined to eliminate Corbin, even if it meant killing him. Predictably, Corbin and Juanita met on opposite sides of a river, with a log bridge between them and rising rapids below. Juanita shot Corbin while falling into the river and was rescued by him, as witnessed by Barr. "Juanita did not quite understand it to be looking up into the forgiving eyes of this man whom a moment ago she had wanted to kill." Barr's response upon wit-

"And on top of a stunted burro, rolled and strapped in his blanket, rode Juanita"

Fig. 1. These illustrations accompanied the story "Juanita," by Richard Aumerle. The odd couple: the young Mexican girl, Juanita, and John Barr, the Irish American frontiersman, in their early years together. *Extension Magazine*, September 1907.

She Could Kill Him Anyway...Her Gun Slipped to the Hollow of Her Arm

Fig. 2. Father Corbin suggested Barr let Juanita go when she reached adulthood. Juanita confronted the priest at the river crossing. Story by Richard Aumerle, *Extension Magazine*, September 1907.

nessing all of this was, "We're needin' you Father."[2] And thus, both Juanita and the old West were saved.

*Extension Magazine*, the official publication of the Catholic Church Extension Society of the United States of America, was one of the most widely read monthly magazines in the United States in the early 1900s. The Extension Society, established in 1905, was designed to serve remote populations throughout the United States, living largely off the contributions of relatively well-off Catholics through special collections and memberships in the society, which included *Extension Magazine*. The magazine existed explicitly to raise funds. Priests in remote, rural parishes, some reached by railroad cars, motor chapels, or even horseback, wrote compelling narratives and shared testimonials of conversion and service to the most needy of America's Catholics and potential converts. *Extension Magazine* featured articles and images of these remote and impoverished communities and, in the case of American Indian and Eskimo communities, substantial photo layouts. The goal was to inspire donations for churches, schools, and liturgical needs for missions in the rural South and West.

Aumerle's Father Corbin bore a striking resemblance to an Extension Society priest.[3] "The Bishop had given him this corner of the state—territory enough for two eastern dioceses—to do what he could for stray Catholics, to put up a little church here and there with what the miners could give him and what assistance he could get from the East."[4] The illustrations accompanying these stories reflected the heroic nature of home mission work: a priest pulling Juanita from the rapids, or in another story, a small chapel glowing in the dark forest, where Illiniwek Indians were rescued from the warring Chippewas by a persistent and forgiving priest.[5] Photos of Euro-American missions showed chapels or schools built with Extension Society funds, while those of black, American Indian, and Mexican missions showed how civilized they had become with proper attention.

Francis Kelley, through *Extension Magazine*, revised the American narrative of the taming of the West and its peoples to a Catholic narrative about saving communities of color from Protestant proselytizers who had no qualms about snatching children from the arms of their parents—in this case, the Catholic Church. This chapter charts the separation of white immigrant faithful from their black, American Indian, and Mexican counterparts in the pages of *Extension Magazine.* It examines the rhetoric and imagery of conversion and the civilizing mission presented through testimonials, short stories, and images. These reports were important in racializing blacks, American Indians, and Mexicans to northeastern Catholics who had interacted with Italian, Slavic, or Polish immigrants but were unlikely to encounter Mexicans or American Indians in their daily lives. This chapter also marks the beginning of the Extension Society's project, when Kelley laid the groundwork for his expanded mission beyond U.S. borders. The foundation for this work was the mapping of the social and geographic space of the U.S. Southwest, which drew on the Spanish Catholic past, thereby legitimizing Catholic ownership of an American narrative of civilizing the land and the people of the West.[6]

The Extension Society converted the civilizing mission from Protestant Americanization to a renewed embrace of Catholicism with a distinctively American bent. U.S. Catholics were provoked into action by the work of Protestant proselytizers with Mexican immigrants in the Southwest. The home mission work of the Extension Society gave them an outlet to address the Mexican situation and affirm their own identities as American Catholics. This Catholic taming of the West hints at Kelley's broader project, which followed American expansion into former Spanish territories to ensure that former Spanish subjects remained Catholic. This Catholic project within the broader American imperial project helped establish the Catholic Church as an American institution. Genealogically, the Protestant-Catholic tensions and rivalry of England and Spain were passed on to the United States and Mexico. This chapter excavates the layers of U.S. history and historiography that have clouded our understanding of Catholicism, Mexico, and the ultimate intersection of the two—Mexicans in the United States.

34

U.S. Catholic history tells the story of foreign missionaries through the mid-nineteenth century but takes a dramatic turn late in the century to the "native" diocesan structures, particularly in urban northeastern and midwestern dioceses. Catholics continued to live in rural and remote areas of the United States, but they have received scant attention in the historical literature. This chapter, much like the Extension Society and *Extension Magazine*, bridges these distinct U.S. Catholic bodies.

U.S. Catholic history in this era is largely the story of urban immigrant Catholics and the development of Catholic school systems. Without a doubt, Catholics were a predominantly urban and northeastern population. But as these urban Catholics became better established in major cities, they built their own infrastructure of organizations, presses, and projects. What little has been written about rural Catholics in the early twentieth century emphasizes the work of Protestants reformers to Americanize outlying populations.[7] Urban Catholics, led by Kelley and the Extension Society, saw a place for themselves in a broader American story: a Catholic history of the West, South, and Southwest shows the maturing Catholic discourse, which envisioned a national role for Catholics in shaping more remote areas of the country. Catholics were in the borderlands of American empire, working to counter the Protestant national project with a Catholic errand into the wilderness.

## Home Missions in a Missionary Land

In America, some of the first ripples of "this new evangelization" began nearly a hundred years ago, when a penniless priest embarked on a cross-country begging circuit.

—Catholic Church Extension Society, *Family Appointment Calendar*, 2002[8]

Until 1908 the United States was officially designated "mission" territory, meaning it had received the gospel relatively recently. The Catholic Church Extension Society of the United States of America, the U.S. home mission society, was tasked with bringing the faith far and wide in this young nation and its territories. Kelley's success in converting the civilizing mission from one of Protestant uplift to one of Catholic defense was shaped by the society's status within the American church as well as Kelley's role in building the Extension Society.

Francis Clement Kelley, born in 1870 on Prince Edward Island, Canada, became one of the most influential Catholic priests in the United States in the first half of the twentieth century. During his first assignment, in Lapeer, Michigan, Kelley found that his own and surrounding rural parishes suffered from a lack of funding to sustain churches and schools. In 1905 he approached Archbishop James Quigley of Chicago with a plan to support such struggling rural parishes by calling on better-off, mostly urban parishes for financial support. The Extension Society was established in 1905 to serve remote populations throughout the United States, with Kelley as president its first nineteen years. The fact that Kelley skirted his own bishop in Detroit suggests his desire to think about this problem on a national rather than a local scale. The society was a joint effort of the archbishop of Chicago, the archbishop of Santa Fe, the bishop of Wichita, and several Illinois Catholic bishops. Catholic leadership from the East was noticeably absent from this project. Chicago, the largest and most stable diocese in "the West," was the natural home for the Extension Society. As part of the thriving Archdiocese of Chicago, the Extension Society was able to gain a national and even international audience, giving Kelley national and international stature as a Catholic spokesman and statesman in spite of his low rank within the Catholic hierarchy.

The generation of bishops leading the U.S. Catholic Church shaped dioceses into a more orderly and efficient era in the first two decades of the twentieth century. The Catholic Church was in a process of reorganization. As it grew rapidly in the United States, Rome was more and more aware of how complicated its very existence was. There was frequent competition from Protestant communities and pressure from politicians to limit the scope of the Catholic Church.

Bishops were charged with the unique task of making U.S. Catho-

Fig. 3. The Extension Society's board of governors, ca. 1908. *Standing, left to right*: George C. Hennessey, chapel car superintendent and Kelley's first cousin; David Smith, Church Goods Department; Rev. Alexander P. Landry, field secretary; Most Rev. William D. O'Brien, diocesan director and director, Child Apostles; Simon Baldus, managing editor. *Seated, left to right*: Most Rev. Emmanuel B. Ledvina, vice president and general secretary; Kelley; Rev. Edward L. Roe, director of the Order of Martha.

lics seem American to the Protestants while assuring Rome that they were still Roman Catholics—a precarious balancing act. In the early twentieth century, U.S. Catholics struggled to establish themselves as both American and Catholic in a Protestant-dominated nation. Immigrants faced challenges to their legitimacy as true Americans. As Catholics, the prejudice against them multiplied. Catholic bishops in the United States faced pressures from the Vatican and from the American public in the late nineteenth and early twentieth centuries. There was concern that a peculiar form of Catholicism was developing in the United States. Pope Leo XIII's 1899 apostolic letter to the U.S. Catholic hierarchy, *Testem Benevolentiae Nostrae*, cautioned U.S. Catholic leaders that "Americanism" was threatening the unity of the church and confusing earthly liberty with the eternal version offered through the faith.

Bishop Peter J. Muldoon of Rockford, Illinois, reported at the Second Missionary Congress, more than a decade later, the expectation that the Catholic Church in the United States attend not only to the spiritual needs of immigrants but to their material needs as well.[9] Within the church, Americanists sought assimilation of immigrants and embraced the constitutional protection of religious freedom as an opening for the Catholic Church in the United States. Conservatives were more cautious and wanted to protect the flock from the dangers to the soul lurking in the United States. *Extension Magazine* came into being in 1906, in the midst of these simmering tensions.

At the turn of the century, mission societies were being created in the United States, and American provinces of foreign mission societies were established. As mission territory, and given the great geographic expanse that needed attention, U.S. territories were magnets for Catholic missionaries. As early as 1909, Kelley sought to establish an American Board of Catholic Missions to coordinate and oversee the varied Catholic missionary efforts. The board did not win approval of the U.S. bishops until 1919, and it was formally inaugurated in 1925 with Kelley, then bishop of Oklahoma, as a member. Through *Extension Magazine*, Kelley did manage to centralize much of the reporting on U.S. Catholic missions, and he distributed funds widely in the name of American Catholics. In some dioceses, the Extension Society was the only domestic missionary organization allowed to visit to raise fund or have special collections.[10]

In 1918, Kelley wrote that the society was formed to assist small missions and parishes in "pioneer sections."[11] In its first thirteen years the society focused on building churches and schools—an amazing seventeen hundred structures from 1905 to 1918. It purchased pews, chalices, altars, and whatever else was needed to turn a "dry goods box with a cross" into a church.[12] The society also provided railroad and motor chapels to those dioceses that had Catholics spread far and wide—particularly in the plains states and the far West. Extension worked collaboratively with dioceses and orders to man the mobile chapels and serve as many Catholics as possible. The society did not provide the personnel to reach remote Catholics. Rather, it provided funds and vital publicity and, most importantly, used Catholics missions to create and sustain an American Catholic ethos of giving to less-fortunate Catholics here in the United States.

*Extension Magazine*, the official organ of the Extension Society, had a rapidly growing audience in its first decade.[13] The magazine frequently contained short stories that produced narratives of faith and conversion of morally impoverished populations in the South, West, and even the rural Northeast on occasion.[14] Kelley fancied himself a novelist and sought to cultivate a cadre of young Catholic writers.[15] He soon found, however, that the most compelling stories came from those "in the field." *Extension* featured articles and photos of remote, impoverished communities and the heroic priests who served them. The magazine was the major source of fund-raising for the society, with personal appeals coming not only from Kelley but also from priests in need around the United States and its territories. Testimonials from those serving communities around the country reported the quantity and quality of Catholics in their assigned territories. Priests and brothers described in painstaking detail the lack of appropriate chalices and vestments, let alone churches or schools. They requested funds for projects such as building or repairing churches or attracting an order of sisters to start a school. Through short stories, testimonials, and editorials, Kelley outlined for *Extension* readers the perils of life in the West, marking the presence of an America Catholic borderlands.

### The West in the Catholic Imagination

Early issues of *Extension Magazine* brought the unkempt and unruly West, in story form, to Catholics in the Northeast and Midwest. In "Lost in the Western Mountains," Chicago novelist Mary Lupton wrote of a trip to Colorado that she hoped would provide "local color" for her new novel. Lupton recalled for her New York friends her adventures in the Rocky Mountains.

> There, just about a stone's throw from me, rode a girl—a beautiful, young girl, mounted also on a burro, and followed by a score of more rough looking individuals—miners, evidently, judging from their dress. "What a curious sight!" I thought. "Where can they be taking her or she taking them. I'll follow to be near, lest they try to do her an injury." . . . I saw myself, single-handed, fighting off those brawny sons of the mountains, and escaping to some ancient castle with my rescued prize.[16]

*Extension Magazine* certainly dealt in rescue narratives, but this was an unexpected take on it: an urban woman imagined rescuing a young girl in the West from the riffraff presumably lurking there. "I saw the mysterious procession stop in front of a rude wooden structure and the men file in one after the other," Lupton continued. "I certainly was not prepared for the shock I received on entering, for I actually found myself inside a Catholic Church."[17] This rendering precisely fit the goals of *Extension Magazine*: Lupton brought the righteous news of a ramshackle Catholic Church in the wilderness, catering to miners and maidens alike, to her friends in the East. It also solidified the Catholic presence in the East; Lupton was civilized, assimilated, and sophisticated—more than worthy of saving the innocent young girl, in both the sacred and secular senses of the word. Such stories demonstrated the importance of the Extension Society's work, taking the faith to the far corners of the burgeoning national landscape. "Western history," Limerick writes, "has been an ongoing competition for legitimacy—for the right to claim for oneself and sometimes for one's group the status of legitimate beneficiary of western resources." For Catholics in the early twentieth century, rearticulating a Catholic history of the West legitimized their claim to Americanness. American Catholics had a place in the epic legacy of the West, not just historically but in the present as well. Far from the Catholic cities dotted with immigrant national parishes, Catholics were indeed part of the American story. Catholic leadership in the West contributed to this narrative as well.[18]

In the fall of 1913, the Second American Catholic Missionary Congress took place in Boston. Catholic priests, bishops, and laypeople from across the country met for three days to discuss Catholic home missions. Archbishop John Baptiste Pitaval of Santa Fe, New Mexico, represented the leadership of the "wild and wooly west."[19] In a speech repeatedly interrupted by bursts of applause, Pitaval compared the ornate cathedrals he had seen in Boston with the sacred buildings that surrounded him in the Southwest: "It is the picture of another glorious edifice, hoary with age, cemented with the blood of many martyrs, with the sweat of countless apostolic men—the picture of the older Church in our great country, but now crumbling into ruin, disintegrating pillar by pillar—nay, stone by stone, moreover exposed to the fierce attacks of a relentless foe. It is our Catholic Church in the Southwest." Pitaval, met with applause, continued his comparison of Catholic life in the East versus the West: "Occasionally I hear from your churches and cathedrals the peal of mighty organs, the strains of heavenly music in praise of the Most High, but it is drowned in the far-off cry of the dark skinned sons of my western desert: 'Behold, our children are crying for the bread of God's Word and there are none to break it to them.'[20] Behold, *we* are being dispossessed of *our* lands; *we* are a doomed and vanishing race." The archbishop seemingly embodied Mexicans or American Indians of the Southwest. He continued, "The white man," presumably referring to Protestants from the East, "is enjoying the fruit of the land that *we* inherited from *our* fathers," subtly transitioning from the dark-skinned "we" to the Catholic "we." "After being robbed of our earthly heritage, are we to be deprived of our heavenly birthright also?"[21] Pitaval began by invoking the seemingly familiar image of the West in the mind of the northeasterner, but he ended by reminding his audience that this territory had a Catholic past and that Protestants were taking the land "we inherited from our fathers." Carey McWilliams writes of the Spanish legacy in the Southwest, "It is only natural that the monuments and ruins should later acquire a piquant antiquarian interest and that the figures of the earlier scene should assume heroic proportions in the imagination of a later period." Kelley used this antiquarian interest to bridge the Catholic Southwest with the Catholic Northeast and Midwest. The embrace of the Spanish Catholic past was an important part of building an American Catholic missionary ethos in the early twentieth century, based in an American Catholic borderlands.[22]

The Missionary Congress was Kelley's creation. His work as editor of *Extension Magazine* sustained a national Catholic conversation about the West. Kelley's audience, both in the magazine and at the congress, was people who for generations had been treated as foreigners. Now they had the chance to declare themselves 100 percent American by carrying out the American agenda, but in a distinctly Catholic way. The influx of Mexican immigrants, in particular, into the Southwest after 1910 gave Catholics of the Northeast and Midwest the opportunity to reframe the message of Protestant uplift and civilization into a Catholic taming and civilizing of the West. This, combined with a recuperation of the Catholic history of the Southwest, allowed for the manifestation of an American Catholic destiny in the borderlands. The testimonials, short stories, and images presented in *Extension* demonstrate Kelley's effort to cultivate an American Catholic discourse that did not simply mimic Protestant efforts. Rather, Kelley wove the Spanish Catholic past into a deeper historical understanding of the United States, particularly the West, as naturally and inherently Catholic.

Kelley sought to develop Catholic writers and published a range of stories in which characters stumbled upon the faith in far-off and unexpected places. As *Extension* developed its voice, however, Kelley recognized the power of testimonials. Priests from throughout the West, South, and Southwest reported the disrepair of churches, the ills of those fallen from the faith, and the constant threat from Protestant proselytizers. It was here that the importance of the Extension Society's work with communities of color became clear to readers.

## The Savage, Made Noble by the Cross

American Indians offered Catholics a unique opportunity to affirm their own modernist credentials by reaching "back" to bring Indians to civilization through evangelization. Philip Deloria suggests, "Native actions have all too often been interpreted through the lens of Euro-American expectations formed, in many cases, in ways that furthered the colonial project."[23] He likely was not thinking about U.S. Catholics as part of that colonial project in the early twentieth century. *Extension Magazine* shared the broader U.S. fascination with American Indians, but its assimilation project was a Catholic one, rooted in the Spanish colonial project centuries earlier, rather than an "American" one. In fact, Catholic missionaries often criticized "whites," meaning Protestant missionaries, for separating Indians from their culture, as well as their faith.[24]

As we might expect in this era, Indians were frequently described as savage or childlike, and, in either case, the better for being found and brought along by the hardworking, earnest priest. Genevieve Cooney offered a tale of Illinois (Illiniwek) Indians rescued from the Chippewas by the "White God," represented by Father Dalvez and his little log church. "Three years they had lived in peace and brotherhood," Cooney declared. However, we learned, American Indians could not stay peaceful for long. "Once more the savage longed for the sullen, sultry sound of the tom tom; for the din din of flying spears and war cries; for the wild hissing whirl of arrows. Once more the tribes looked forward to the dizzying war dance."[25] Nature, in the form of a flood, conspired with the savages to produce a perfect storm that left Ponwaka, the Illiniwek chief, in search of a sign from the heavens about where to lead his people. "Looking up to the murky sky, to the home of the Great Spirit, he sought an answer there, but none came. . . . Down the road, he saw the little church again, saw the tiny light and in his heart a ray of hope was born." This Easter morning, symbolically enough, Father Dalvez was lighting the candles in the church. Ponwaka greeted the priest, "Me pray to Christian God. He send light. . . . You white medicine man bring light. . . . Christian God he friend of Red man" and the Illiniweks were saved from the warring Chippewas. Where there had been the darkness and violence of the indigenous past, there was now the white, peaceful light of God. This Catholic modernity narrative came at the expense of any possible discourse on Indian modernity. These stories and, to some extent, the testimonials from the field represent the classic rescue narrative of (in this case) white Catholics priests saving their lesser neighbors, American Indians, presented here.[26]

Once American Indians were converted to the faith, they still needed to be guarded closely. Aloysius Vrebosch, a missionary with the Crow Indians in southern Montana, reported, "Our Catholics are not specially pious, since many of them are yet struggling against their old habits of paganism." The Crows were willing, however, to go great distances in subzero temperatures to get to Mass on Sundays. Vrebosch reported that the Crow tribe numbered 1,700— 700 Catholic, 100 Protestant, and 900 pagan—demonstrating the success of paganism and proselytizers against Catholic missionaries. Vrebosch faced competition from two government schools and a Baptist school on the reservation. As another missionary put it, "No missionary expects results from his work among the Indians or pagans without Catholic schools." With Catholic schools, Indians communities could be converted in one generation.[27] Vrebosch reported that most of the Crows in the government schools were Catholic, though he had no doubt "that the children educated at the Mission School make better Catholics, inhaling, as they do, every day, the spirit of Catholicity, and every day hearing Mass and saying regularly their morning and evening prayers." Still, the Extension Society's assistance was needed. Vrebosch requested "'Bible History' illustrated" for his mission, as "reading helps the Catholic instructed Indian." In spite of the apparent successes of the mission school, Crow children faced ridicule from their pagan parents and from whites for practicing Catholicism. "Many whites instigate the Indians to act thus," Vrebosch noted, but the children who attended the mission school remained Catholic, even if they

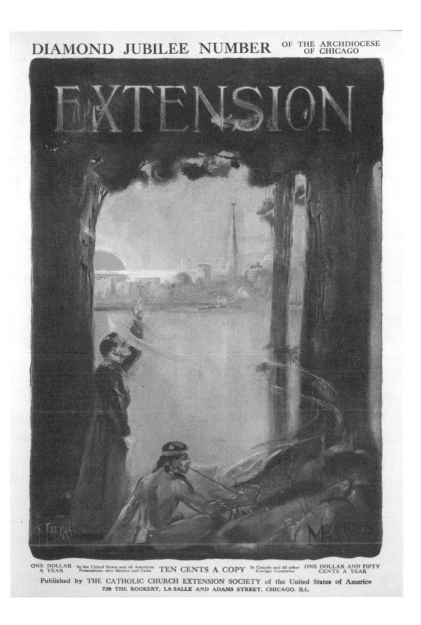

Fig. 4. The May 1908 cover of *Extension Magazine* illustrated the powerful
pull of the mission priest working to bring American Indians into the modern
American town across the lake and, more important, into the Catholic flock.

"go astray for a while." Recounting the history of the area, shaped by railroads, irrigation work, and finally the army, the missionary lamented the immorality that resulted and that "the Indians became greatly prejudiced against every white."[28] The society's work, then, was designed to counter the history of American expansion, which came at the expense of the Spanish Catholic and American Indian legacies in the region.[29]

The Knights of Columbus offered another intriguing take on Indians. A 1905 article in *The Columbiad* brought a report out of Ann Arbor, Michigan, likening Ojibwe Indians to the villagers of Oberammergau, Bavaria, who celebrated God's sparing them the bubonic plague by performing "The Passion of Jesus Christ" every ten years, beginning in 1634. Although the Ojibwes featured in the story were in Desberats, Ontario, their annual reenactment of Henry Wadsworth Longfellow's "Hiawatha," honoring the leader of the Iroquois Confederacy, was considered "An American Oberammergau." The comparison is an odd one, yet it confirms the fascination of Catholics, like others in the United States, with American Indians.[30]

Evangelization of American Indians allowed Catholics to take a heroic turn in the role of civilizing the earliest Americans by rescuing them from not just other hostile Natives but from Protestants as well. As Deloria suggests, "cultural expectations and social relations exist in dialogue with economic, political and legal structures."[31] Intercultural expectations are also shaped by those same factors. Joseph Crimont, the prefect apostolic of Alaska, described the work of proselytizers with the Inuit: "Some apostles of a certain Christian denomination were not slow to caution the natives in contact with them against Catholic influence." Crimont repeatedly described the Eskimos as hungry for Catholicism: "The Chief of the King Island Eskimos has entreatingly asked the missionary over and over again to come and live with his people in their sea-girded realm."[32] The mission parish at Mary's Igloo built their own schooner, named *The Immaculate*, to support the community's fishing and hunting needs. "Our idea," Crimont reported, "is to make

46

the natives self-supporting—a problem quite hard to solve since the whites destroyed the fish and game around Nome." Presumably "whites" was a reference to Protestant or other invaders of the sacred and isolated community. Crimont's account suggests Catholicism and culture enriching each other, much as Pope Benedict XVI described St. Kateri Tekakwitha at her canonization in 2012.[33]

Rare were the mission parishes that served more than one ethnic group, but Gisleen Haelterman, a missionary from Santa Cruz, New Mexico, reported on both American Indians and Mexicans in his mission: "The Mexican children mature much earlier than the others; they are sensible little men and women at an age when other children still attend school and think nothing of it." This seeming compliment may reflect the fact that Mexican children often labored with their parents in the fields or other workplaces. The government schools, Haelterman reported, posed a threat to American Indian children, as some teachers "are desirous of perverting the Indians," that is, separating them from their Catholic faith. Fortunately, Haelterman continued, "race suicide" (a euphemism for the use of birth control) is not common among the Indians, thus the stork is "an annual visitor, but the yearly visits of scarlet fever, diphtheria, etc., carry off so many children." Several Mexican women had married non-Catholics, but they still attended Mass and offered "their services whenever needed in cleaning or decorating the church." Haelterman bemoaned life in the territories: "If our pastors in the States would acquaint themselves with the actual conditions of the Catholic missions in America," as of course *Extension Magazine* did, Catholic leaders "would not hesitate to use their influence in arousing their parishioners to prompt action in behalf of the missions."[34] Haelterman understood what was at stake, and Kelley succeeded in raising funds for American Indian, Mexican, and black missions, in some cases with support from other notable Catholic leaders such as Mother Katharine Drexel.[35] This national project was led by Kelley, who, through *Extension Magazine*, had a broad audience invested in an American Catholic civilizing project, enhanced by the Spanish past in these Catholic borderlands.

## Evangelizing the South

The Spanish and French Catholic past in the South made the Extension Society's work in the region a natural recovery of the Catholic faith. By restoring Catholicism to blacks in the South, *Extension Magazine* readers participating in the national civilizing project in the early twentieth century. Priests and brothers funded by the society consistently reported on the inability of black missions to financially sustain a priest. There were some chapels, but as often as not, Mass was offered in something "more like a stable or a chicken-house than a house of the Most High." Even those missions that had chapels suffered from lack of vestments and century-old missals.[36] The Extension Society not only helped to build churches and schools but also provided Mass kits with chalices, liturgical garments, and texts for impoverished parishes. Smaller expenditures such as these provided opportunities for donors of smaller amounts to feel they were making a difference in the society's mission. In a 1909 editorial titled "Negro Missions," Kelley made clear the role of the Extension Society in mission efforts with blacks. "We do not believe in promiscuous giving," he reminded his readers. "It is the duty of a society, or of a bureau, to find where the greatest need is: only in that way will the medicine reach the afflicted part." Implicit in this was the understanding that funding for black missions could be channeled through the Extension Society.[37] The Catholic Board of Negro Missions, founded in 1907, was the central organizer of work with black Catholics, but the Extension Society was more than happy to collect funds on the board's behalf. The evangelization mission in the South had two components: converting and sustaining black and other Catholic populations, and combating anti-Catholicism in the region.[38]

Kelley and Extension Society priests in the South outlined the special case of the South to appeal to *Extension* readers. Rev. H. A. Spengler shared in great detail his time in Rodney, Mississippi, working with blacks. Spengler sprinkled in phonetic spellings of dialogue with "darkies" and shared superstitions common in the community.

Still, he knew his job was to remind Catholics of their charge in the South: "The people are very indifferent but perhaps they are not to blame, for a priest visits them only a few times a year." This recurring theme urged readers to provide funds to support more missions in remote areas of the country. Spengler lamented the fact that the mission at Rodney did not raise any funds itself and thus could not get a priest of its own. "The Rt. Rev. Bishop has determined the amount each mission should contribute but though this is small, it is never given at Rodney." As such, priests from the diocese rotated through the missionary rolls. "I almost rejoiced that it would not be my turn next time," Spengler wrote. "While the prospect of a visit to Rodney is not particularly exhilarating, the fact remains that there are souls to save there and they must be saved, at whatever cost in personal sacrifice."[39] Overall, his tone was one of pity rather than distaste—a poignant reminder to *Extension* readers that Catholics had urgent obligations in the South. In southeast Arkansas, Rev. John Albert, whose order was brought to Pine Bluff to work with blacks, noted that most of his Catholics were converts and were housed in a separate church that was "erected through Northern generosity to take care of the colored portion of the flock." The attached school was doing exceedingly well with both enrollments and conversion.[40] Such comments affirmed for readers that their contributions were already making a difference for black Catholics in the South.

In rare instances, writers other than priests chimed in about the importance of Catholic missions. Ralston J. Markoe of Minnesota wrote an article titled "Can We Save the Negroes of the South?" in which he detailed the "scientific" nature of his study: "The following observations are the result of a personal study on the ground, of existing conditions in the south, during two different visits, covering an aggregate period of over two years."[41] Markoe, a well-known attorney and the son of an Episcopal minister, had the reputation needed to make an impression on *Extension* readers. The notable poverty of blacks in the South presented an obvious funding challenge. Markoe proposed that Catholic orders expelled from France or the

Philippine Islands, who likely had funding from home orders, take on the black missions and set up industrial schools so as to become self-supporting as soon as possible. Rev. Spengler agreed with this assessment: "France, Portugal and even Italy, careless of their treasure, openly expel religious orders, or hamper them in their retired life. . . . Here they could find peaceful spots in healthy places, workshop God as the rule orders, save their souls and bring down abundant blessings upon the land."[42] Donations from *Extension* readers would sustain the missionaries until the industrial schools could provide for the missions. Markoe's vision was never quite achieved, but it indicated the clear need for Catholic missions in the South from both a scientific and a non-Catholic standpoint.

The distinction between blacks and Creoles, meaning blacks whose language and culture were marked by the French Catholic past, was frequently addressed by authors in *Extension Magazine*. Much as the Spanish Catholic past was embraced in the West and Southwest, the French and Spanish Catholic legacies in the South were noted in the better quality of black Catholics in the Louisiana region. As Rev. H. A. Spengler put it, "France and Spain are the father and mother" of these Catholics.[43] Markoe detailed the effects of slavery on the black family and explained the Spanish and French uses of the Creole language in marking the population in Louisiana. Markoe declared that stereotypes of blacks as dangerous and rude were mistaken and noted that the communities he visited were uniformly welcoming. He knew of "one efficient and competent remedy which can be applied to the existing evils of the negro race in this country. This remedy is the application to the lives of the negroes of the precepts of Jesus Christ as taught by the Catholic church." Markoe affirmed the distinction between blacks in Louisiana and those elsewhere in the South. "That this remedy would be effective is clearly demonstrated by the very superior character of the 'Creole negroes' before referred to, who were reared in the midst of Catholic influences and surroundings." The French and Spanish Catholic influence in Louisiana elevated Creoles above black converts. More importantly for *Extension Magazine* readers, the Catholic past in the region reinforced the natural place of U.S. Catholics and their mission there in the early twentieth century. These Catholic borderlands legitimated Catholic claims to the South as part of their natural recovery of the Spanish and French Catholic past.

Like American Indians in the West, blacks in the South were marginalized and damaged by the surrounding "white" communities. Rev. Albert noted the need for a Catholic hospital for colored people, as the local hospitals begrudgingly attended to blacks but "visiting relatives are treated discourteously and physicians of color are absolutely excluded." Catholics, according to the missionary, were more accepting of blacks than were surrounding Protestant communities. In Cameron Parish, Louisiana, the Baptist minister was "devilishly" perverting black Catholics. Rev. G. J. Buissink reported that the 1910 Rand-McNally pocket map of Louisiana listed Cameron Parish with a population of 4,288, of whom more than half were Catholic. A Catholic school and two Sisters would be the best protection against further poaching by Protestants in the area.[44]

The Extension Society's mission in the South was occasionally supported by Protestants. In Mansfield, Louisiana, for example, Protestants merchants and townspeople contributed three-quarters of the funding needed to build a Catholic church, with the Extension Society contributing the remaining funds.[45] Missionaries noted that Protestants regularly had segregated churches for blacks. Catholic missionaries, often from other parts of the country or outside the United States, were less committed to such segregation, but they found it necessary to build separate churches for blacks due to the expectations of surrounding communities. The poverty of black mission communities was frequently remarked upon.

Mansfield's support for a Catholic church, however, was exceptional. The Extension Society and other Catholic organizations were more often fighting anti-Catholic writing and activity in the South. Anti-Catholicism was openly tolerated in many areas of the South. A 1911 report in *Extension Magazine* described a pamphlet titled "The Shame of It!" circulated by the International Catholic Truth Society regarding the activities of Thomas Watson. Watson, a prominent

Georgia politician and publisher attacked the Catholic Church in the pages of *Jeffersonian Magazine* with articles such as "The Roman Catholic Hierarchy: Deadliest Menace to Our Liberties and Our Civilization" in August 1910. Rev. Lucian Johnston called on Protestant ministers to stand up to Watson's attacks, arguing that "the effect of such persecution and malice in the long run will be as detrimental to Protestantism and their common Christianity as to the struggling Catholic community in their midst."[46] It is unclear to what extent Protestant ministers accepted Johnston's charge.

In 1924, Kelley wrote a lengthy article on "How a Catholic Feels about It," referring to the Ku Klux Klan. The Second Klan, founded in 1915, promoted itself as a Protestant organization, but many Protestant writers and ministers publicly distanced themselves from the Klan. Kelley also separated Klansmen from Protestants. "Two thirds of the anti-Catholic agitators of the day rarely go near a Protestant church," he wrote. While Kelley took issue with much of the work of Protestant proselytizers, he seemed to recognize they were not supporting the Klan—at least not openly. To "sincere" Protestants, he concluded, the Klan "is the outbreak of a cancer diagnosed long ago." Kelley gave Protestants the benefit of the doubt, perhaps to flush out potential allies against anti-Catholicism in the South.

Catholics, Kelley believed, actually benefited from the attention brought by the Klan. Rather than scaring off Catholics, Kelley reported, the "Klan has strengthened the same Church in the heart of its people, to the surprise and gladness of Catholic leaders. I do not know of a single Catholic who has deserted his Church because of the Klan; but I know a lot who came back because of the hooded brothers of the lash and the pitch-pot." Kelley wanted to encourage Catholics to speak out against the Klan and, if possible, discourage the attacks by Klansmen on all things Catholic in the United States. "The Klan has put the name of the Catholic Church into the mouths of millions," he wrote. "To Catholics, it is a blessing disguised in a night-shirt." Kelley embraced the despised status granted by Klan attention. He resisted the presumption that Catholics would not want to be associated with blacks and Jews, other common targets of the Klan. "The one who belongs to that universal brotherhood—the Catholic Church—cannot very well object to being associated with 'just Niggers and Sheenies' or he simply would not belong to it at all." Whatever ire Kelley had for non-Catholics in his other projects was suppressed in the face of the bigotry of the Klan.

Kelley's biggest concern, however, was that the Catholic Church in the United States was not fighting back against the Klan and other anti-Catholics. "The Catholic Church in America is not well organized on the propaganda side. She has been quite content—and for that I criticize her—to take care of her own and let outsiders take care of themselves." Kelley saw the need for a more public Catholic agenda, but the church was "too busy assimilating the floods that come over the seas to advertise. She writes few books here, for she is busy laying many bricks." Describing his own contribution to the Catholic propaganda project, Kelley continued, "But she has within her in America the elements of a great and effective missionary body. She has a mighty story to tell of achievements in education." Certainly this was one of the Extension Society's strengths, having built hundreds of schools. "She had enemies who tell better than her sons the tale of her working for civilization." Kelley was determined to tell this story—the Catholic Church's contributions to civilization in the United States. This Catholic history had its roots in the Spanish and French civilizing mission, but these were enhanced by U.S. Catholic contributions in the early twentieth century, led by Kelley.[47]

### Extension Society Work with Mexicans

By mid to late 1913, reports about Mexican immigrants appeared regularly in *Extension Magazine*. The union of former Spanish subjects with former Spanish territories sealed the Catholic claim on an American Catholic borderlands. This territory and its people were historically Catholic, so the society's work there was more than justified. The fact that Mexican refugees were fleeing an anticlerical revolution furthered this commitment. American Catholics assisted in the broader civilizing project with Mexicans, but they did so through a distinctively Catholic mission.

The August 1913 issue of *Extension Magazine* offered brief reports from Galveston and Brownsville on the spiritual needs of Mexicans who had fled the Mexican Revolution. E. de Anta, an Oblate missionary in Galveston, remarked, "How sad is their lot in this country! They crossed the Rio Grande in search of comfort, but . . . they have found . . . nothing but labor and sufferings." De Anta noted the material reality of Mexicans, laboring in Texas and beyond, before moving on to the more base experience of Mexican immigrants: "They came, hopeful of finding respect and love, but there is no love—only contempt and hatred. 'Greasers' they are called, and looked down upon and considered pariahs." De Anta captured more than a century of tensions between Anglos and Mexicans in Texas. The Oblate missionaries, committed to working with the poorest of the poor, took a particular interest in Mexican immigrants in Texas.[48]

In the same issue, the vice president of the Extension Society, Emmanuel Ledvina, offered a field report on one of the society's motor chapels near Brownsville. "We of the United States have a grave duty toward these poor Mexican people. Their souls will be on our consciences if we let them fall prey to the systematic efforts of the proselytizer," he wrote, referring to Protestant missionaries in the area. Ledvina knew this was cause for alarm, especially among Catholic populations. "I would like to tell the Catholic people of our land what a great charge we have on our hands right now within the borders of our own country," he wrote, urging concern at home, not across the border or the ocean. "We took the State of Texas from the Mexicans," he wrote, hinting at the Catholic past of the region, "and now every effort is being put forth by the Protestants of the United States to rob them of their Religion, and we Catholics are quietly and indifferently allowing proselytizers to steal these children from before our very eyes."[49] It is unclear whether "these children" were indeed young people, or Mexicans as a community, but the message was clear: these are *our* Catholics, who are being perverted by proselytizers. Ledvina's desperate plea was near the beginning of a wave of concern on the part of American Catholics for the souls of their Mexican brethren. An appeal in September 1913 recognized that, at least in some areas, Mexican Catholics were the future of the church. "Two thousand Mexicans are living in a town in Arizona with a small number of American Catholics. Fine prospects for the future but a chapel must be built."[50] The Extension Society's persistence was rewarded by the constant flow of funds to support such appeals.

The following month, as anticipation grew for the Second American Missionary Congress, an article previewed the gathering in Boston. "At this meeting also, the greetings of the Hierarchy of Mexico will be presented by the Most Rev. Archbishop Gillow, of Oaxaca, who will speak, in particular, on the Mexican Immigration Problem in our own country."[51] Ultimately, the panel on immigration did not include a representative from Mexico, though the American bishops did comment on Mexican immigrants in a number of sessions at the congress.

Bishop Peter Muldoon of Rockford, Illinois, wove together an American Catholic identity and a concern for immigrants in his opening remarks on the immigration panel at the congress: "[Immigration is] a most important subject, whether we consider it as American citizens, interested in the growth and permanent welfare of our country, or as Catholics who love their Church and are happy only when her tents are extended, and who believe that it is their bounden duty to welcome the foreigner of every nationality."[52] With this, Muldoon affirmed the quintessentially American nature of the Catholic missionary project: it was committed to expanding and strengthening both the United States and the health of the American Catholic Church. Muldoon warned, with an emphasis on the Catholic borderlands, "The action of the Protestant sects in the South and West towards the Mexicans, who are coming to our country in no inconsiderable numbers . . . should make us very apprehensive of the future of the faith of many Mexicans." Echoing reports from priests in the field, Muldoon noted the substantial funds Protestant denominations were spending on churches, schools, and social work

Fig. 5. The rear of the motor chapel opened to form an altar, elevated enough for missionary parishioners to see the priest leading Mass. Motor chapels allowed priests to cover large mission fields in areas of the South and West. Salado, Texas, 1913.

Fig. 6. Motor chapel, Belto's Mine, Texas, n.d.

"to attract the Mexican laborer and his children."[53] These native Catholics were being stripped of their Catholic faith by the devilish proselytizers. The bishop proposed the formation of a Catholic Immigration Bureau to centralize Catholic efforts and prevent the loss of immigrant souls to the lures of the proselytizers and socialists recruiting at every turn. Saving the fictional Mexican child, Juanita, however, was very different from serving Mexican immigrant families in the flesh.

Kelley and Ledvina romanticized Mexicans in the pages of *Extension Magazine*, but the missionaries who dealt with Mexicans on a daily basis were less charmed by the experience. Mexicans, particularly those in Texas, challenged Extension Society missionaries. One 1915 report read, "The more I have to deal with these Texan Mexicans the more I doubt their former practices," casting aspersions on their native Mexican exercise of Catholicism. "Brought up in the States bordering either side of the Rio Grande, they are far less religiously inclined than those I knew for years farther south in the interior of Mexico."[54] One wonders if the subtext here is that proximity to Protestantism is the problem or if it is the Mexicans themselves. European Catholics, even those from southern and eastern Europe, were models of the faith compared to Mexican Catholics. Slavs were described as faithful and devout in one 1915 report.[55] A few months later, Mexican Catholics were presented in a very different light. "The ignorance of these poor Mexicans is appalling. Pictures of saints seem to mean religion for them," M. A. Dombrowski wrote, referring to the devotional character of Mexican Catholic practice. Echoing decades-old complaints about many European Catholic immigrants, he continued, "a priest is lucky if he finds [Mexicans] acquainted with the Apostles' Creed, the Ten Commandments of God and the precepts of the Church."[56] Mexicans in Texas, whether they had been present for generations or were recent immigrants fleeing the Revolution, were cast in a questionable light. At the edges of the American empire, Catholic borderlands were even more important to sustaining not just the faith but a broader civilizing influence.

Mexicans were frequently underappreciated as Catholics, and they did not compare well to European American Catholics. A 1919 guest "chat" by Arthur Drossaerts, bishop of San Antonio, made explicit the differences between Mexican and European immigrant Catholics. Drossaerts described Belgians as "all good Catholics" with large families, whereas Mexicans were described as ignorant and indifferent to the faith. "Indeed, the priests working among [Mexicans] need almost superhuman courage and a limitless, angelic patience," the bishop said.[57] Photos of Euro-American missions generally showed neat, little chapels or schools built with Extension Society funds, while those of Mexican missions almost always focused on the people, in their Sunday best, illustrating how civilized they had become with proper attention from Extension-funded missionaries. On occasion, they were in front of the Extension-funded altar, church, or school.[58] Ultimately, Drossaerts declared, the "Mexican problem" is "a *national* problem; the problem of our American Catholic people, and, as such, one that should appeal especially to the Extension Society."[59] He reminded urban Catholics in the Northeast and Midwest that their legacy was not just in their national parishes but in Catholic borderlands within the American empire where Catholicism was being threatened. Kelley's choice of Drossaerts for the guest chat denotes the emphasis the Extension Society had placed on supporting Mexican Catholics in the United States. The Diocese of San Antonio consistently received substantial funds from the society, confirming Kelley's assessment that need there was great—especially for the Mexicans.

In their appeals, priests who were supported by the Extension Society often noted the elaborate, modern churches, schools, and services available from Protestant proselytizers in their areas. They emphasized Protestants' support of their missionaries, challenging Catholics to contribute to the upkeep of their own home missions. The pressure to keep Protestants at bay fed pleas to *Extension Magazine* readers, as illustrated in the case of Clifton, Arizona. Rev. Emile Barrat reported, "My Bishop has sent me here experimentally to see whether it is possible for a priest to remain and live, and

Fig. 7. A procession of Mexican Catholics in Benavides, Texas, in 1915, likely celebrating a saint's day.

Fig. 8. St. Patrick's Chapel, Bynum, Montana. A typical photo of an Extension-funded church in a white parish. Missionary priests in white communities took photos of Extension Society–funded churches and altars to appear in *Extension Magazine*.

Fig. 9. Joseph and Theodore, altar boys. Mary's Igloo, Alaska, 1914.

so keep the people from falling away from the Faith."[60] Barrat outlined his costs and his income, which made clear the need for additional funds. He warned *Extension* readers that if he were to leave,
the Protestants would make sure that Mexicans were lost to the
church. "The Protestant minister has his residence about 100 yards
away from mine. . . . He is a Mexican, and should I go away would

Fig. 10. Extension priest with music class, Pine Bluff, Arkansas, 1917. Priests working with communities of color often sent photos of their parishioners in front of the buildings funded by the Extension Society in order to show *Extension Magazine* readers the civilizing effect of their donations.

no doubt carry on a successful campaign of proselytizing among my poor, uneducated people." The call for funds to compete with Protestants was constant. It was not often that the Protestant minister lived near the Catholic priest, and even more rare that the minister was Mexican. Surely this made the urgency even greater for *Extension* readers. Barrat continued, noting his understanding of the principle of the Extension Society, that "later on, if I have charge of a larger parish I will point out what the Society has done for this mission." Barrat noted the poverty of the Mexican miners and that even his best families were unreliable in attendance, unfamiliar with Mass Intentions, and likely to leave for a "more prosperous place" after a short stint mining in Clifton.[61] Barrat, an immigrant from France, was likely unfamiliar with the labor migration patterns Mexicans had followed for decades. Likewise, he seemed unaware that Mexicans generally faced greater prejudice in border states and would have good reason to continue the journey north. Mexicans discovered both better wages and less prejudice further from the border.[62]

Figs. 11 and 12. Rev. Emile Barrat of Metcalf (Clifton-Morenci), Arizona, mapped the location of his crumbling residence on the edge of town in reference to the Catholic church and the well-maintained home of the Protestant minister in his appeal to *Extension Magazine* readers. March 1908.

A. Priest's palace, B. Business trail, C. Catholic church, D. Minister's house, E. Room of priest, F. Catholic church, G. Company store, H. Minister's residence

Mexicans were portrayed by Extension missionaries in Texas as feckless in the face of proselytizing by Protestant missionaries. The Extension Society was fairly aggressive in its attacks on Protestant missionaries poaching "our Catholics" and doing a poor job of keeping former Catholics in the Christian fold. In Texas, a Passionist missionary wrote that if he "had the zealous support that the Protestant proselytizers receive from their missionary societies in the North, many difficult phases of Catholic life would be solved. In fact we could help establish real Catholic life in a real Catholic community."[63] Where the Protestants succeeded in "perverting" Mexicans, such as in Banquete, Texas, Extension Society priests noted the ultimate failure of the proselytizers' work. Rev. Isidore Dwyer wrote in 1915 that American Bible Society members "cannot make good Protestants out of Mexicans; they can transform them into indifferent Christians."[64] Dwyer condemned Mexicans who had left the church as unworthy: "By claiming the name Catholic they brought much more dishonor than they ever did credit to the Church . . . anything they may become hereafter, in the way of members of some sect . . . will hardly be a step down from their former condition of worthlessness."[65] Dwyer's contempt for Mexicans was unusual. Most Extension Society priests believed that Mexicans could be saved, particularly as they were at least nominally Catholic. "Being as he is, easily led to good or evil by his surroundings," Dwyer wrote, "the Mexican in the United States finds himself exposed to every influence calculated to pervert his mind, estrange him from all religion, and unleash his every vicious inclination."[66] Dwyer portrayed Mexicans as readily susceptible to influences, good or bad, thereby leaving room for *Extension Magazine* readers to swoop in and provide good influences to save the Mexicans in Texas. This responsibility to Catholics in the borderlands helped strengthen an American Catholic ethos built on sustaining the faith in every corner of the American empire.

This was in stark contrast to Ledvina, who also saw Mexicans being lured away by proselytizers but viewed the circumstances quite differently. "Their hearts are not easily won by the gift-offering proselytizers," he wrote, "but their poverty and their great pride in their children . . . drives them to secure like advantages for their own offspring, blindly accepting inducements at the sacrifice of their Faith."[67] Ultimately, Dwyer and others painted a fairly consistent picture of Mexicans in the Southwest: without the intervention of American Catholics, Mexicans were at risk of being lost to the church. This situation allowed U.S. Catholics the opportunity to affirm their American identity through claiming and saving the Mexican immigrant. The Extension Society's attention to the Southwest allowed for an even stronger case to be made for an American Catholic borderlands that simultaneously affirmed both the right to evangelize the Southwest and the American identity of Catholics in the Northeast and Midwest. Their investment in the civilizing project made them consummate Americans.

The early narratives of the Spanish past were very much like "American" narratives, though Spain was presented as hero, not villain.[68] As the Extension Society found its audience and refined its point of view, its "special work" gave it an edge to claim both an American and a Catholic identity. Its discourse glorified the Catholic history of the American continent and cast Protestants as the dastardly foes corrupting the Catholic purity, or pagan simplicity, of Mexican immigrants. The Extension Society worked to demonstrate the need for its presence, without denigrating the needy. The ultimate mission of *Extension Magazine* was to generate donations for mission projects. As editor, Kelley masterfully balanced the dramatic imagery of Catholic decline with the enduring hope that a few dollars in each of these missions could save the at-risk souls in the far reaches of the United States.[69]

### Regaining Catholic Title to the West

The Extension Society's work in the Southwest transcended many of the boundaries that existed between the United States and Mexico, and Kelley created a new national narrative, a Catholic national narrative, with trans-imperial and transhistorical grounding and relevance. "Spain's imprint on national imaginations has been resilient," notes John Nieto-Phillips, and Kelley used that imprint to create "new historical memories" for U.S. Catholics. Through *Extension Magazine*, Kelley mapped Catholicism into the cultural geography of the U.S. Southwest, a Catholic borderlands.[70] A 1907 article titled "Some Notable Catholic Landmarks" informed readers of the Catholic past on the continent, in the form of Spanish missions, at risk for destruction in the early twentieth century. "Neglect has lost to America many of her most precious historical relics, the Catholic missions, which marked, like milestones, the progress of the pioneers in every quarter of the continent," wrote Thomas O'Shaughnessy, a *Chicago Daily News* artist. He warned of further neglect and reminded readers that Catholics had arrived first: "To the indifference of the present generation may be charged the destruction of two of the first fourteen churches built in America, San Yldefonso and Santa Clara, which were standing . . . when the first protestant colonist set foot upon this hemisphere."[71] O'Shaughnessy was driven both by a desire to preserve the missions and by the overwhelming desire for Americans to acknowledge "the sublime story of the Catholic parentage of America" buried in the ruins of Spanish missions, which "were all standing in 1617, three years before the first non-Catholic had set foot on America."[72] Of course, by "non-Catholic" he meant Protestant, as there had been non-Catholics in the hemisphere for centuries before the Spanish arrived. Still, O'Shaughnessy clearly staked his claim for an American Catholicism, "indigenous" to the continent, or at least antedating the Protestant presence. More importantly, it was the responsibility of U.S. Catholics to care for "our" relics, as Protestants were not invested in preserving this history.

The legacy of the Black Legend in the American historical imagination leaves little doubt why American Protestants had little interest in invoking this past.[73] The civilized past of the Spanish friars, however, gave American Catholics a deed to this territory and this work. A 1922 article by a California missionary made explicit the link between the Spanish past and Kelley's contemporary project. "To associate the work of the Extension Society with this land of fantasy would seem incongruous, for it is a far cry from the modern deluge of Eastern Catholic tourists and home-seekers to the days of Father Junípero Serra and his first Extension Society among the Indians. And yet his modern Chicago successor," the missionary wrote, referring to Kelley, "has found arid spots in this land of milk and honey upon which to rain its gifts, and this appeal is voiced that a forgotten corner of the Golden State may not become spiritually what it is materially, a desert waste."[74] The preservation of these Catholic borderlands and their relics was critical to marking the U.S. Catholic inheritance in the U.S. West.

*Extension Magazine* brought the Spanish Catholic past of Mexico into conversation with the U.S. Catholic present in the early twentieth century, with an eye toward the Spanish and Roman Catholic empires, which had global reach and impact. Advocates of *hispanismo* argue that the loss, in 1898, of the last Spanish territories in the Western Hemisphere strengthened the *spiritual* dimension of the Spanish presence—the shared language, history, culture, customs, and religion—especially in contrast to and solidarity against the new empire on the block, the United States.[75] Kelley invoked that spiritual connection to Spain to challenge the imperial and national narratives operating in the United States regarding the Southwest. Historiography and nation-building are closely tied, Schmidt-Nowara notes in reference to Spain.[76] The same applies to U.S. historiography and nation-building. The historiography of Prescott's era was tied to Manifest Destiny, with Spain's decline juxtaposed against the rise of the United States. In the era of the Monroe Doctrine, as the United States was pursuing means and methods of expansion across the continent, Prescott documented the failings of Spain, which had dominated the Western Hemisphere for the previous three centuries. Although many of these visions were designed to embrace the California missions and the heroics of Spanish friars, they rarely embraced Catholicism. Kelley produced a strictly Catholic inheritance for *Extension Magazine* readers, as always, designed to raise funds for U.S. Catholic missions.

The natural Spanish Catholic past was also gauged in the peoples of the Southwest presented in *Extension Magazine*. Those present-day

Catholics who could demonstrate Spanish ancestry were admired and held up as examples for Mexicans. Brother Lawrence reported from Louisiana that his mission was divided into three groups. "The first and smallest division is composed of descendants of the original Spanish colonists, who have preserved the purity of their blood and their racial integrity," he began, echoing centuries of racial hierarchies enforced in New Spain.[77] "Those of mixed Spanish and Indian blood constitute the second and largest division; and the last division and by far the most miserable, consist of those of pure Indian blood, descendants of the aboriginal inhabitants."[78] Brother Lawrence's description could have been written in 1716 rather than 1916. The "Americans," as Lawrence called the Protestants, referred to all of these groups "contemptuously" as Mexicans, "though neither they nor any ancestor of theirs ever saw Mexico. They are accorded less social and civil recognition than negroes."[79] Lawrence dramatically simplified a diverse and complex social system in an area that had seen more imperial hosts than most parts of the present-day United States. The hierarchy, however, was clear: Mexicans—at least in Lawrence's eyes—were at the bottom. Similar observations of the Spanish legacy were more often reflected in New Mexico, where Rev. Estvelt reported on the land struggles of the Spanish dons in Union County in 1917. These Spaniards, likewise, were seen as noble, pious, and reserved—meaning not Mexican. They were also an anachronism, as much of the land transfer Estvelt described had happened in the previous century. Estvelt likened them to Longfellow's Acadians, "Honest, upright, Godfearing, they think no evil, because their hearts are pure." Forty Protestant ministers had descended upon Union County in the previous two decades, Estvelt reported, putting the Spanish Americans' faith at risk.[80]

Isidore Dwyer, writing of Bluntzer, near Corpus Christi, Texas, reported the similar Spanish past and, more notably, the efforts of the early colonial families to stem the tide from the unnamed North: "The pioneer settlers of this neighborhood were sturdy Catholics, who were brought over by Spain in the early part of the last century, as an English-speaking element to hold the territory against the anti-Spanish settlers from the North, who were trenching on Spanish domains, and working to wrest territory from Spain."[81] No doubt they were likewise wresting souls from the Catholic Church. The Extension Society's "special work," then, was not unlike that of these pioneer settlers—holding off the Protestant proselytizers who were trying to poach Catholics from along the contested religious borders at the edges of civilization, the borderlands of American empire. All of these accounts echo Spanish missionary reports written centuries earlier. The Mexican presence, even in earlier American eras, seemingly evaporated.

The enduring influence of the early, hardy Spanish families on subsequent Mexican immigrant settlers was significant, according to Dwyer. He described generations of Mexican families who "were born, have lived and died in the service of the same families of Catholic ranchers." The patronage labor system common in Texas at the time allowed for such sedentary lives. Dwyer continued, the "effects of such Catholic influence surrounding them, the sympathy shown them, were evidenced in the fervor with which they attended services, some of them driving six miles each night for the privilege."[82] As was seen in Clifton, Arizona, Mexicans at this time were perceived as not inclined to attend Mass regularly. However, when provided with the Spanish example of religious practice, Mexicans could learn to be obedient Catholics. These Tejanos, settled in to the Spanish patronage system, were protected from proselytizers. The Arizona miners, on the other hand, had little protection for their jobs or their souls, both of which needed reinforcements from *Extension* readers. In either case, the message was clear: fund the missions to save the Mexicans in these Catholic borderlands.

*Extension Magazine* provided important historical pieces for readers, further girding the Catholic foundations on the continent. O'Shaughnessy drew extensively on the work of Charles Lummis—a non-Catholic, he noted for good measure—who was doing justice to the heroic deeds of Spanish missionaries. Lummis, a journalist, photographer, and adventurer, was his era's "most active exponent of Southwest culture." He wrote extensively of his travels in the West for assorted newspapers, sharing his views of the people, the natural scenery, and the Spanish missions with those still anchored in the East. Lummis was not always highly regarded, but his knowledge of the Southwest was well established.[83] O'Shaughnessy's use of this "authority" on the American Southwest bolstered *Extension Magazine*'s claim to an inherently American Catholic story.

The taming of the Indians who spilled "the blood of martyred priests" was intimately tied to American Catholic history. These churches, O'Shaughnessy wrote, "had been built and the . . . Indians won to civilization and to the Church not without sacrifice." In the process, he reminded *Extension* readers, "forty priests had been put to death by the Indians in the pueblos." However, once the Indians had been claimed for Christianity, they guarded the missions zealously.[84] There was little history, as told by *Extension Magazine* chroniclers, between these Spanish colonial stories and the present-day Mexicans. Perhaps Ledvina described it best: "One can imagine what inspired the early missionaries who labored so perseveringly among the aborigines of this land. . . . The childlike simplicity of the people and the characteristic devotion of these descendants of the Aztec Indians of Mexico disclose the inspiration of the early *padres* who penetrated the wilds of Mexico and of the Rio Grande valley, and along the Pacific coast in California, to bring them the glad tidings of the Christian Faith." Ledvina reduced hundreds of distinct indigenous cultures and histories to a singular Mesoamerican population. At times it is unclear if he was speaking historically or about the Mexicans he encountered in Texas a few weeks earlier. The same themes resound, however: the heroic Catholic missionaries sacrificed to bring the Indians and Mexicans along in the faith. Ledvina managed to connect the American historical narrative of devotion to God and taming the wild landscape to the Spanish Catholic mission centuries earlier. "Conditions in Texas," he wrote, "emphasize strongly the necessity of erecting and maintaining Catholic schools; and that, too, without delay. The Protestants are cunningly concentrating their whole efforts in establishing schools." There was hope, however, and the Extension Society could deliver it: "If we Catholics would erect Catholic schools, though only humble buildings, and supply Catholic teachers, the Mexicans would prefer to come to the Catholic schools."[85] Without a doubt, the future of Mexican immigrants rested solidly in the hands of Catholic missionaries, dependent entirely on the goodwill of U.S. Catholics and the hard work of Extension Society priests and missionaries. Funding the Extension Society, then, was the way to save Mexican immigrants *and* the West. This important missionary work with communities of color throughout the South and West affirmed U.S. Catholic identity by giving them a place and a voice in a broader American discourse focused on curbing the wild and uncivilized corners of the nation. These Catholic borderlands could be sustained by the good intentions of American Catholics.

Extension Society support for missions in the South and West invited U.S. Catholics to engage in broader American projects to lift up the ragged edges of the nation. In the Southwest and in work with Mexicans, the Spanish colonial past was entangled with the U.S. imperialist present in the work of U.S. Catholics. As the Extension Society grew in power and geographic reach, it increasingly encountered nominally Catholic populations. The next chapter outlines a framework that negotiated a Spanish colonial past, which remained present through Catholicism, and the U.S. imperial present, including Protestant missionaries, in the Philippines, Puerto Rico, and Mexico. This Protestant activity provoked U.S. Catholics to act, but they were enabled by an expanding vision of Catholic borderlands. The Catholic mission mimicked the Spanish past but was enabled by the "grace" of the American empire.

# 2

## The Devil Is Having a Great Time

*The U.S. Catholic Civilizing Mission in Puerto Rico,*
*the Philippines, and Mexico*

In a 1909 report, Francis Kelley warned *Extension Magazine* readers that Catholic souls were being lost in Puerto Rico. Protestant missionaries, he wrote, were using deceptive means to lure Puerto Rican Catholics away from the church. The proselytizers "said that this new religion was American; that all Americans belonged to it; that this religion meant progress and all that went with it." According to Kelley, they used strategies such as "putting up statues and altars," which Protestants in the United States considered idolatrous. These statues and altars, of course, mimicked traditional Catholic paraphernalia, which was often under attack by Protestants on the mainland. Kelley claimed the proselytizers succeeded by associating the new, Protestant faiths with wealth, while "Catholicity meant Poverty." "The Devil," Kelley claimed, "is having a great time in Porto Rico."[1] Kelley, through *Extension Magazine*, sought to reverse the formula, born in the Reformation era, that associated Protestantism with progress and Catholicism with backwardness. This divide was exacerbated by British and Spanish colonial competition in the era of exploration and, during and after the Spanish-American War, by tensions between the United States and Spain.

Colonial annexation raised anxiety for Americans who believed the United States was foundationally distinct from European powers; the republican principles that guided the United States did not include expansion beyond the continent. In contrast, colonialists argued that it was necessary for responsible nations to expand their reach to less fortunate peoples of the world. "Many people," James LeRoy wrote in *Atlantic Monthly* in 1902, "find in our occupation of the Philippine Islands the threat of a radical change in American character and ideals." LeRoy, however, could not imagine "how American character and social ideas can thus be radically altered."[2] LeRoy, an 1896 graduate of the University of Michigan, accompanied William Howard Taft on two visits to the Philippines and was Taft's personal secretary when Taft was secretary of war. In his extensive writings, LeRoy portrayed the Philippines as "a spiritual colony of Spain." He lamented the lingering pre-Spanish structures that interfered with the successful implementation of Taft Commission recommendations designed to modernize and restructure the government and economy of the Philippine Islands. However, he consistently framed Spanish missionary work as a factor in beginning the process of civilizing Filipinos. Whereas the Spanish had failed militarily and economically, they had succeeded in converting tens of thousands of pagans to Christianity.[3]

The Philippine Islands, as they were referred to at the time, were an archipelago, parts of which had been colonized by the Spaniards, while the southern part was considered "untouched" by Christianity and civilization. Perhaps it was his time spent in the Philippine Islands that convinced LeRoy of the progress made by Spanish missionaries. "Spain . . . did accomplish in the Philippine Islands . . . what no other European nation has ever done in the Orient, and did accomplish it without crushing the people under her heel." The conversion en masse of large segments of the Philippine Islanders to Christianity was accomplishment enough, in LeRoy's eyes. The "semi-feudal" social institutions and "half-developed languages" that lingered were issues for American occupiers to solve. American Protestants went abroad in significant numbers to support the Americanization project in the Philippine Islands.[4]

Inter-imperial cooperation between the United States and Britain provided important justification for colonial expansion: it gave such expansion the weight of "the logic of history," in the words of Senator Albert Beveridge. Paul Kramer demonstrates that the racial thinking which linked British and U.S. imperialisms at the beginning of the twentieth century had implications for both the rhetoric at home and actions abroad. This normalization of overseas expansion provided the racial and philosophical framework for the strengthening of U.S. global power and reach in the early twentieth century. The mass immigration of foreign bodies to the United States and the expansion beyond the continent revealed tensions between U.S. confidence abroad and parochialism at home.[5]

During and after the Spanish-American War, the discourse of Spanish failure in contrast to Anglo-American triumph strengthened. Echoes of this narrative were seen in the religious tensions at home, which marked American Catholics as foreigners and their loyalty to the United States as suspect. Kelley united the seemingly divergent U.S. and Spanish empires in his own imperial expansion, layering a U.S. Catholic missionary practice on top of the Spanish missionary work centuries earlier. The Spanish civilizing mission was reinforced and reaffirmed by American Catholics in Puerto Rico and the Philippines in the early twentieth century, creating an overseas Catholic borderlands. These Catholic borderlands used the expanding United States to strengthen the Catholic legacy left by the Spanish missionaries in the Caribbean and the Pacific. This American Catholic claim to new U.S. territories also strengthened Catholics' claim to being fully American.

By its fourth volume, in 1910, *Extension Magazine* trailed only *Columbiad* (the Knights of Columbus magazine) in circulation among Catholic monthlies.[6] In the previous chapter we examined the rhetoric and imagery of conversion and the civilizing mission presented in *Extension* in the United States. This chapter considers work beyond the continental United States. The Extension Society was negotiating a far more complex set of narratives as it increasingly turned its focus to the "Special Work of the Society," referring to work with former Spanish subjects.[7] Catholic borderlands, in the shadow of American empire, extended beyond the continental United States. There are multiple, at times conflicting, narratives presented in *Extension Magazine* about colonial Spanish Catholicism. Much of this was fed through Mexico, as was the Spanish empire, but the Philippine Islands, Puerto Rico, and Latin America more broadly made appearances as well. The discourse on former Spanish territories moved beyond a simple racial or imperial formula of backward versus modern. "It was not simply that difference made empire possible," Kramer notes. "Empire remade difference in the process."[8] American Catholics were remade by U.S. imperial expansion: as part of the American empire, they had a new role to play in the transformation of the Philippines and Puerto Rico. Former Spanish subjects now under the official or unofficial influence of the United States lived on the cusp between the Spanish past and the American future, as well as the Catholic past and the Protestant future. The Extension Society's mission had now expanded beyond the borders of the United States and into a more explicit battle against Protestant poachers. Protestant missionaries, as William Appleman Williams and others have noted, have "tended to operate on an assumption quite similar to the frontier thesis."[9] However, Williams and others overlooked the role of Catholic missionaries in the expanding American empire. As the United States continued to covet former Spanish territories, the Extension Society's work was not just about saving souls; it was also about preserving the legacy of those Spanish friars and all of their sacrifice civilizing the Philippine Islands and its people. Under Spanish rule, church and state were deeply connected, providing a Catholic education for Filipinos and Puerto Ricans. As Kelley portrayed it, the American-led schools, populated by Protestant teachers, threatened to deny children of their Catholic faith. It was incumbent upon *Extension Magazine* to take the story far and wide to Catholics across the United States: Catholic missioners were needed in areas of U.S. expansion to counter the U.S. imperial mission with its promise of wealth and success through conversion to the American, and thus Protestant, way. American Catholics had the opportunity—nay, the obligation—to sustain Catholic borderlands in U.S. territories abroad. This vital work affirmed their Americanness by scripting their role in American empire and their prior claim to Puerto Rico, Latin America, and the Philippine Islands for the Roman cause.

Kelley's mission in U.S. territories was to undermine the Protestant Americanization of Catholic peoples. This international work on behalf of the U.S. Catholic Church also enhanced the process of Americanizing U.S. Catholics by creating an explicit role for them in the global U.S. imperial project. There are extensive reports from the Philippines, in particular, that stake out the U.S. Catholic mission. The American imperial project continued to envelop former Spanish territories, making Kelley's mission of saving Catholics souls that much more important. In order to honor the Spanish civilizing mission of centuries past, Kelley had to protect Puerto Ricans, Filipinos, and especially Mexicans from proselytizers who were threatening to separate unsuspecting Catholics from their faith. Wherever the U.S. expansionist project went, Kelley followed to subvert the Protestant mission with his Catholic one.

### The Latin American Mission

Although the Extension Society was the Catholic home mission society of the United States, Kelley found ways to extend his work beyond the continental United States. Theodore Roosevelt, in his 1901 State of the Union address, suggested that the civilizing process was a prerequisite for peace, particularly in Asia.[10] Missionaries, as John Fairbank and William Appleman Williams declared, had already undertaken that task on behalf of American empire. Yet missionary contributions were rarely acknowledged. If the missionary in general was invisible in U.S. history, the *Catholic* missionary was even further from the center of the American narrative.

The Extension Society was conscious of casting its missionary work and those it served differently from Protestant proselytizers. A 1916 *Extension Magazine* editorial lamented the Panama Conference, a project of Evangelical missionaries who gathered to talk about mission work in Latin America. The conference was a response to the 1910 World Missionary Conference in Edinburgh, Scotland, which declared Latin America off limits for evangelical missionaries, as it had already been Christianized by the Spanish and Portuguese. The Panama Conference, Kelley suggested, would produce tensions between the United States and Latin America. "Latin American sentiment is against us," he wrote. "These suspicions are fed by the type of missionaries American religious sects send to Latin America; and even by the fact that so many of us consider Latin America a missionary field at all." Kelley continued with an air of expertise, "The Latin is proud. He doesn't care to be classed with darkest Africa, and he objects to being paraded as a 'Christless' individual before his North-American brothers."[11] Kelley reported that his fears were confirmed after the meeting. Americans, he wrote, "cannot expect to win the friendship of a people whose religion we abuse."[12] The Extension Society swiftly adopted the role of defending the civilized nature of the former Spanish territories and protecting those peoples and their needs from greedy and misguided American Protestant denominations. Catholic missionaries working with Mexicans, Latin Americans, or Filipinos had to demonstrate how much they were needed without insulting the Spanish Catholic past or sounding too much like Protestant missionaries who criticized seemingly adulterated forms of the faith practiced by these Catholics.

Two months after Kelley's report on the devil's work, the bishop of Puerto Rico, William Jones, wrote a letter to the Extension Society that graced the pages of *Extension Magazine*. "Accept my congratulations, as well as my thanks, for your well-presented article in *Extension* on behalf of Porto Rico," the bishop wrote. He, like Kelley, appealed to the historically minded reader: "It is a singular coincidence that your youthful society, established for the extension of God's Kingdom in the United States of America, should find a place in your charity to admit Porto Rico, which is the most ancient diocese within the domain of the Stars and Stripes." Jones noted the 1511 founding of the See of San Juan and acknowledged how grateful he was for the Extension Society's attention so that "the cradle of Christianity in America" may celebrate its fourth centenary in 1911.[13] In 1917, Rev. Domingo Miro described a visit to one of the oldest churches in Puerto Rico. "Centuries have brought this once beautiful church to the condition shown in the picture," he wrote. Adding insult to injury, "the place where the first Catholics preached the true Faith is now an important field for Protestant endeavor."

Miro recognized the Catholic borderlands in Puerto Rico: the long-standing Spanish Catholic presence, which needed the support of U.S. Catholics to remain standing. Miro requested funds to rebuild this important Catholic relic and vestments for the priests to man the church.[14] This refrain about the deep Catholic roots in the hemisphere lent legitimacy both to the Catholic Church as an American institution and to Catholic mission work in these historically Catholic areas within the U.S. domain. Above all, it was designed to get U.S. Catholics to invest emotionally and financially in the Extension Society's mission projects, in this case in Puerto Rico.

At Bishop Jones's request, the Extension Society funded a school in Puerto Rico and found a group of Sisters to teach there. The "pioneering" Franciscan convent in Buffalo, New York, set out for Puerto Rico to "fight the efforts of the proselytizers among the little tan children," as Kelley told it.[15] Warning that the Porto Rico Fund was inadequate even to finish a school year in Puerto Rico, he asked that "each and every subscriber remember the Porto Rico mission by some little gift." Kelley emphasized that the "pioneering" Sisters and their missionary spirit was all that stood between Puerto Rican children and the proselytizers. In the borderlands of the empire, the faith was at risk: U.S. Catholic pledges were desperately needed.

The American schools, which removed children from the Spanish religious education system, reinforced the work done by Protestant proselytizers. Kelley combed Protestant missionary publications to demonstrate to his readers the Protestant successes on the island, and he featured quotes that denigrated Catholicism. *The Christian Missionary* reported that "Porto Rico has caught a faint glimpse of a greater light than has been given by its Roman Catholic paganism," suggesting that Protestant missionaries were accomplishing what Spanish Catholic missionaries did not.[16] The devil, indeed, was having his way with Puerto Ricans. In essence, as Kelley presented it, the U.S. presence in Puerto Rico was endangering Puerto Rican souls, and the work of the Extension Society was more urgent than ever. The ragged edges of the Catholic borderlands needed to

Fig. 13. Church ruins in Puerto Rico represented the historic Spanish Catholic presence in the New World. These relics reminded *Extension Magazine* readers that the Catholic faith was in danger.

be sewn up by hardworking priests and nuns supported by *Extension Magazine* readers.

A decade later, following a 1919 earthquake, Extension-funded priests and brothers in Puerto Rico reported the growing threat to children: "Old classrooms have been remodeled temporarily so as to continue our school, with the only and main object to keep a hold on the children. . . . The Sisters of Charity, from St. Louis Province, have a great influence over the children, and through their untiring efforts succeeded in bringing many back."[17] The unnamed priest reported that children and parents continued to ask when a new school and new church would be built. Kelley detailed the efforts of Bishop Jones in establishing schools in Puerto Rico but warned that the faith "of little ones" was "being made the object of heretical onslaught. The island . . . is well supplied with Protestant mission schools." The parents want their children to learn English, he continued, and would gladly send them to Catholic American schools. "Each school we open," Kelley claimed, sharing his strategy with his readers, "means a check-mate to the proselytizer."[18] Once again, readers' generosity was needed in Puerto Rico to counter the American proselytization project. If American Catholics could not reach the children of Puerto Rico, the faith was within a decade or two of dying out after having sustained the island for four hundred years. This important Catholic legacy in the New World had been deeded to U.S. Catholics; they could not afford to let the work of Spanish missionaries go to waste. A 1919 "missionary chat" with Kelley reminded readers that Puerto Rico was the first diocese in the New World, established in 1504. "For over four hundred years the union of Church and State, as recognized by the Spanish law, took care of the material welfare of church and clergy." When the United States took over, "self-support" could not sustain the Catholic Church in Puerto Rico. American Catholics had to "prevent the light of Faith from being extinguished" on their watch.[19] Puerto Rico was the anchor of the faith in the Western Hemisphere! The Philippine Islands were likewise a Catholic outpost on the edge of the American empire in the Pacific.

"Only Three Centuries Distant from Idolatry and Savagery"

President William McKinley declared in 1898 that the U.S. mission to the Philippines was one of benevolent assimilation, designed to protect the natives' rights. Still, questions lingered about whether these foreigners were ready for the kinds of liberties Americans had. Catholics were not entirely convinced that U.S. interests in the Philippines were altruistic. In 1907, *Extension Magazine* readers were introduced to the Pacific world by Frederic Lloyd, who wrote "The Truth about the Philippines as Told by Archbishop [Jeremiah] Harty." Harty, the archbishop of Manila, portrayed Filipinos as intensely musical, alert, docile, and keen to learn. Most importantly for this audience, the "Philippino is Catholic to the soul." Lloyd's article clearly was in response to what was being reported elsewhere about Filipinos. Lloyd noted that the Filipino "trusts his spiritual father," while "from others he shrinks." Benevolent assimilationists, however, portrayed the Filipino "to the world in awful caricature rather than in faithful portrait." The first step in getting *Extension Magazine* readers to support the Extension Society's projects in the Philippines was to counter these unflattering representations. This was about humanizing Filipinos, but it also involved demonstrating that they were "Catholic to the soul," and thus civilized, and worth rescuing from the impending Protestant invasion. There was hope for Filipino Catholics, but American Catholics needed to step in to prevent the loss of souls to the Protestants in these Catholic borderlands.[20]

U.S. occupation of the Philippine Islands allowed for the Extension Society's intervention there. In 1915, the society's vice president, William O'Brien, reported that the bishops of the Philippine Islands were writing frequently to make the Extension Society aware of their needs.[21] Filipino Catholics were in danger of being perverted not only by Protestant missionaries but also by lay Protestant teachers in the American schools. Rev. J. A. Zandvliet, writing in a special issue of *Extension Magazine* dedicated to education, quoted Rev. Philip Finegan's writing on the Philippines: "A nation that is only three centuries distant from the habits of idolatry and savagery can-

Fig. 14. This procession of children includes numerous banners to saints.
Note the American flag in the center. Ilocus, Philippine Islands, 1918.

not be removed from daily religious education and still be expected
to prosper."[22] Zandvliet feared that U.S. public schools would separate Filipinos from their faith, since the great majority of teachers
would be Protestant. Spanish Jesuits in the Philippines appealed to
the Extension Society using the same language, characterizing Filipinos as "but a few generations removed from paganism" and "in
need of constant care."[23] When Spanish Jesuits referred to Filipino
Catholics they sounded strikingly similar to Catholic missionaries
in the United States speaking of Mexicans. "They want to be recognized as Christians," William Finneman wrote of the islanders,
"although their knowledge of the tenets of Christianity is not even
rudimentary."[24] It was important to remind *Extension Magazine* subscribers that Filipinos were Catholic and wanted to be better Catholics, yet they needed more priests and nuns to make that a reality.
This could only be accomplished with funds from the Extension Society. But Kelley and his authors had to walk a fine line, not sounding
too much like Protestant missionaries or benevolent assimilationists
in casting the Filipinos as uncivilized or un-Christian.

Fig. 15. The priest who sent this photo to the Extension Society described the subjects as "newly baptized Tiguian savages." Although they were no longer pagan, it appears they were still considered savages.
Tiguan, Philippine Islands, n.d.

One 1912 pamphlet brought together a multitude of voices concerned about U.S. activity in the Philippine Islands. "Following the Flag—Religion or Infidelity?" was produced by Colonel Thomas Mair, assistant director of the Philippine Constabulary, and circulated by Archbishop Harty, among others. Mair wrote, "The attack on our faith is fed by money sent here from the United States; the attack can be repelled only by contributions from our loyal Catholic brethren at home." As a member of the U.S.-imposed government structure in the Philippine Islands, Mair brought a worldly view to Catholic concerns. "What some Americans are trying to pull down," he continued, "let other Americans strengthen and build." One of the questions circulated at home was whether the U.S. Constitution should follow the flag to the Philippine Islands, to provide the same rights that were enjoyed at home. Mair cited an editorial from *America*, a Jesuit publication, to urge Catholics to "get together and defend the helpless Catholic youth of the Philippines, whom God has given to share with them the blessings of an American protectorate, against the hostility and religious aggressiveness of the Y.M.C.A." In spite of race, climate, and customs, Mair noted, the unity of faith was supreme and demanded the protection of Filipino Catholics. The cry for help from U.S. Catholics could not be overstated.[25]

The Philippine Islands, like Puerto Rico, had their fair share of natural disasters. A 1912 typhoon led to even more requests for support from the Pacific. Father Verbrugge, superior of the Mill Hill Missionaries, appealed to Catholics as Americans. "America has undertaken," he wrote, "to lead these people on, and educate them, until they can look to their own interest," echoing benevolent assimilationists. Verbrugge sharpened his approach: "Should the American Catholic not also take part in this glorious work, by trying to safeguard our Holy Father in these unhappy islands?"[26] Indeed, the occupation by the United States created a role for the Extension Society and American Catholics in the Philippine Islands. American responsibility, however, was only part of the story.

Bishop Dennis Dougherty of Jaro, Philippine Islands, reminded *Extension Magazine* readers several months later that the "archipelago was civilized and Catholicized by Spanish friars, who had left their homes and their country in order to devote the remainder of their lives to the welfare of that far-off land." It was the very transfer of the Philippines from Spanish rule to U.S. rule that left so many Catholics vulnerable to the Aglipayan schismatics, along with the Protestant proselytizers.

The Aglipayans, named for their first supreme bishop, Gregorio Aglipay, were an independent Filipino national Catholic Church formed in 1902. Americans were uniformly suspicious of the Aglipayans in the early twentieth century. British writer John Foreman suggested that Filipinos, having been accustomed to the Catholic Church for centuries, were taken with the "glamour and pomp" of religion and were "ever prone to stray toward the idolatrous." He concluded that "their adhesion to the [Aglipayan] movement is merely a natural reaction following the suppression of sacerdotal tyranny." The

U.S. occupation had freed Filipinos from Spanish Catholic tyranny. The Aglipayans, Foreman suggested, were following a natural path away from Catholicism, much like Europeans during the Protestant Reformation.[27]

Catholicism was under attack from multiple sides, then, in the Philippines. "As soon as the American flag was hoisted in the Philippines," Bishop Dougherty announced, "the Episcopalians, Methodists, Baptists, Presbyterians . . . flocked to that country . . . in order to wage a war against the Catholic Church."[28] The various denominations collaborated to ensure the undoing of the Catholic Church in the Philippines. They divided the territory into "distinct zones of propagandism" so they would not overlap or clash with each other. This strategy, according to Dougherty, ensured "that the natives might not behold their mutual dissensions and doctrinal differences."[29] He detailed the methods used by the proselytizers: preaching on street corners and in marketplaces and distributing Protestant Bibles and anti-Catholic materials, including literature by Maria Monk.[30] Rather than promote their own denominations, Dougherty noted, they were intent on destroying the Catholic Church, especially through the establishment of Protestant schools.

Without the Spanish Catholic infrastructure, Dougherty claimed, more than forty parishes were vacant and over one hundred thousand Catholics had been abandoned. The bishop offered a subtle critique of Spanish rule: the links between church and state in the Spanish colonial era meant Filipino Catholics were "never habituated to the maintenance of religion"; they did not have to financially support their churches. Under U.S. authority, "it will be extremely difficult to accustom them to support religion. . . . The American bishops cannot look to the mass of the Philippine people for the upkeep of the Church." Dougherty made clear, however, that this challenge could be overcome with support from *Extension Magazine* readers.[31]

Dougherty's report transitioned seamlessly into a plea for Catholic schools in the Philippines by Rev. Lawrence Rogan. Rogan reiterated a claim published previously in *Extension Magazine*, namely, that "the public schools through the length and breadth of the Philippine Islands are Godless, and now they are consequently drawing away from the Holy Church the rising generation of Filipinos." He noted the massive numbers that Catholic churchmen were trying to keep in the faith. His parish alone numbered seventeen thousand, most of whom were children "growing up without any knowledge of God." The "present generation of Filipinos is growing up quite pagan . . . without any knowledge of the Religion to which they are heirs," Rogan warned, echoing the calls of Extension Society missioners in the West. Historically, these were a Catholic people; therefore, under the American flag, it was the obligation of U.S. Catholics to restore and maintain the faith among Filipinos. Rogan had recently received word that a Mill Hill father would join the parish to teach the children, but Rogan still needed funds to support a school. He nicely combined Kelley's key themes: the responsibility of American Catholics to support "tan" Catholics in need and the powerful reminder of the work of Spanish friars in this far-off land. Catholics in the United States must sustain the missionary work in the Philippines that their Spanish forebears had started centuries earlier. American Catholics inherited the mantle of Spanish Catholicism around the world, not just at home in the American West. The Philippine Islands represented the far eastern outpost of the Spanish Catholic empire, and now the American Catholic empire. These Catholic borderlands were made possible by U.S. expansion and were cultivated by American Catholics in the early twentieth century.[32]

American Catholics' support was necessary politically as well as financially. In a 1916 editorial, Kelley mourned the moral decay evident in the U.S. political sphere. "Many Catholic voters will . . . always vote with their party," he lamented, referring to the Democratic Party, led by President Woodrow Wilson. Kelley dared enter terrain that for generations had worried Protestants: clerical interference with the U.S. government. "Loyalty to the politician and to public office will often outweigh loyalty to God, to religion, to true liberty and to common decency," he wrote. As national debates turned toward a presumed future Philippine independence, Kelley worried that "cutthroats, in spite of protests of decent elements

Fig. 16. Missionary priests pose with child actors in character
for the Nativity play. Tamag, Philippine Islands, 1916.

among the Filipinos themselves," would start a revolution putting
religion, liberty, and decency at risk. He pointed to a present-day
example of this chaos. "The flag of the United States has covered
the most damnable outrages," he wrote, referring to U.S. support
for Mexico's post-revolutionary governments. "Catholic members
of Congress and the Senate openly stand behind this attempt to
make a desert waste of our neighbor to the South," he warned. This
turn toward Mexico noted Kelley's expansion beyond the United
States and its territories. Mexico was not part of the United States,
but it fell within the social, economic, and now religious sphere of
U.S. influence. Kelley's expansion into Mexico took Catholic borderlands to a new level, one that was not dependent on U.S. political ownership of former Spanish territories. The crisis to the south
was Kelley's most important project, the one that defined his leadership of the Extension Society and his life's work.[33]

### The Extension Society beyond U.S. Territories

By 1913, in the face of anticlericalism present in many factions of the
Mexican Revolution, the Extension Society was expending consider-

Fig. 17. This photo showed *Extension Magazine* readers what was possible if U.S. Catholics succeeded in their mission in the Philippine Islands. Eventually, the islands would produce their own priests and nuns. Philippine Islands, 1917.

able resources in support of Mexican Catholicism. In *The Book of Red and Yellow*, Kelley described in excruciating detail the experiences of Mexican clergy and the actions taken by various revolutionary governments in Mexico. According to Kelley, the Constitutionalists destroyed three-fourths of the church in Mexico by forcing priests into hiding or out of the country.[34]

Most of the priests who fled Mexico headed for Cuba or Texas. Father Henry Constantineau, the Oblate provincial, sheltered many of the exiled Mexican priests and their flocks in San Antonio, Texas. In need of assistance and support, he sought out the archbishop of Chicago, "who promptly sent [Kelley] to the border with orders to go to Vera Cruz or anywhere else [he] was needed."[35] The exiled priests reported to Kelley their efforts to avoid imprisonment, death, or the punishment of their parishioners for defending their priests. Kelley accepted the mission of educating the American public, particularly American Catholics, about "the Mexican situation." He reported to Catholics and other Americans on the harrowing journeys of priests across the border to seek refuge from the violence. Increasingly, Kelley looked beyond Mexicans in the Southwest to Mexico itself. On December 14, 1914, he was appointed to represent the Mexican Catholic Church in the United States.[36] This elevation in the secular hierarchy of the United States gave Kelley an audience beyond his readers in *Extension Magazine* and other Catholic publications.

The Extension Society mirrored what Walter Nugent calls "Empire II," the early-twentieth-century emphasis on controlling, rather than acquiring, strategic territories.[37] "Mexico has been transformed from a land of hope to a land of grim and black despair," Kelley editorialized. Mexico, however, did not create this despair on its own. "If Mexico has sinned it has paid a horrible penalty," Kelley preached, "but can we afford to pay our share of it?" Kelley was persistent in attacking the U.S. government for recognizing Mexican governments that did not explicitly protect the Catholic Church. He accepted a portion of the blame himself, as well. "Fear of mixing politics and religion has purchased silence too long. I, myself as editor, of this Magazine, have allowed such considerations to influence me." Kelley

# Read Up the Mexican Situation

The Mexican question is to the front and will be to the front for a long time to come. It is the one absorbing question of the hour around which political controversies are, and will be, raging. Even after the battle at the polls November next, whatever party assumes the administration of affairs will still have its most interesting action in the final settlement of the Mexican question.

Already the enemies of the Church and all religion are accusing the Catholic Church, bound and powerless for fifty years, of responsibility; denying the outrages against her and, by misrepresentations and falsehood, seeking to discredit her with both American and Mexican people.

Last month a petition was sent to the President, charging that Catholic Church authorities in the United States are plotting a new revolution, and have raised fifty millions of dollars to aid it. As a matter of fact the only money collected for Mexico by the Church here was for the relief of the poor refugees.

Every one of these anti-Catholic movements is financed and exploited by a revolutionary junta in New York and Washington. Millions of dollars are at its disposal for purposes of slander. These desperate men, foreseeing the doom of the persecutor, are now appealing to the bigoted element of Americans.

Don't be deceived. This situation will grow worse, instead of better. The order of the calumniator has gone forth. There is money in plenty to see that the mails are filled with falsehoods. Only recently two large secular magazines accepted and paid for stories inimical to the Church in Mexico.

It behooves Catholics to know the truth and to be on the alert. Question after question will be asked of us every day; not all in malice, but WITH A REAL DESIRE TO LEARN THE FACTS. We ought to be able to answer.

The best and fullest book of information on the religious question in Mexico is that of Mgr. Kelley, called "THE BOOK OF RED AND YELLOW, a story of BLOOD and a YELLOW STREAK." It has had one edition after another in both English and Spanish, in Chicago, U. S. A., and Barcelona, Spain, till its sales have almost reached the 125,000 mark.

We have a new edition now off the press in English, ENLARGED to over 150 pages. This book gives facts, figures and proofs. It treats the question exhaustively. You need it. The new part contains a reply to Luis Cabrera, the Minister of Finance in the Carranza cabinet.

The truth is told in an addendum entitled "AN OPEN LETTER TO AMERICAN MASONS," on the relation of Masonry to the Revolution; but without abuse or anger. You can show it with pride to any American Mason — and you ought to. Send for the new edition of "THE BOOK OF RED AND YELLOW." It is an investment you will not regret. Read it and pass it on to your non-Catholic friends. Help to spread the truth. We are face to face with the fact that we are going to be — we are being — attacked. Let us meet the accuser with the FACTS.

Write for prices in quantities. We will quote you at special rates for all orders over six.

## READ *THE PROOF*

We are prepared and ready to send out the Truth. We need only the help to circulate it. Send 35 cents for *"THE BOOK OF RED AND YELLOW"*—NEW EDITION. Address

Book Department of EXTENSION MAGAZINE, Brooks Building, Chicago, Ill.

Fig. 18. Advertisements for Kelley's *The Book of Red and Yellow* appeared regularly in *Extension Magazine*. In this June 1916 version, Mexico's national imagery is inverted, with the serpent strangling the eagle, rather than in the eagle's mouth. The text warned that anti-Catholics in the United States were discrediting the church in both nations. Below, the death and destruction wrought by the Mexican Revolution are displayed.

steered away from blaming others, though, and turned toward a call for action.[38] The proximity of Mexico, along with Kelley's appointment to represent the Mexican hierarchy in the United States, provided the perfect opportunity for him to legitimately cross into the terrain of U.S. politics, as well as across the political boundaries of the nation and its territories. Kelley's new role also furthered U.S. Catholic interest in Mexico and renewed the emphasis on the shared religious heritage of the United States and Mexico as former Spanish territories, the Catholic borderlands.

Kelley outlined his strategy for enacting this important mission. A passive plan of watchful waiting had not met with success, he argued, so Catholics must be more aggressive. "We believe that the President and Secretary of State are most anxious to do what is right; but they have been misinformed and badly advised. We believe that they know this themselves now."[39] Kelley certainly did his best to advise the Wilson administration, with support from an array of allies in business and politics. Colonel Joseph A. Robertson, a Texas businessman working in Mexico, and Dudley Field Malone, a New York politician, had arranged for Kelley, as representative of the Mexican hierarchy, to meet with Secretary of State William Jennings Bryan and President Wilson.[40] Kelley had received repeated assurances that the administration would only support Mexican governments that guaranteed religious liberty. After Wilson recognized the anticlerical Venustiano Carranza, Kelley continued to "keep the truth before the Catholic public by the circulation of *The Book of Red and Yellow*."[41] Kelley also continued to push his claims in *Extension Magazine*.

The editorial pages of the magazine each month were peppered with reports about Mexico. One 1917 piece, "A Voice Out of Mexico," described the dearth of priests in the Diocese of Campeche: "one priest was allowed to return and since then only three have entered" to serve a population of eight thousand Catholics.[42] The magazine regularly reported violations of the Mexican constitution to American Catholics and compared Mexican governing bodies to those of Russia.[43] Kelley's goal was to keep Mexico on the minds of

American Catholics even after many of the refugees had returned to Mexico. This campaign reinforced the idea that Mexico, as a Catholic territory under threat, was deserving of American Catholic attention and concern. It was their right and their duty to protect the faith in Mexico.

In order to secure the future of the Catholic Church in Mexico, Kelley pushed for a seminary in exile. A Mexican seminary in the United States would allow for the continuous training of priests for Mexico while seminaries were not permitted to operate or were unsafe in Mexico. Kelley first raised the topic in October 1914. To build momentum, he discouraged the Knights of Columbus from pursuing an investigation of the anticlericalism in Mexico and suggested they support Mexican refugees and a seminary for training Mexican priests.[44] In June 1915, *Extension* introduced readers to "The Exiled Mexican Brothers of Mary." The Extension Society rented buildings from the Sisters of Divine Providence in Castroville, Texas, to start San Felipe de Neri Seminary. As the seminary closed in 1918, Kelley wrote, "These young Brothers of Mary carry many hopes for the future of Catholic education in poor Mexico. . . . [W]hen peace returns to that stricken land they will return equipped to reopen their schools and colleges." American Catholics, then, were responsible for sustaining the hopes of Mexican Catholics. Catholic borderlands only existed where U.S. Catholics could take a role in sustaining the faith: their investment in San Felipe de Neri was all that was protecting Mexico from the godlessness of the Revolution. The seminary remained active through June 1918, funded by the Extension Society and the U.S. and Mexican hierarchies. Kelley and other American Catholic leaders grew frustrated with the seminary faculty and students who returned to Mexican when it was opportune to do so rather than as the seminary calendar dictated. More than eighty priests were ordained at San Felipe de Neri, thanks "to the readers of this Magazine, who constantly and persistently sent their pennies."[45] Kelley kept the seminary in the pages of *Extension Magazine* to remind readers that the training of Catholic priests was vital to sustaining the faith of Mexicans, this time *in Mexico.* Catholic borderlands entitled U.S. Catholics to engage in spiritual warfare to save the church, but it also required them to sustain that fight with donations to the Extension Society.

In subsequent months, Mexico remained central to Kelley's agenda. In a special issue of *Extension Magazine* he commemorated the life of the late Archbishop Quigley to recount how the Extension Society learned about the Mexican Catholic Church. Quigley never lost interest, Kelley reported. "It was he who directed the efforts of the Society made for Mexico. . . . It was he who directed the campaign which culminated in letters from the Department of State, promising that all the influence of the United States Government should be used in securing liberty of conscience for Mexico."[46] Kelley overstated Quigley's role, but his effusive tribute linked the important prelate of the largest archdiocese in the country to the Mexican project, elevating its importance locally and nationally.

As representative of the Mexican hierarchy in the United States, Kelley was free to speak and write about politics. In the pages of *Extension* he openly criticized Joseph Tumulty, President Wilson's personal secretary, for minimizing the outrages against priests and nuns in Mexico, and took this opportunity to revisit claims made in *The Book of Red and Yellow*. "Father Juan Alanis, Pastor of Camargo, left his exile in the United States and went back to his parish. He was practically put in a chain gang to work in the streets, until he escaped into American territory again." Although the United States served as a refuge for Catholics fleeing Mexico, Kelley implicated the U.S. government for the Mexican situation. Since Wilson formally recognized the Carranza government, "even the cemeteries have been desecrated and the walls thrown down," according to Kelley. Publications across the country were attacking the Catholic cause in Mexico, he noted. Tumulty became representative of anti-Catholicism in the United States. "Mexico is at our doors. Her misfortunes are largely, God forgive us, our own fault."[47] Politicians were certainly the ones most responsible for Mexico's great losses, and Catholics had to take a stand to protect Mexico's Catholic Church. Challenges to the faith were everywhere; U.S. Cath-

Fig. 19. At the opening of the San Felipe de Neri Seminary in Castroville, Texas, January 1915. *Left to right*: Mexican students of the seminary, Rev. Henry A. Constantineau, OMI, Bishop Juan Herrera (Tulancingo), Kelley, Bishop Miguel de la Mora (Zacatecas), Bishop Fernandez, Archbishop Leopoldo Ruiz y Flores (Michoacán), Monsignor Edward F. Hoban, Chancellor (Chicago), Archbishop Francisco Plancarte y Navarette (Linares), and Bishop Maximino Ruiz y Flores (Chiapas).

Fig. 20. Mexican seminary students ready to start their coursework in exile in Castroville, Texas, ca. 1915.

Fig. 21. Mexican nuns were in exile staying at San Felipe de Neri Seminary.
They likely attended to the seminary students. Castroville, Texas, ca. 1915.

olics had to be ever-vigilant to protect the Catholic legacy in the New World.[48]

The Extension Society created a Mexican Relief Fund for the seminary in Castroville and the general care of exiled priests and nuns. Periodically, Kelley warned readers that the fund would run dry within weeks. "We don't want to go from door to door to beg, but we MUST if necessary," he wrote. In April 1916, readers were offered *The Book of Red and Yellow* in exchange for donations to the relief fund. They were asked to educate not only themselves but also their friends and neighbors on the dangers in Mexico. A gift of *The Book of Red and Yellow* would be suitable for doing just that. It is unclear to what extent subscribers believed Kelley's every word. Circulation leveled off from 1915 to 1917, but growth continued from 1918 on, and Kelley did not seem to have trouble funding his Mexican projects.[49]

Mexico offered a renewed opportunity to invoke the long-standing Catholic ownership of the continent. Protestants were "getting a lot of consolation now out of the Mexican situation, dreaming of 'open Bibles' and open Sunday schools for the Mexican children," Kelley reported. Protestant claims that Catholics did not know the Bible were rooted in the commitment of Catholic authorities to teach the Bible and its lessons rather than have lay Catholics read it for themselves. However, Kelley reminded both his readers and Protestants that Mexicans "had Bibles before Plymouth Rock and all sorts of schools before Harvard." Those schools, of course, were run by Catholic orders. Kelley challenged the credentials of Protestant proselytizers in Mexico. Methodists reportedly wanted "to help conserve child life in Latin America," especially Mexico, but "the only interest they have in Latin-American children," Kelley wrote, "is to take their religion away from them." The result, according to Kelley, was the deaths of thousands of Mexican children from typhus and starvation. The implication was that the Catholic Church had tended to the health and welfare of Mexicans and other Latin Americans, whereas Protestants had not. He congratulated the Protestants on "increasing the child population of the Kingdom of Heaven; for it has been increased greatly during the last five years of bloody desolation in Mexico, encouraged by the missionaries who want to 'beat out the Catholic Church.'" Catholics, on the other hand, attended to the material as well as spiritual needs of the faithful.[50] Anticlerical government leaders in Mexico often embraced Protestants to prove they were not curbing religious liberty. The severity of religious repression varied based on location and local and national governance, but Protestants were treated much more reverently than Catholics. This likely was due to concerns that their home orders, based in the United States, might push for U.S. interference if the Protestant missionaries were not protected.[51]

Martyred Mexico, which had occupied the editorial pages of *Extension Magazine*, took center stage in the April 1917 issue dedicated to the religion trouble to the south. The cover image portrayed a haunting vision of Cristo Rey—Christ the King—hovering over Mexico, with priests and families fleeing and a Spanish colonial church behind them. Kelley once again identified multiple publications that questioned the legitimacy of persecution claims. He offered an extensive history of Mexico that countered the Black Legend, offered by the likes of Prescott, with a White Legend of the heroics of Spanish priests in saving the Aztecs.[52]

Kelley relied on the extensive writings of Eber Cole Byam, a disgruntled American businessman with interests in Mexico. Byam was Methodist and a Mason yet was very concerned about anticlericalism in Mexico. Like Kelley and O'Shaughnessy, Byam pointed to the legacy of a civilized North America provided by Spanish friars. Byam reiterated in graphic detail the significant gains made by the Spanish friars in Mexico. Through devotion and self-sacrifice, the church in Mexico cleansed the Indians "of the blood of human sacrifice, raising them from the unutterable depths of cannibalism to the impressive heights of Christianity." Evangelization was just the beginning: the church educated the masses, printed the first books in the Americas, and trained surgeons. All of this was undone first by independence, reinforced by Juarez's reforms of the mid to late nineteenth century, and finally destroyed by the Revolution. "A hundred years of 'Liberty' and 'Democracy' have left the Mexican Indians deprived of their knowledge of how to read and write," Byam wrote.[53] This history, like the Spanish history north of the border, served to remind readers that Mexicans were inherently Catholic; Mexico was a Catholic nation long before the Protestant United States was established, and long before the anti-Catholic and anticlerical Revolution emerged. The natural order included a Mexican Catholic Church and a Catholic presence on the continent, started with the daring evangelization carried out by the Spanish friars and reaffirmed by the noble work of the Extension Society, on behalf of and supported by U.S. Catholics in the early twentieth century.

President Wilson's tolerance of the Carranza administration's anticlericalism endangered the Mexican Catholic Church but brought the American Catholic Church to life. American Catholics embraced the charge issued by Kelley and other Catholic leaders to hold the U.S. government responsible for the tragedy of martyred Mexico. In 1919, as many Mexican priests and bishops returned to Mexico, Kelley kept the campaign alive. "In spite of all published interviews

The Tragic Story of Martyred Mexico in this Number

EXTENSION·MAGAZINE

April, 1917    The World's Greatest Catholic National Monthly    Vol. XI. No. 11

Fig. 22. The April 1917 issue of *Extension Magazine* was dedicated to the
Mexican situation. In this cover image, a saddened Christ looks down
upon Mexico as priests and Catholic families flee Mexico.

from persons in Mexico or out of it," he wrote, "there has been no change in the persecuting laws against religious liberty in that country. We state this with full knowledge of the situation." He reminded readers that he was the *only* person authorized "to speak to Americans on behalf of the Church in Mexico" and took the liberty of speaking *for* American Catholics on Mexico: "The tolerated return of the exiled Mexican bishops changes nothing so far as American Catholics are concerned. . . . The one thing that interests American Catholics is this: Have the persecuting laws been changed?" Kelley informed his readers that nothing had changed in Mexico and that the campaign must continue. Although priests and nuns were being allowed to return, without changes to the constitution or other assurances for the safety and prosperity of the church, Catholic borderlands were still threatened.[54]

The Extension Society navigated and negotiated Spanish colonial narratives and U.S. imperial discourses masterfully to provoke U.S. Catholic support for projects in the Philippines, Puerto Rico, Mexico, and the southwestern United States. These missionary projects gave U.S. Catholics ownership of the Americanization agenda, an agenda they often consciously countered. Kelley worked to undermine Wilson's efforts and reputation where Mexico was concerned, and he invited U.S. Catholics to do the same. This served to reinforce the growth of an American Catholic identity.

While the United States and Great Britain were making their marks around the world and tidying up their justification for doing so, American Catholics, led by Kelley, were implementing a project to undermine or redirect some of those "American" activities in the West and in other U.S. territories. This American Catholic project hinged on connecting present-day Catholics not to the American—that is, Protestant—empire but to the Spanish Catholic empire, which had prior claim to the "new" American territories in the Caribbean and Asia. This American Catholic project, then, predated the American Protestant one, not only in the Spanish borderlands of the West but in Puerto Rico, the Philippines, and all of Latin America.

# 3

## Religious Monroeism

*U.S. Catholic Influence and Intervention in Mexico*

In April 1916, Gilbert Nations, of the Free Press Defense League in Washington, DC, wrote to President Wilson warning that the U.S. Catholic hierarchy had been attempting for more than a year "to bring about a state of war between the Republic of Mexico and the United States of America." After secret meetings in New York, Baltimore, San Antonio, and New Orleans, Nations claimed, twenty thousand armed men in Mexico were awaiting the word of the hierarchy to attack.[1] Nations was not alone in reporting the activities of the U.S. Catholic Church to the federal government. H. M. Andrews, a self-proclaimed Catholic Democrat, reported to Wilson's secretary, "I am enclosing you a pamphlet . . . being sent broadcast from Chicago all over the country. . . . Don't you think for the good of the party some action of refutation should be taken?"[2] The pamphlet criticized President Wilson, American Federation of Labor president Samuel Gompers, and Mexican president Venustiano Carranza and included commentary by Eber Cole Byam, a Kelley collaborator.[3] Although Nations's letter might strike the reader as more dangerous than the pamphlet itself, the real war was the one being coordinated out of Chicago. Kelley, in defense of Mexico, was urging American Catholics to defend their faith in the Catholic borderlands.

Mexico had been invaded by the United States in 1848, losing half its territory, and again in 1914 and 1916 with U.S. occupations of Mexico during the Mexican Revolution. Mexico's position in early-twentieth-century U.S. foreign policy was different from that of other Latin American countries. "It was intimately bound up with the character of that country's regime, and the regime was intimately bound up with that country's proximity to the United States," according to Peter Calvert.[4] The series of regimes ruling Mexico from 1910 to 1929 sought to redefine Mexico as a nation and to find pride and glory in that new nation. Most of the leadership of Mexico during and after the Revolution imagined a community whose new identity included being anti-foreign, especially anti–United States. Despite Mexico's desire for separation from the United States, and U.S. claims to be simply a concerned neighbor, the Revolution had a tremendous impact on the United States. Mining, oil, and agricultural interests in the United States had significant landholdings and personnel in Mexico. Public interest in the United States focused less on business and commerce than on religion. It was no surprise that Monroeism reappeared when Mexico was vulnerable, but it operated in unexpected ways.[5]

This chapter analyzes the role of U.S. officials in supporting Catholics and Catholicism in Mexico. U.S. individuals and organizations sought ways to direct U.S. control over Mexico, based on the assumption that the United States ought to have strong and direct influence over Mexican policy decisions. Calls for U.S. interference in the Mexican religious situation, or "religious Monroeism," as two Catholic activists termed it, came in a variety of forms: U.S. Catholics urged the U.S. government to restrain the Mexican government; U.S. anti-Catholics declared that the Mexican church was getting what it had long deserved and implored the U.S. government to let the Mexican church be dissolved; and Mexican Catholics attempted to shape Mexican policy through U.S. government officials.[6] Religious Monroeism, or more accurately, Catholic Monroeism, also contributed to the developing Catholic confidence in an American identity and Catholic investment in the expanding American empire. Catholic borderlands can be understood as a Catholic strategy to sustain the faith in Mexico, a historically Catholic nation. Catholic Monroeism shows a broader U.S. Catholic disregard for national boundaries as well as a Mexican Catholic investment in a weakened, permeable border. U.S. State Department correspondence regarding Mexico demonstrates that the "religion question" was central in the diplomatic concerns of the U.S. government. Within the metropole, correspondence between U.S. Catholic organizations and the U.S. government shows that government officials were responsive to Catholic concerns, even if they did not act as Catholics hoped. State Department and other officials understood that Catholics were a growing and significant political presence in the United States, especially in the urban Northeast and Midwest. On more than one occasion, the United States intervened in cases involving U.S. and other foreign Catholics in Mexico.

The concept of "religious Monroeism" rests on a broader definition of intervention that considers not only the U.S. military presence in Mexico but also the impact of U.S. social and cultural interventions. In the growing American empire and the similarly growing Catholic borderlands, Mexico was fair game for Americans. Even groups with quite different policy goals acted in ways that showed broad consensus about the right and responsibility of the United States to shape the religious landscape of Mexico.

### U.S. Intercessions in Response to the Outrages

Liberty is being crucified at our very door.

—Archbishop Arthur J. Drossaerts[7]

U.S. ambassadors, consuls, and special representatives in Mexico kept a close eye on the religion question. Religious repression in Mexico was a recurring theme in State Department correspondence from 1914 to 1918 and again from 1926 to 1929. The outrages, defined by one priest as "the afflictions and persecutions suffered by the Catholic Church in Mexico," consisted of exiling priests and nuns, in some cases after raping the women.[8] Priests were often held hostage until their parishioners raised a given ransom, after which the priest was forced to leave the country.[9] The revolutionaries' initial emphasis was removing the foreign clergy, but as time went on, Mexican priests were often imprisoned or forced into exile as well. It is important to note that anticlericalism and anti-Catholicism did not always work in concert. As one Mexican put it, "to believe in god [*sic*], I do not need the priests."[10] Although Mexicans over-whelmingly considered themselves Catholic, many did not see their religious practices or beliefs limited by the absence of priests. Mexican practices such as home altars and celebrations such as *días de los muertos* did not require the presence of clerics.

The State Department most likely recognized the connection between social stability of the Catholic Church and political and, therefore, economic stability in Mexico. U.S. consuls in Mexico were expected to report on the outrages against Catholics in correspondence with the secretary of state. U.S. representatives in Mexico understood the importance of gathering information on the religion question, whether Catholic pressure in the United States or another political agenda drove this activity. As early as 1914, much of the news being reported to the State Department from Mexico was on the church struggle. Philip Hanna, consul in Monterrey, reported on the "great prejudice against the catholic [*sic*] church" and described the spiraling effect of this prejudice. "Bitter attacks on the church and clergy and also the Catholic schools are made in the newspapers in Monterey [*sic*], and the very fact that the same appear in the press convinces the public that it meets with the approval of the authorities." U.S. representatives in Mexico were charged with interpreting the actions of Mexicans with little or no knowledge of Mexican history or customs.[11]

American officials were committed to religious practice, but many expressed a distaste for Catholicism. Consul James Silliman was in some ways sympathetic to the Catholic plight in Mexico. In describing events in 1918 in Guadalajara, Jalisco, he wrote: "Today, policemen have been stationed at the doors of the churches who suggest to persons who carry the mark the advisability of removing it immediately." The "mark" was the sign of the cross on the foreheads of the faithful on Ash Wednesday. Silliman continued, "If the suggestion is not complied with, the persons are taken to the police headquarters and required to remove it, and in addition, pay a fine." Silliman reported that such a "*constumbre sucia*—a filthy custom" was what the Mexican government was trying to eliminate when prohibiting outward signs of religious faith.[12] This, of course, is an oversimplification of the anticlericalism present in Mexico at the time, but it confirms Silliman's sense that Catholicism was behind the times. In this case, the Mexican government and the U.S. government were in alliance to curb this unclean, antimodern practice by Catholics.

Silliman, stationed in what is considered the most Catholic state in Mexico, understood the broader ramifications of the religious situation even if he did not understand Catholic practice. A 1918 report to Secretary of State Robert Lansing described a Catholic boycott in Jalisco in response to government repression of Catholics. This is one way Catholic women, in particular, exerted their power at the local level. "Retail businesses and public entertainments such as picture shows, theatres, etc., continue seriously affected by the continued seclusion of the women of the city. It is believed in well informed circles that before the end of the month the Government will be obliged to recede from the position it has taken." The following decade, Consul Dudley Dwyre reported on subsequent boycotts organized by Catholics in Guadalajara. The economic boycotts were often successful in Jalisco, where Catholics harnessed their economic power to influence local governments, but correspondence suggests that such orchestrated movements by Catholics either did not exist or lacked significant impact in other areas of the country.[13]

Mexican Catholics along the border capitalized on the Mexican Catholic presence north of the border. Consul Oscar Harper reported from Piedras Negras that Mexicans often crossed the border into Eagle Pass to attend Mass on Sundays. In 1927, as a result of increased tension between the Catholic Church and the government, Mexican immigration authorities warned that if Mexicans attended Mass in Eagle Pass they would not be allowed to return. Harper reported that according to the director of the Mexican immigration service, the concern was not to curtail churchgoing but rather "to prohibit their receiving anti-Mexican propaganda which was being spread by the priests across the border."[14] Again, according to the immigration official, this border inspection was not anti-Catholicism, but anticlericalism at work. In spite of this state-sanctioned religious repression, religion flowed freely in these Catholic borderlands. Mexican worshippers most likely attended Masses celebrated by exiled priests, who were not imagined to be citizens in the community of revolutionary Mexico. Thus even the Mass itself could be considered "anti-Mexican propaganda." That the presumed transgression toward the nation happened on U.S. soil only fed its anti-revolutionary quality.

Most U.S. representatives regarded religion as a powerful and positive force, yet their biases against both Catholicism and Mexico were evident in their correspondence. Consul Hanna in Monterrey reported: "As to the religion, among the people, they are, for the most part, Catholic in name, however, more catholic [sic] than anything else as generally speaking the catholic religion is the only religion that they really understand and it really seems to be the most suitable for them and most natural." Hanna's tone is simultaneously uncertain and absolute in describing Mexican Catholic practice. As Catholics "in name," it appears their practice was not very convincing to the consular official. Yet, they seemed well suited to the presumably backward religion. Hanna continued, "Without its practice it is feared that the majority of the Mexican people would practice no religion which would, of course, bring grave disaster."[15] Clearly, religious and national biases were interwoven for Hanna. Catholicism was better than no religion. Without the Catholic Church, Mexico would be subject to moral ruin. Hanna, like many others, believed the foreign presence in Mexico was vital. "With the help of high foreign clergy the church people would be able to upbuild their church and bring it to a high standard and in that way be able to assist greatly in the regeneration of [Mexico]." Hanna was seemingly unaware that foreign clergy—Spanish, in particular—had been in Mexico for centuries. Presumably he was calling for the support of U.S. clerics. In a later report, Hanna declared that Mexico's system of education would be destroyed if the U.S. church properties— Protestant, of course—were nationalized. All the work U.S. churches had done on behalf of Mexicans would be lost.[16] Mexico could not, in his eyes, educate its own people. It needed the guidance of U.S.-

run schools to make modern citizens. This discounted the extensive Catholic school systems, including universities, that had existed in Mexico since before Jamestown was settled. Catholic schools, however, would not produce the modern citizens that U.S. Protestant schools, under the canopy of American empire, would. Although Hanna was not invested in a *Catholic* borderlands, he too saw the ways the United States could step in to help neighboring Mexicans achieve a more progressive destiny.

There were other U.S. representatives who were suspicious of the anticlerical forces of the Mexican Revolution. John Wood, consul in Veracruz, suggested in 1927 to U.S. Ambassador to Mexico James R. Sheffield that the anti-religious campaign was an attempt to divert attention from land and oil issues. Wood's inability to understand the seriousness of the Cristero Rebellion reflected a poor understanding of the nation in which he was stationed. His counterpart in Guadalajara pondered links to the Soviets: "Capital has been attacked and severely punished," wrote Consul Dwyre. "The second stage is the attack on all religion. . . . Can it be a coincidence that the Soviet program is the same?"[17] Thus the anti-Catholicism in Mexico posed an indirect threat to the United States. A decade later, the Knights of Columbus were also sure that Mexico had been invaded by Bolsheviks, as described in their pamphlets "Red Mexico" and "Mexico: Bolshevism the Menace."[18] Whether based on religion or economics, suspicion of the true agenda of the Revolution abounded in the United States. Indeed, the suspicion was that Mexico did not have its own agenda, making it ripe for U.S. intervention. Decades of upheaval and change were not about creating a new nation, according to these Americans, but the result of Bolshevik agitators. Such reports reinforced the understanding that U.S. interest in Mexico was about sustaining an American empire and making sure Mexico remained part of it. The role of U.S. Catholics in this project was to sustain the faith in these Catholic borderlands, in support of U.S. empire.

In contrast, John Lind, President Wilson's special representative in Mexico, found the role of the Catholic Church to be the downfall of Mexicans. In a letter to Secretary of State William Jennings Bryan, he wrote, "The tale of these unfortunate people brings back the dark ages. . . . They are naturally an intelligent, virile race which has enabled them to survive the sufferings of centuries to rise against their oppressors." Although Lind cast Mexicans as intelligent and virile, since they were Catholic, this only enabled them to suffer, not to free themselves.[19] Lind's appointment as Wilson's special representative in Mexico in 1913 was problematic, as he was openly hostility toward the Catholic Church. Some Mexican leaders appreciated his support on this issue, but his presence in Mexico and his tendency to use inflammatory language did nothing to enhance U.S.-Mexican relations.

U.S. observers also asserted Mexico's racial inferiority. *Current Opinion* reported on discussion in the U.S. Senate on Mexico's plight. "The existence of appalling conditions in Mexico . . . is due, according to Senator [Augustus] Bacon (D-Georgia), chairman of the Senate Committee on foreign affairs to just one thing—the cowardice or supineness of the white citizens of Mexico who have education, wealth and social standing. But who refuse to risk their own blood to restore order to their stricken country."[20] Lind seemed fixated on the *mestizaje*—the racial mixing—of the non-white Mexicans. Upon returning to the United States, he made a career out of philosophizing about Mexico based on his eight-month stay. Lind theorized about the racial composition of Mexicans in "The Mexican People," a speech he gave at the Chicago Industrial Club in December 1914. "I venture to say that . . . the Mexican people . . . are more homogeneous than our people," he said. "This is the more remarkable as it is confessedly in a people of mixed bloods that a fixed type is rarely found. Whether this is owing to the fact that the original mixture proceeded almost wholly from fathers of Spanish blood and Indian mothers I will not assume to say." He concluded that Mexicans were "a people *of great promise*." For Lind, Mexico would only be able to achieve its full potential if the yoke of Catholicism was not weighing it down. He received support from the Mexican consul in New York, and of course the ire of Catholics, for his anti-

Catholic stance in "The Mexican People."[21] Lind saw Mexico as an opportunity to help a "virile race" achieve its promise. The role of U.S. empire in saving Mexico was not in doubt in Lind's thinking. He imagined a secular salvation, however, rather than the Catholic one outlined by Kelley and other U.S. Catholics.

Within the United States, the State Department was often called upon to clarify the situation in Mexico. In 1915, Representative James Maher (D–New York) requested information from the State Department about outrages against Catholic priests and nuns in Mexico. Secretary of State Bryan responded that five priests had been executed in Zacatecas but that other outrages had not been substantiated.[22] The State Department later included translations of the Constitution of 1917 and other relevant documents in responses regarding Mexico. This likely was to show concerned Americans that Mexico's constitution was not being violated. State Department representatives walked a fine line, assuring Catholic citizens and organizations that they were being vigilant regarding the outrages, and assuring non-Catholic and anti-Catholic groups and individuals that their government was not pandering to the Catholics. U.S. citizens and officials were very invested in the outcomes of the Revolution and the Cristero Rebellion.

U.S. officials even reached out to Catholic leaders in this era. Secretary of State Robert Lansing, in 1915, thanked Rev. Thomas Shannon of the *Catholic World*, the official newspaper of the Archdiocese of Chicago, for his information regarding the concerns of U.S. Catholics, and requested his continued advice on Catholic public opinion. It seems unlikely that Lansing was soliciting input from Catholics in general. Rather, he saw the value of telling vocal Catholics what they wanted or needed to hear. Catholics were scrutinized by their neighbors, who wrote to U.S. government officials questioning the patriotism of Catholics. Most often, those who wrote the letters were informed that the matter would be considered carefully. This mixed record of the State Department demonstrates that the views and concerns of Catholics were being considered like those of other groups. The primary goal of the State

Department was not to upset any letter writers concerning the religion question in Mexico.[23]

The government largely allayed the fears of Catholics in the United States, but at times it took the offensive when Catholic organizations charged that the United States was not doing enough. In 1926 the Knights of Columbus were taken to task for accusing the president and secretary of state with fomenting and approving the "evils at our own doorsteps." The representatives of the Knights of Columbus who met with Secretary of State Frank B. Kellogg were quick to acknowledge that the language was perhaps too strong. Both parties agreed, however, that to retract the statement or otherwise draw attention to the document could cause more harm than good, especially in Mexico.[24] Kellogg surely recognized the importance of the Knights of Columbus as a national Catholic voice, and he sought to shape its message in whatever ways he could—in this case by being accessible to the Knights of Columbus. The Knights' campaign during the Cristero Rebellion demonstrated their commitment to a Catholic body that transcended the U.S.-Mexico border. The Catholic Church was considered unsuccessful in achieving its goals concerning the U.S. government.[25] Still, Catholic interest and activity forced the religion question into U.S. government discussions of the Revolution and the Cristero Rebellion, and on more than one occasion, U.S. Catholics did get the U.S. government to act on their concerns.

Informal inquiries seemed to be enough to secure the residence of one U.S. Catholic priest in Mexico. Rev. Francis J. Krill had been stationed at a church in Córdoba, Veracruz, until 1917, when his church was closed. In the mid-1920s he accepted a position as manager of a coffee finca owned by U.S. interests near Fortin, Veracruz. He began saying Mass in a chapel on the property for the other employees, and eventually for Catholics from neighboring fincas as well. On February 28, 1926, it was reported, Krill was roused by armed men at 3:30 a.m. and asked to surrender. He escaped and later walked to Orizaba, Veracruz. The chapel on the property was reportedly closed and sealed. John Wood, consul in Veracruz, reported this to Ambassador Sheffield and suggested that since Krill was on private—and even U.S.-owned—property, he should not be subject to Article 130 of the Constitution of 1917, which stated that "Only a Mexican by birth may be a minister of any religious creed in Mexico." Mexican Catholic officials in Veracruz suggested to Krill that he return to the United States and conduct a propaganda campaign on their behalf, an idea that was most unpalatable to Krill. Sheffield contacted Aarón Sáenz, the secretary of foreign relations, requesting protection for U.S. churchmen. Within twenty-four hours, Krill consulted state authorities in Jalapa, Veracruz, and was informed that he could stay.[26] The legal standing of the coffee finca, as property "owned" by U.S. interests, was in doubt given the Constitution of 1917. Yet, this concession to the U.S. government suggests a desire by Mexican officials to calm relations between the two countries—or at least to choose battles carefully. Sheffield's request that U.S. clerics be exempt from Mexican policies shows the political power of the expanding American empire. Although Mexico was still not formally part of that empire, it was subject to U.S. influence—to the pull of Catholic borderlands. Krill's case was not unique in the level of official U.S. involvement or the nature of the intervention. There is no record of it in State Department correspondence, but it is possible that the United States was particularly attentive to Krill's case because the Mexican Catholic officials in Veracruz wanted him to return home to work for their interests in the United States. Both the U.S. and Mexican governments preferred that he remain in Mexico, preaching. This possible violation of the Mexican constitution seemed less damaging than the alternative. Representatives of the United States made similar interventions in other cases.

In 1914, during the U.S. occupation of Veracruz, several hundred priests and nuns were evacuated to Galveston with the financial support and encouragement of Kelley and the Extension Society. The U.S. government absorbed most of the expenses associated with the removal, though the Extension Society contributed to the priests' escape with funds from *Extension Magazine* readers. The Extension Society provided support and helped relocate priests and nuns throughout the United States, reporting to the president and the

State Department at every opportunity. In this instance, the Catholic borderlands project and American empire worked together toward the same end, bringing priests and nuns to safety.

The Catholic Church was not able to influence major U.S. policies toward Mexico, yet it could and did pressure the State Department to act in specific cases. Catholics were able to keep religious liberty central to the discussion of the Mexican situation, much to the dismay of anti-Catholics. U.S. Catholics had the confidence to demand the attention and actions of the U.S. government. They recognized, in this moment, that they belonged in the United States and that their concern—religious liberty—was every bit as relevant and legitimate as the concerns of other Americans. They shared with other Americans the assumption, rooted in ideas that had coalesced around the Monroe Doctrine and the Roosevelt Corollary, that the United States had a responsibility to nurture and protect an "improved" Mexican Catholic Church. This religious Monroeism in the Catholic borderlands was an expansion of the Monroe Doctrine beyond economic and political concerns.

### Alms for Mexico

The Mexican leaders will certainly know that in order to command the sympathy and moral support of America, Mexico must have, when her reconstruction comes, true freedom of conscience and worship.

—State Department memorandum[27]

This 1926 State Department memorandum laid out the U.S. position on the religion question in Mexico. The *actions* of representatives of the United States were not always so clear, however. President Wilson and subsequent presidents, as well as State Department officials, were often placed in the position of defending U.S. government decisions and denying the level of influence that many believed the United States had in negotiating with Mexico's leaders. Oilmen had little hope that the U.S. government would address their needs, and they resorted to dealing directly with the Mexican government on issues of land use, protection of U.S.-owned property, and policy.[28] However, regardless of which side they were on, U.S. citizens believed their government should be directing Mexican policy on the religion question. Mexican Catholics and diplomats from other nations also expected the United States to dictate Mexican policy on religion. This recognition of U.S. influence over Mexico affirmed Mexico's station in the U.S. sphere of influence as declared by the Monroe Doctrine. The presumption by other nations that the United States had some say in the direction the Mexican government took affirmed the rise of American empire and the view that Mexico was part of that empire; that the United States would intervene on behalf of the Catholic Church affirmed the existence of Catholic borderlands, a space in which a U.S. Catholic agenda, within the American empire, could be enacted to preserve the Spanish Catholic legacy in Mexico.

President Wilson attempted to downplay the power Catholics believed he had in Mexico. He wrote Cardinal James Gibbons in 1914, "I am sorry to say it is not true that 'one word from me to the Constitutionalist leaders would have a great effect and would relieve the sad condition of affairs' in Mexico with regard to the treatment of priests." Wilson tried to reassure the prelate, "I have spoken that word again and again. My influence will continue to be exerted in that direction and, I hope, with increasing effect."[29] Wilson simultaneously tried to lower expectations and assure the cardinal that they were on the same side. For the next decade, Catholics attributed power over Mexican policy to the U.S. government. Kelley often led the charge against the State Department, accusing it of sacrificing religious liberty as it dealt with Mexican officials. In response to his concerns, the Division of Mexican Affairs of the State Department reported: "At every turn of affairs . . . and upon every report of persecution, [the administration] has advised and warned those who were exercising authority of the fatal effect any disregard for the lives or rights of those who represented religion or any attack upon the liberty of conscience or of worship would have upon the opinion of the people of the United States and the world."[30] Such rhetoric, it seems, was rarely used on the Mexicans. In the words of Ambassador Sheffield, "it will be much more effective to handle specific cases informally and to make general representations in the form of formal notes."[31] As the case of Father Krill demonstrated, this was how the U.S. government chose to deal with Catholic issues in Mexico.

Advice and warnings from U.S. authorities did little to change the overall anti-foreign anticlericalism of the Revolution, though reprieves were sometimes granted on a case-by-case basis. This is perhaps best demonstrated in the case of Archbishop George Caruana, apostolic delegate to Mexico in 1926. On May 1, the chief of the Division of Mexican Affairs in the State Department, Franklin Mott Gunther, met with the Mexican ambassador to the United States. Gunther shared with the ambassador letters from Catholic individuals and organizations in the United States expressing concern over the religion question in Mexico. Gunther made passing reference to Caruana, a U.S. citizen, and the ambassador reported his understanding that Caruana was doing well. On May 12, Archbishop Caruana, who had been able to work across Catholic divides in Mexico, received word that he must leave Mexico within six days. He sought the support of Ambassador Sheffield, who contacted the secretary of foreign relations, Aarón Sáenz Garza. Interventions in both the United States and Mexico were unsuccessful, and Caruana was forced to leave Mexico. In recognition of U.S. Catholic concerns and power, Secretary of State Kellogg shrewdly reported his and Ambassador Sheffield's actions on behalf of Caruana to the National Catholic Welfare Conference (NCWC). NCWC news releases appeared in Catholic newspapers across the country, reinvigorating Catholic concern over the Mexican situation while also assuring Catholics that high-level officials in the U.S. government were on their side. Certainly Caruana's status as a papal representative did not help his case in Mexico, but it is also possible that Gunther's inquiry initiated the case against Caruana.[32]

In the Caruana case, official U.S. attention did not help, and perhaps even harmed, the Catholic cause. However, earlier requests for diplomatic intervention were more successful in at least drawing attention to Catholic concerns. Consul Philip Hanna forwarded an article from a San Antonio Spanish-language newspaper which reported that Mexican Catholic refugees in the United States were calling on the U.S. government to withdraw recognition of Carranza. Mexican Catholics recognized that they were part of the American empire and sought a firmer hand from their imperial host. "The article says that their petition asks our Government that 'Carranza be abandoned to his own luck.' I send this without comment," Hanna wrote, "further than to state that it is well known that many Mexican catholics [sic] have been compelled to leave Mexico and many who are now in the country claim that their religious rights are denied them."[33] U.S. Catholics were making similar claims. T. J. Walsh of Baltimore later petitioned Secretary of State Bryan with this desperate telegram: "Make all possible representations to arrest threatened execution of Bishop of Guadalajara." Mexican authorities must know, Walsh continued, that "the world" would condemn them "for putting to death a great prelate because of the religious views he holds."[34] Walsh was not exaggerating when he suggested that the (Catholic) world was counting on the United States. Similar sentiments came from abroad.

In 1915, the Brazilian minister in Mexico, on behalf of "the French Minister, Vicar General and other respectable persons," appealed to the Secretary of State Bryan to intervene in Mexico because foreign clergy were being expelled and Mexican clergy imprisoned if they did not pay levies to the government. Bryan responded by asking President Carranza to "prevent the arrest of any American priests . . . and provide every possible assurance of protection for any foreign priests."[35] The U.S. consul in Mexico City, James Silliman, contacted President Carranza and suggested that foreign priests be excluded from these proceedings. Representatives from other governments believed that the U.S. government had extraordinary influence over Carranza.[36] Whether or not Carranza acted on this request, it was clear that other nations recognized that Mexico was part of the expanding American empire. Catholicism, unexpectedly, had become an important part of the imperial body.

The Spanish ambassador to the United States also called on Bryan to assist in reversing a 1915 order expelling Spanish priests.[37] The involvement of U.S. officials in discussions between the Spanish and Mexican governments was particularly ironic. In this moment, Spain acknowledged the cultural transfer of its most important colony, Mexico, to the United States, long after the economic and political ties were loosened. A Spanish plea to the United States to protect the Catholic Church affirmed the existence of Catholic borderlands: the United States now had a compelling interest in supporting Catholicism as part of its imperial project. In light of U.S. interest in numerous former Spanish territories, this interaction must have produced waves on both sides of the Atlantic Ocean.

In 1925, as tensions between Catholics and the government again increased, Ambassador Sheffield reported to Secretary Kellogg: "So great has this anxiety become that the Embassy has been approached both by important Catholic laymen and by the diplomatic representative of His Catholic Majesty, the Spanish Minister, with the apparent thought that it may become appropriate for me on behalf of the United States to intervene in the situation."[38] The British Embassy also wrote the State Department concerning the expulsion anew of foreign clergy, wishing to know the U.S. position on the matter. The Division of Mexican Affairs issued an internal memorandum to remind staff of the U.S. stance on Mexico: "[The U.S.] Government has not taken any stand on the Constitutional provision to which [the British ambassador] referred, although *it has from time to time advised the Mexican authorities to exercise moderation in dealing with members of religious organizations.*"[39] Sheffield, like his predecessors, made suggestions to the Mexican government regarding the treatment of foreign clergy. U.S. officials were notably influential in U.S. Catholic cases, though in most others, it seems, their suggestions were ignored. It seems unlikely that French, Spanish, and British officials who turned to the United States did so in deference to the Monroe Doctrine. They clearly believed that the United States would have the most success in trying to reason with Mexican officials, as it was within the U.S. sphere of influence. Mexican officials recognized that their long-term survival was rooted in support from the United States and acknowledged U.S. investment in the Catholic Church in Mexico.

Even the Vatican recognized the role of American empire in shaping post-Revolution Mexico and understood the Protestant nation's interests in Catholic Mexico. A 1917 telegram from Pope Benedict XV to President Wilson brought the most surprising appeal for U.S. intervention in Mexico. It was unprecedented for the pope to contact the president directly, as the United States did not have diplomatic relations with the Vatican. Pope Benedict XV implored, "We pray with all our souls that your excellency will use your high influence on Mexico to avoid the condemnation of religious personages inspired perhaps by political passions." This communication sent the State Department into a tizzy, with department heads meeting to determine the best way to respond. The pope was provided the same assurances as others who asked about the religion question, namely, non-interference and encouragement of moderation in dealing with the religion question. It is notable that throughout this era, the Vatican acknowledged the Catholic borderlands: Mexico fell within the American empire, and as such, Catholic concerns there were to be addressed in the United States.[40]

Although foreign clergy were no longer welcome in Mexico, members of U.S. orders and organizations seemed to believe this restriction did not apply to them. They found a special calling in Mexico in response to the issue of religious repression. When announcements were made regarding the required departure of foreign religious leadership, U.S. missionaries assumed that these notices were meant for European religious.

The State Department provided documentation for a group of American citizens affiliated with St. Catherine's Convent in Washington, DC, to go to Mexico to "bring certain members of religious orders in that country to the United States."[41] Numerous convents and Catholic schools in Mexico had the backing of or were directly affiliated with U.S. Catholic orders or were the U.S. provinces of European orders. As such, these institutions expected the U.S. government to protect their property and work in Mexico. In another case, the Ursuline Convent in Puebla sought the support of U.S. chargé d'affaires Arthur Schoenfeld. Senator Joseph Ransdell (D-Louisiana), lobbied the secretary of state for the preservation of the school and property of the Ursuline Sisters. In the eyes of the Ursuline headmistress, the power of U.S. influence was second only to divine power. "After the help of God," she wrote, "the American flag which we continually keep near our entrance door has saved us from many annoyances." If God's own protection were not enough, in other words, the safety of nuns in the Catholic borderlands was assured by the American flag![42]

Catholics in the United States were often seen as un-American, while American Catholics in Mexico seemed to be over-identified with their home country. U.S. Catholics in Mexico felt the same entitlement that other Americans in Mexico felt, reflecting their strengthening American Catholic identity within the American empire. Others made testimonials to U.S. officials. Katherine Stecker reported seeing nuns who had been outraged by revolutionary soldiers, and she knew of further outrages against nuns. Similar affidavits were submitted by priests arriving in Tucson in 1915. In more than one case, the United States then asked for Mexico's protection of U.S. interests or the interests of U.S. citizens.[43] The expectation was clear: the policies regarding religion were meant for the European clergy, not for religious orders from the United States, as ordained by the Monroe Doctrine and the Roosevelt Corollary. Religious Monroeism required Mexico, in the shadow of American empire, to provide cover for U.S. religious bodies to intervene in Mexico, to save it from itself. As part of the Catholic borderlands, Mexico was open to U.S. religious intervention.

The protection of the U.S. government was sought by Protestants as well as Catholics. The Social Gospel movement, which saw improving the surrounding environment as critical to the work of conversion, was well established in Mexico by the mid-1910s. The Social Gospel allowed—in fact, required—Protestant missionaries to lobby the U.S. government to improve conditions in Mexico through recognition, intervention, and the like. They also turned to the U.S. government to intervene on their behalf, as needed, when economic or military pressure disrupted their missions.[44]

Ambassador Henry Fletcher reported to Secretary of State Robert Lansing on a conversation with Protestant representatives in Mexico City in 1917. He assured the Protestants that the U.S. government was sympathetic, and he promised to intervene on their behalf or the behalf of other U.S. citizens when it would be diplomatically appropriate to do so. In the early 1920s, Louis Fritts of the Congregational Church felt that the limitations placed on foreign churchmen were too restrictive and lobbied President Coolidge to support his work. "If I am not asking too much, will you please call the attention of the Commissioners in Mexico City to these points? We are sincere friends of Mexico but feel *as American citizens* we should have a larger measure of liberty in our work." Similarly, Mormons, Methodists and Mennonites working in Mexico sought the permission and protection of the U.S. government in the maintenance of their missions.[45] Sentiments of Manifest Destiny, in an explicitly religious sense, and American exceptionalism motivated many U.S. religious in Mexico. The special project of Protestant denominations was to modernize Mexico. Liberalism, with a specifically anti-Catholic bent in Mexico, guided their mission work. American denominations saw their presence in Mexico as a natural extension not only of their religious commitments but of their national ones as well. Catholicism was antiquated, and modernity was tied to the American empire.

Mexican priests also saw the unique role the U.S. government could play in their protection in Mexico. In 1914, Bishop Miguel de la Mora of Zacatecas, residing in San Antonio, requested U.S. support through Cardinal Gibbons of Baltimore: "I beg of your Eminence's kindness and charity to make every effort through the President of the United States, to see that permission be given to at least a few of the priests of Zacatecas to return to the abandoned city."[46] In response to a subsequent letter from Gibbons, Secretary of State Bryan reported that "the Department of State has for some weeks past advised the Constitutionalist authorities in Mexico to exercise justice and moderation in their treatment of persons and properties belonging to religious organizations." Such statements were repeated in numerous letters to U.S. citizens concerned about Mexico's religious question. Regardless of who expressed the concerns, U.S. officials presented a uniform response of awareness and frequently expressed concern for religious liberty in Mexico.[47]

Mexican Catholic women were savvy about the influence of the U.S. government in Mexican decision making. As early as 1922, a group of Mexican Catholic women in Mexico City lobbied Mexican politicians and drew public attention to the plight of Catholics. By 1926 they were appealing directly to U.S. authorities in Mexico. Bartley Yost, consul in Torreón, Coahuila, wrote Secretary of State Kellogg about a group of Mexican women who had visited the consulate to complain about religious persecution. Yost told them that he would report their grievances to the U.S. government but said that the government could not interfere with Mexican internal affairs. The women, according to Yost, responded that "the only salvation of their country was the intervention of the United States, which they hoped and prayed for." Within their families, women worked to achieve their own political goals. According to a 1926 report from Torreon consul Bartley Yost to Secretary Kellogg, "the women in Mexico had been endeavoring to create discord in the Army, with a view to bringing about a revolution to overthrow President Calles." In 1927 the American Club of Mexico City appealed to Sheffield on behalf of "afflicted mothers" whose sons were being deported to Islas Marias—an island prison of sorts—for outward expressions of Catholicism.[48]

Mexican appeals to the U.S. government projected a protective role onto the Colossus of the North. Pedro Rentería and C. Martínez wrote to Ambassador Sheffield, "The Mexican society sees in you a guarantee of order, your presence here represents civilization and humanitarianism." Rentería and Martínez seemed to be reading the minds of U.S. government officials and the broader public. "You are without doubt the rein which holds these demagogues in check in their criminal course," they continued. "When you leave us we will be helpless and hopeless because your presence inspires respect."[49] It is unclear whether Rentería and Martínez believed this or were merely appealing to U.S. paternalism toward Mexico, but their posture affirmed the presumption that the United States was looking out for Mexico. Catholic borderlands provided a context for Mexican Catholics to gain support—if not from their own government, then from the United States; that the United States even received such pleas confirmed its own interests in playing this role.

Mexican Catholics cultivated U.S. public support for religious expression in Mexico. In 1924, U.S. chargé d'affaires Schoenfeld was invited to sit on the dais at the benediction of the National Eucharistic Congress of Mexico. The Mexican Catholic laypersons who invited him indicated that his presence would send a strong message to the Mexican people about U.S. support. At this same time, the U.S. Embassy was asked to safeguard Mexican Catholic jewels, a request it denied. Still, Schoenfeld accepted the invitation to further a U.S. public presence in support of Catholic religious expression, well aware that Mexican Catholics saw this as U.S. backing for their cause.[50]

Mexicans used U.S. newspapers as a medium for debates between Mexican Catholic and government leaders. The *New York Times* most often served this role through its letters to the editor. In 1928 the Committee of Catholics of Mexico prepared to approach the Mexican Congress to ask that the constitution be amended to allow the Catholic Church to return to prominence in Mexico. Information on their plan appeared in the *New York World* before it appeared in Mexico.[51] Such deliberate displays of Mexican Catholic goals for the U.S. public demonstrate how powerful they believed U.S. influence to be.

Some in the U.S. government saw the United States setting an example for Mexico on religious tolerance. Ambassador Sheffield reported on the response to the International Eucharistic Congress held in Chicago in June 1926: "The enthusiastic reception accorded . . . to the Papal representative and to the other cardinals attending the conference have produced a profound impression in

Mexico." As proof, he continued, "an editorial which appeared in *Excelsior* on June 15 commented on the praiseworthy spirit of tolerance on the part of a Protestant country giving so warm a welcome to the high dignitaries of the Roman Catholic Church."[52] Sheffield commented that many in Mexico were hoping such a demonstration would have a positive impact on the Mexican government's thinking on religion. Of course, this made no discernible difference in the treatment of Catholics in Mexico. Given such displays, though, the United States was seen by some as a neutral yet positive force in these discussions. In 1929, Cardinal Secretary of State Pietro Gasparri suggested Washington, DC, as the site for talks between Mexican leaders and Vatican officials regarding the settlement between church and state in Mexico. Gasparri also sought the assistance of Georgetown professor Father Edmund Walsh in these talks.[53]

In the end, though, U.S. government officials—at least privately—understood and accepted their role as Mexico's closest and most powerful neighbor. In a rare rant to Secretary of State Kellogg, Ambassador Sheffield decried the religious repression that emerged violently in 1926 and the role the United States had played in bringing about and sustaining this particular Mexican government. "I would not want you to feel that I am advising interference with the purely domestic affairs of another country," he wrote. "Surely there must be some way, even within the limitations of diplomatic intercourse by which we could point out and protest the folly of denying to children the right of religious education." Commenting on the Calles Law, which further limited the role of the Catholic Church in Mexico, he continued: "I am not surprised that the question has been raised in the United States of continued recognition of a government capable of promulgating a penal statute of the character under discussion. Kept in power by the aid of the United States, we have, at least, some moral responsibility for men in government in Mexico whose official existence depends in large part on our friendly acquiescence and support."[54] Sheffield, not known for his subtlety, had the pulse of the Mexican hierarchy. His plea was written less than a week before the Mexican bishops declared the church strike, which led to the Cristero Rebellion. A month later, Secretary of State Kellogg seemed to have calmed Sheffield. Kellogg reported to President Coolidge that Sheffield "agrees with our attitude on the religious question and that it would not be useful or beneficial to send a note to Mexico on this subject. It would switch the issue from one between the Catholic Church in Mexico and the Mexican Government to one between the Mexican Government and foreign interference and would probably unite sentiment behind Calles." U.S. officials understood their own power in Mexico, and they only supported the Catholic agenda if it suited their purposes. Still, Catholics were able to keep such concerns and strategic issues on the table. Kellogg was pleased that Sheffield had cultivated positive relations with the Mexican government despite the continuing anti-American feeling in Mexico. He indicated to President Coolidge that Mexico seemed to be trying harder to please the U.S. government. As Sheffield reported, however, the situation only worsened in the months to follow. He and U.S. consuls throughout Mexico reported on the escalating violence against clergy, nuns, and lay Catholics.[55]

Ambassador Dwight Morrow, who replaced Sheffield during the Cristero Rebellion, became intimately involved in the settlement between Mexican Catholics and the Mexican government. In 1927, Arthur Bliss Lane, chief of the Division of Mexican Affairs in the State Department, was in contact with Manuel Sierra of the Ministry of Foreign Relations. Sierra hoped that Morrow would be able to reason with President Plutarco Elías Calles regarding the religious question. According to Morrow's notes, Sierra reported that "the pressure which had been put on the Mexican Government in the religious question by the church was similar to that exerted by foreign petroleum companies during the oil controversy. As long as such pressure was asserted by foreign oil companies, the Mexican Government could not yield as a matter of national dignity." Morrow's role was to divert the pressure from the church to allow for a settlement that did not challenge Mexico's independence or constitution.[56] It is intriguing that oil and religion were recurring points of conflict between the United States and Mexico. In both cases, U.S. interests feared they lacked the ear of the U.S. government and conducted their own foreign policy as they deemed necessary. Catholics had the same idea, as they continued their project of direct influence in Mexico.[57]

American Catholics also appealed to Morrow as a go-between in the settlement of the religious question. In 1928 Morrow met with representatives of the National Union Party, a group of lay Catholics, who demanded a role in any settlement talks to ensure themselves special rights. "Any settlement made without guaranteeing a strong Catholic lay organization in Mexico would make the situation worse than ever," they claimed. Morrow found this approach problematic and assured these men that the return of the Catholic Church to Mexico could only enhance and support the work of an organization such as theirs. During this same period, correspondence between the Vatican and Catholics in Mexico regarding a settlement with the Mexican government outlined the role of the United States in not only solving the problem, but creating it: "It must be borne in mind that the Government of the United States, the purveyor of arms and money to maintain the revolutions in Mexico, has failed in moral and material support (of the Catholics)." The U.S. government had received blame from many factions by the time the Revolution was over. As the imperial overseer, the United States had ultimate responsibility for Mexico. U.S. Catholics were more than happy to accept this burden. They believed in Catholic borderlands and the charge that came with it.[58]

Morrow was held in high esteem by many Mexicans. An article appearing in 1928 in *El Universal Gráfico* called him "without any doubt, the most distinguished representative which the United States has had in Mexico. There have been lawyers, politicians, business men and diplomats, some of them very intelligent, but no one crossed the border with the baggage of good will as did Mr. Morrow." The article described the faults of previous U.S. representatives in Mexico and noted, "Personal friend since childhood of the present American President, [Morrow] has known, with all discretion, how to make use of this influence, and has thus been able to clear up the situation between the two governments."[59] *El Universal*

*Gráfico* seemed to note the historical reality that U.S. ambassadors to Mexico often saw themselves as superior to Mexicans, straining relations with bitterness and mistrust.

The standard line of the U.S. government was to extend its good offices on behalf of church leaders and advise Mexico on the treatment of foreigners. However, U.S. administrations took much more responsibility behind the scenes. When it came to religion, the world depended on the United States to secure the safety of the faithful in Mexico, its Catholic borderlands. Some even held the United States directly responsible for the happenings in Mexico. This was, of course, in keeping with the general thrust of American foreign policy within its hemisphere—the Monroe Doctrine was understood to have established U.S. responsibility for stability throughout Latin America.

By 1910 the United States, in the name of the Monroe Doctrine and the Roosevelt Corollary had cast its shadow far and wide in Latin America and the Pacific. U.S. officials might refer to the Mexican Revolution and the Cristero Rebellion as internal matters for Mexicans to negotiate, but those same officials could not keep from assisting, most often against Mexico's wishes. Annexationists hoped that the Mexican Revolution might lead to a U.S. intervention that would start with the annexation of Baja California and end with the occupation of Panama and eventual control of the Panama Canal. Ultimately, despite claims to the contrary from both sides, the United States, particularly Woodrow Wilson, was held responsible for much of the Mexican Revolution, which was seen as limiting Mexico's liberty, not enhancing it. North Dakota bishop Vincent Wehrle wrote to Wilson, "We must declare to you . . . that by recognizing Carranza you participate in making our own Country, the Country of true liberty, participate in robbing Mexico of true liberty." Catholics became experts at the use of such patriotic rhetoric. "By reason of the Monroe Doctrine," wrote Charles Denechaud, president of the American Federation of Catholic Societies, "the civilized Nations of the world look to the United States of America to exercise its great power for the preservation and maintenance of the fundamental rights of mankind on the American Continent."[60] This sentiment did not end with Wilson's administration. In 1926, William Russell, the bishop of Charleston, South Carolina, wrote to Secretary of State Kellogg, "The least the United States can do in self-respect is to mitigate the evils which have been brought on Mexico by the dictatorial interference of an American President."[61] It seemed no matter how the U.S. government responded, U.S. Catholics were rarely satisfied. Conveniently, this provided continued opportunities for Catholics to pursue their own goals in Mexico.

Through the U.S. government, Catholics kept religious liberty on the front burner throughout the 1910s and 1920s, and hence sustained a Catholic voice and vision in Washington. Catholic bodies transcended political boundaries in multiple directions, resulting in U.S. protection of the Catholic Church in Mexico. This U.S. Catholic claim on Mexico was rooted in the same Spanish past that made the U.S. Southwest, Puerto Rico, and the Philippines inherently, naturally Catholic. This religious Monroeism could not have existed without the leadership of Francis Kelley. His political work is the subject of chapter 4.

# 4

## An American Catholic Diplomacy

*Expanding Catholic Borderlands*

From 1915 to 1918 the Extension Society funded San Felipe de Neri Seminary in Castroville, Texas, outside San Antonio. At the height of the anticlericalism in Mexico, seminaries across the country closed. San Felipe de Neri served as a seminary in exile to train priests, thus sustaining the Mexican Catholic Church for the future. In April 1918, weeks prior to the seminary's planned closing, Francis Kelley wrote to Archbishop George Mundelein in Chicago regarding the possibility of using Spanish priests who had taught at the seminary as missioners in the West, which was still dominated by French priests. Conditions in Mexico had improved to the point where seminaries there could reopen, Kelley reported, but "none but native-born Mexicans may return." Kelly envisioned housing the Spaniards in Chicago and assigning them to work with Mexican laborers across the West. There is no indication that Mundelein moved forward with Kelley's proposal.[1]

Eight months after his initial letter to Mundelein, Kelley sent a follow-up. "I had no idea there were so many Mexicans here," he exclaimed, indicating that one of the Mexican archbishops was told by his parishioners that there were more than three thousand Mexicans in Chicago. "Now it appears the Presbyterians say there are double that number," Kelley continued. He seamlessly transitioned to his earlier plea. "You may remember that our board favored the idea of securing two Mexican priests to look after these scattered Mexican laborers. The proper place for these priests to live would be Chicago. I was instructed to see if I could get co-operation from railroad men. Several have promised to assist."[2] Kelley's turn to help

Mexicans in Chicago years after first engaging "the Mexican situation" abroad and in the larger region reflected his realization that the people he had invested so much time and energy supporting were closer than he thought. This proximity gave him an opportunity to apply his mission concept close to home. It is striking that the Spanish priests of the April letter had "become" Mexican priests by December. This sleight-of-hand by Kelley was likely deliberate, and perhaps designed to gain diocesan support for a more localized project, over a plan to send Spanish priests to the West. Catholic borderlands, as this chapter shows, extended not only to former Spanish territories but also to other Catholic parts of the United States and the world.

The Extension Society's mission was to bring the gospel to the unfortunate in the United States, but Kelley's vision often wandered outside of the United States. This expansion of mission mirrored the expansion of American empire. The acquisition of more territories in the late nineteenth century had given way to a grasp for global power and influence after World War I. Catholic borderlands followed this same model, allowing Kelley to further his own work in reinforcing Catholic borderlands beyond the Spanish-U.S. borderlands model. Kelley took every opportunity to expand his reach well beyond the explicitly domestic agenda of the Extension Society, often to the dismay of Archbishop Mundelein and Vatican officials. His constant desire to reach farther—though often for good causes—earned him a reputation for dishonesty and meddling.

Alongside Kelley's political mission was a uniquely American mission: to bring civilization to war-ravaged Europe or "backward" and "primitive" Mexico. During his diplomatic missions, Kelley was in contact with, and surely a thorn in the side of, U.S. officials. Although his position as part of the American empire gave him access to powerful leaders, he maintained his Catholic mission to counter the empire's Protestant bent. There is a wonderful irony to all of this. The original global, transnational, imperialist entity—the Catholic Church—was in alliance with perhaps the most powerful imperialist entity—the United States—in the person of Francis Kelley, a

Canadian priest. Kelley embodied the greatest fears of revolutionary Mexico—the Catholic Church, the United States, and foreign interference. He justified those fears by intervening in Mexican affairs on multiple levels. In the Catholic borderlands, Kelley was able to access assorted powerful entities, often against the wishes of U.S. government officials, the Vatican, the Archdiocese of Chicago, and even the Mexican archbishops whom he represented. As long as the United States was active, Kelley was present to protect and sustain the Catholic faith in Catholic borderlands around the world.

The rise of the Archdiocese of Chicago was foundational to Kelley's success as president of the Extension Society in Chicago and his subsequent mission work in Europe. This chapter shows Kelley's willingness to go anywhere to continue this mission. The work of the Extension Society continued to shadow U.S. power, in this case in Europe, where Kelley's goal remained the preservation and protection of Catholic missions with the implicit opportunity provided by his identity as an American Catholic leader.

### George Mundelein and the Rise of the Archdiocese of Chicago

In the early twentieth century, U.S. Catholics struggled to establish themselves as both American and Catholic in a Protestant-dominated nation. Immigrants, in particular, faced challenges to their legitimacy as Americans. As Catholics, the prejudice against them multiplied. The generation of bishops that ushered in an American Catholic identity fought all of these forces—some more successfully than others. Chicago's George Mundelein was among the most successful.

The Diocese of Chicago was founded in 1843 and was elevated to archdiocese in 1880. For most of the twentieth century, it was the largest archdiocese in the country.[3] While most eastern dioceses were dominated by one ethnic group, usually the Irish, Chicago had nearly equal numbers of Irish, German, and Polish immigrants.

Cardinal George Mundelein, who led the archdiocese from 1916 to 1939, shepherded the Chicago Catholic community through many local, national, and international changes. He was a New Yorker, and his appointment aroused suspicion among many Chicagoans. He was the youngest archbishop ever appointed in the United States, and the first cardinal in the West. Mundelein was in good standing in Rome. He was of the generation known as "consolidating bishops," leading the diocese into a more orderly and efficient era in the 1910s and 1920s. The Catholic Church was in a process of reorganization. As it grew rapidly in the United States, Rome became more and more aware of how complicated its very existence was. There was frequent competition and pressure from Protestant communities and politicians to limit the scope of the Catholic Church.

One of the changes Mundelein ushered in was the decrease in the creation of new churches, particularly ethnic or national parishes, which preserved the language and culture of the homeland. Archbishop James Quigley, who preceded Mundelein, commissioned the building of many churches. He devised a territorial plan, indicating the need for a Catholic parish every square mile within the archdiocese. These territorial parishes were interspersed with national parishes, in which the homily and confessions were heard in the "home" language. National parishes also served as social gathering places for immigrants, attempting to counter the work of Chicago's famed settlement houses.

Beginning in 1918, in an attempt to lessen the appearance of the Catholic Church as the immigrant church in the United States, the Vatican required that dioceses request special permission for the creation of additional national parishes. Mundelein and others of his generation were also known as Americanization bishops due to this kind of work. Despite pressure from Rome to eliminate national parishes, Mundelein did allow for some to be created. Parishioners could make a strong case for a national parish, but Mundelein resisted most of these overtures. For example, the Polish, as a newer immigrant group, were concerned about maintaining their ethnic identity in a still somewhat hostile environment. In 1921 a group of Polish Catholics in west suburban Bellwood sent $25,000 to Mundelein asking for a parish for one hundred Polish families. Mundelein returned the funds and told them to see their local pastor. German Catholics, in contrast, had lessened their ties to nationality during World War I. They were generally earlier immigrants as well, so they were more content to pass into the territorial parish system. Between 1916 and 1929, of the forty-two parishes commissioned in the archdiocese, only nine were national parishes.[4] This was in stark contrast to the period under Archbishop Quigley, which was defined by the founding of national parishes. Although fewer and fewer national parishes were established, the lines of demarcation between parishes remained. John McGreevy's study of race and Catholicism in twentieth-century cities in the North confirms the strength of the national parish system in supporting segregation and separation of various ethnic and racial groups. Parishes remained closely linked with neighborhoods, solidifying the racial and ethnic character of both simultaneously.[5]

The Catholic leadership of Mundelein's time was charged with the unique task of making U.S. Catholics seem American to the Protestants, while assuring Rome that they were still Roman Catholics—a precarious balancing act. Until 1908 the United States was considered "mission" territory by the Vatican, meaning it had received the gospel relatively recently. Still, there was concern in Rome that a peculiar form of Catholicism was developing in the United States. Pope Leo XIII's 1899 call to the U.S. Catholic hierarchy warned U.S. Catholic leaders that "Americanism" was threatening the faith.[6] Within the church, Americanists sought assimilation of immigrants and embraced the constitutional protection of religious freedom as an opening for the Catholic Church in the United States. Conservatives were more cautious and wanted to protect the flock from the dangers to the soul lurking in the United States. Kelley worked, through *Extension Magazine*, to carve out a role for American Catholics that embraced their ties to the universal church but also emphasized the Americanness of Catholics and Catholicism.

The Catholic Church was still perceived as the immigrant church in the early twentieth century. Anti-Catholic fervor in the United States was focused on more recent Catholic immigrants from southern and eastern Europe in the East and on those from Mexico in the West. As newer immigrants and as Catholics, these recent immigrants were culturally and racially suspect and were perceived to be loyal to the pope before their new home, the United States. The anticlericalism of the Mexican Revolution and the public perception of the U.S. government's tacit support for such activity contributed to a revival and strengthening of anti-Catholic sentiment in the United States.[7]

Mundelein and other Catholic leaders were quick to support the U.S. declaration of war in 1917. "We stand seriously, solidly and loyally behind our president and his congress," Mundelein announced at the opening of Catholic Charities of Chicago four days after Congress declared war. "In this hour of crisis," he continued, "I pledge the loyalty of our Catholic people to our flag." U.S. Catholic bishops challenged detractors to publicize this patriotic effort as they had the church's presumed anti-American work with immigrants.[8]

Mundelein's governance was also marked by the strengthening of the Catholic Church within Chicago circles, national political ranks, and the Vatican. In Chicago, Mundelein built political ties with local Democratic politicians. The power of the Irish in ruling the city was slowly growing. Although Catholics were not the majority in Chicago, they dominated the Democratic machine during Mundelein's era, and he cultivated powerful alliances, which made Chicago Catholics very visible. Mundelein garnered support in the state legislature as well. As nativism was reaching an all-time high in 1919, the Illinois General Assembly was under pressure to pass legislation regarding language use in the schools. Eventually, it passed an Americanization law, but Mundelein ensured that more extreme measures, which would have forbidden all foreign-language instruction, were not passed. While he did want ethnic Catholics to Americanize, he did not believe it had to cost them their heritage.[9]

Mundelein financed a massive seminary complex, St. Mary of the Lake, in northwest suburban Chicago. He enlisted the support of the local business elite, including the Armour meatpacking family and the Hines lumber family, for this and other causes. The community in which the seminary was built was largely Protestant, and Lake County officials challenged St. Mary of the Lake's tax-exempt status in court. The church prevailed, and in 1925 the residents of the nearby town of Area voted to rename the town Mundelein. His stature remains legendary, as captured in *Commonweal* more than six decades after his death: "Cardinal Mundelein, who styled himself 'Prince of the West,' built a large mansion, a copy of Mount Vernon, above his private lake at Saint Mary of the Lake Seminary." Mundelein's Mount Vernon affirmed an American identity, but one built on entirely Catholic ground. "In his black limousine with the number one license plate, he would be driven into Chicago in solitary splendor. He and his successors seemed quite princely." Mundelein was a larger-than-life character, but most importantly, a Catholic one.[10]

Nationally, Cardinal Mundelein developed close ties with President Franklin Roosevelt. Over the course of several years, Roosevelt's assistant Thomas Corcoran and Mundelein's lawyer, William Campbell, made frequent trips between Chicago and Washington, DC. Mundelein provided public Catholic support, especially important when prominent Catholics like Charles Coughlin challenged the New Deal as communistic. Mundelein relished his role as the most liberal Catholic bishop in the country. Chicago, and the country at large, had a Catholic and world leader to claim as its own.[11]

Mundelein also built connections with labor in the region and across the country. Addressing diocesan priests at the height of the 1919 steel strike, he invoked the spirit of Leo XIII's *Rerum Novarum*. "In a crisis of this kind the Church must be on the side of the workingmen, on the side of the poor," he said. "The workmen must feel . . . that we are not controlled by big interests to be used as watchmen over them."[12] Catholics in the Archdiocese of Chicago were largely working men and women; Mundelein made sure his priests understood his commitment to this population. In April 1926 the Workers Party of Chicago declared its support, on behalf of American labor, for the expulsion of Catholic officials in Mexico. Frank Duffy, second vice president of the American Federation of Labor, assured

Mundelein that this public decree of labor's support for Mexico's anti-Catholic stance was not the work of the AFL. "'Does the American Federation of Labor back up the Mexican President in his policy of religious persecution,' . . . as Vice-President of the American Federation of Labor and thereby a member of its Executive Council, I answer, without reservation, No."[13] In his lengthy statement, Duffy explained that the AFL had gone to great lengths to avoid the appearance of collusion with the regime. He valued Mundelein's support and opinion, and he did not want to be construed as an enemy of the church. Organized labor, like Mundelein, served many working Catholics, and Duffy recognized the importance of staying in Mundelein's good graces.

The climax of Mundelein's career in Chicago came in the years immediately after his 1924 elevation to cardinal. In 1926, Chicago became the first city in the United States to host the International Eucharistic Congress. The majority of the activities took place in Chicago's Soldier Field. On the final day, close to a million worshippers attended a procession on the grounds of St. Mary of the Lake Seminary, thirty miles northwest of the city. The congress was recognized as a once-in-a-lifetime media event for the Catholic Church in Chicago. The *Chicago Tribune* presented a welcoming editorial to those attending the Congress in which it accepted the honor of being the chosen site and recognized as an all-American city.[14]

During Mundelein's time as leader of the Catholic Church in Chicago, Catholics in the United States took dramatic steps toward legitimate citizenship. Upon Mundelein's death, Winthrop Hudson, historian of American Protestantism, wrote that "it was impossible to imagine that the death of any Protestant leader could command the attention that accompanied the death of an American Cardinal."[15] Mundelein was known for his fine business sense, his strong leadership, and his ability to put Chicago Catholicism on the map. The rise of Chicago as a national Catholic force enabled the Extension Society and Kelley to find a place of prominence in national Catholic circles.

## Francis Kelley and the Extension Society

As part of the thriving Archdiocese of Chicago, the Extension Society was able to gain a national and even international audience, giving Francis Kelley national and international stature as a Catholic spokesman and statesman. Kelley exploited that exposure to create a narrative of American Catholic belonging and responsibility. As Matthew Redinger writes, "Kelley's work accomplished far more for Mexican Catholics than did the best efforts" of more senior prelates.[16] During his first assignment, in Lapeer, Michigan, Kelley found that his own and surrounding rural parishes suffered from a lack of funding to sustain churches and schools. In 1905 he approached Archbishop Quigley of Chicago with a plan to support such struggling rural parishes by calling on better-off, mostly urban parishes for financial support. In the words of Kelley's biographer, Father James Gaffey, the Extension Society found "their opportunity in the countryside and their material support in the cities."[17] Over the next nineteen years, Kelley was president of the Extension Society, a joint effort of the archbishops of Chicago and Santa Fe, the bishop of Wichita, and several Illinois bishops. Catholic leadership from the East was noticeably absent from this discussion. As the largest and most stable diocese in the West, Chicago was the natural home for the Extension Society. Kelley parlayed this simple idea of urban parishes funding rural parishes into an American Catholic vision and ethos to sustain a national and international project of uplift and outreach in conjunction with the American empire.

In a report to Pope Benedict XV in 1918, Kelley wrote that the Extension Society was formed to "assist small missions, embryo parishes, chiefly located in pioneer sections, to secure the necessary Church buildings which are required for the Holy Sacrifice, the education of children and the residence of a priest."[18] It also provided railroad and motor chapels to dioceses that had Catholics spread far and wide—particularly in the plains states and the far West. The Extension Society provided the funds, while orders and dioceses provided the personnel to manage the mobile chapels and serve as many Catholics as possible.

Kelley directed the society until 1924, when he became bishop of Oklahoma. He continued to serve on the American Board of Catholic Missions, presided over by Mundelein, which oversaw the Extension Society. Kelley's time as president of the Extension Society coincided with a unique setting in which the Archdiocese of Chicago wielded significant power on the national, international, and Vatican levels. Due to Kelley's persistence, the anticlerical activities of Mexico's revolutionary administrations received special attention from Mundelein, hence national and Vatican attention as well. While the Extension Society was based on noble work, when it moved outside its original calling it entered into the political realm—a dangerous territory for Kelley, yet vital in terms of his broader mission. Kelley's political maneuverings enabled him to combine his two major concerns: shadowing the territorial expansion and growth in political power of the United States, and countering that work by sustaining Catholic populations in those areas. Catholic borderlands extended beyond the American West and beyond former Spanish territories into a broader international project sustained by the cultural entitlement Kelley embraced as part of the American empire.

### Kelley's Diplomatic Missions

The Extension Society existed to serve a uniquely domestic agenda, though Kelley saw his mission as much broader. Kelley's diplomatic missions were not limited to Europe. He sought a role in negotiations between the United States and Mexico numerous times during the Revolution. Kelley's biographer describes his life's work as a series of accidents, but it was no accident that he was always seeking a larger audience and a "higher" power. Kelley frequently overextended his reach and authority in order to accomplish his goals. Much to the chagrin of Quigley and Mundelein, Kelley became the Archdiocese of Chicago's unofficial minister of foreign affairs, and in true Catholic fashion, the United States was one of the "foreign" governments he addressed.

One of Kelley's earliest diplomatic missions was to Rome after the death of Archbishop Quigley in 1915. His goal was to secure support for the Extension Society, and the appointment of Chicago's next archbishop would certainly have an impact on the society's future. He understood the perception his frequent visits to Rome gave, yet his desire to protect the Extension Society drove him there. Three years earlier, he had written to his Vatican confidante, Sante Tampieri, "Frequent visits to Rome might be misunderstood."[19] Kelley's second five-year term as president of the Extension Society was about to expire, and he wanted to ensure his reappointment. His involvement with the Mexican hierarchy and his lack of success in negotiating with the U.S. government on their behalf compelled him to bring "the Mexican situation" to the Vatican's attention.[20] In addition, his desire to protect the future of the Extension Society led him to lobby for the appointment of Peter Muldoon, bishop of Rockford, Illinois, and co-founder of the society, as archbishop of Chicago. He was disappointed and discouraged when a New Yorker, Mundelein, was named to the post. This brought Kelley's first diplomatic mission to a less-than-auspicious close.

Kelley's next mission to Europe was in the aftermath of World War I. He made several trips to war torn areas to meet with religious men and women. Kelley attended the peace talks in Paris in 1919 as an informal liaison for the Mexican hierarchy. He pushed for the inclusion of a religious liberty clause in the peace agreements so that he could later use this to pressure U.S. officials to respond to the outrages against Catholics in Mexico. Kelley visited U.S. troops to make sure Catholic clergy were being provided for the soldiers, and he sought to secure the German mission territories in Asia and Africa.[21] He did so with tremendous gusto, raising funds across the United States to support European Catholics, potentially risking the financial stability of the Extension Society. With this, Kelley expanded Catholic borderlands beyond former Spanish territories. Here, Kelley's U.S. affiliation allowed him to speak for German Catholic orders, seeking to maintain their placements after the end of German dominance in their missionary fields.

The 1919 Paris peace agreements required Germany to give up control of its overseas colonies. The transfer of these territories allowed for the Allied and Associated powers to repatriate the missionaries and confiscate the missions. After extensive negotiations, the Holy See convinced Allied leaders that Catholic mission properties really belonged to the Vatican, but it reluctantly agreed to the staffing requirements outlined by the Allies, which led to the removal of many German missioners. American Catholic leadership, including Mundelein, worked to maintain German missions in China, in particular. In a letter to Acting Secretary of State Frank Polk in March 1919, Mundelein wrote: "In the recent expulsion of Germans from China, which is now going on under pressure we are told from the allied powers, it is proposed to include these missionaries according to the purely pagan and commercial code that the missionary is the forerunner of the trader." Mundelein rejected the notion that the missioner and the imperialist were partners in civilizing the barbarians. He also alluded to the political and economic power of one million Chicago Catholics. He wrote that he hoped to report that his appeal "on behalf of interests so dear to their hearts received a favorable consideration on the part of their Federal Administration." Were the German missions to receive the protection of the federal government, Mundelein could assure Catholics in his diocese that "the missions which their money has built up received the needed protection at this critical and dangerous time."[22] As early as 1916, Mundelein had chosen not to allow other foreign missionaries to have special collections in the archdiocese. Solely the Extension Society and the Divine Word foreign missionaries were to benefit from the generosity of Chicago Catholics.

In 1920, Kelley arrived in London to "assist" the British Foreign Office in discussions of the German missionaries in the British empire. Paul Kramer noted inter-imperial alliances between Britain and the United States at the end of the nineteenth century; Catholicism was certainly not part of that link. Kelley garnered the attention of the British as a prominent U.S. Catholic spokesman. From the church's perspective, missionaries were world citizens, responsible to a higher power than those involved in the war. As participants in the colonizing and civilizing efforts of the Germans, however, the missionaries were spoils of war, and the British were determined to remove them after the dust had settled. Kelley was aware of this issue long before his visit to England. He had received reports before the United States entered the war indicating that the Portuguese were imprisoning German missionaries in Africa as enemy aliens. He did his best to leak such outrages to the U.S. press, but he was not able to bring light to the issue. He wisely chose not to use *Extension Magazine* as a vehicle for this project, as the United States was technically still neutral in the conflict.

The British reputation in the United States was damaged by the removal of missionaries from German and French territories. In addition, the British had postponed Home Rule in Ireland, angering Irish American Catholics. The British Foreign Office perceived Kelley as "unreliable and slippery," based on his self-given title as "official liaison of the exiled Mexican hierarchy" at the Paris peace conference.[23] The Mexican hierarchy had dubbed Kelley their spokesperson in the United States but had not given him authority to negotiate on their behalf, a fact later uncovered by the British. In spite of these issues, they recognized that Kelley had an important national Catholic audience, a group they otherwise were not able to pacify. British officials seemed to understand that feeding Kelley's ego was the best way to do this.

After initial investigation of the German mission question, Kelley visited the Vatican to seek guidance on the staffing issues in question. For the first and only time, he received a diplomatic rank and was authorized to assist British cardinal Francis Bourne in negotiations with the British government on behalf of the Vatican. Kelley drafted a protocol that allowed for American or British missionaries to replace the expelled Germans, reproducing a Catholic borderlands in these territories by maintaining a Catholic missionary presence in spite of Germany's losses. In a July letter to Sir William Tyrell of the British political intelligence department, he wrote that "the [British] Empire's task of advancing [Africans and Asians] in civilisation is one that cannot be lightly considered." In regard to the U.S. role in the civilizing mission, he wrote, "outside of sections of our own country and of the Philippine Islands, there is no missionary territory under American control. We must go beyond our limits for Mission work."[24] Although Kelley was only in charge of home mission activities, he was ready to commit U.S. Catholic resources to foreign mission and imperial activities—areas that were clearly outside his authority.

Kelley considered the mission to England a success and was buoyed by the Vatican's confidence in him. He immediately tried to dampen any anti-British, pro-Irish movements that were afoot in U.S. dioceses. In a report to Cardinal James Gibbons, leader of the U.S. bishops, he wrote: "The best help we can get now is by not saying anything to make matters worse. . . . If a resolution has been suggested on this subject, the Holy See would be pleased if it were tabled."[25] It is unlikely that Kelley was empowered to speak so directly on behalf of the pope. Nevertheless, his efforts to contain U.S. Catholic aggression toward the British were largely successful. Before Kelley's protocol could be implemented, however, the Vatican balked at signing an agreement, fearing this would set a precedent whereby Catholic missions served at the whims of changing governments. The Holy See refused to allow the British to decide who would staff the missions; and even if it did, there were not enough British Catholic missionaries to fill the positions to be vacated by the Germans. In the end, Kelley's diplomatic successes were shattered.

Kelley's trip to Paris accidentally embroiled him in yet another diplomatic mission, the conclusion of which came a decade later. Since 1870, the Vatican had been "occupied" by the Italian government, which refused to grant the church the sovereignty it had enjoyed since the eighth century. While Italian leaders were willing to grant tax-exempt status, they still considered the Eternal City to be Italian property that the pope was allowed to occupy. Pope Pius IX (1846–78) and Pope Leo XIII (1878–1903) secluded themselves in the Vatican City and forbade Italian Catholics to participate in the government. Pope Pius X (1903–14) was more interested in a settlement, and he carefully explored the possibilities of negotiating with the Italian government. World War I had further isolated the pope due to travel difficulties in Europe, which limited pilgrimages to the Holy City.

Despite attempts by Cardinal Secretary of State Pietro Gasparri, there was no official Vatican representation at the Paris peace talks. Tension between the United States and Italy grew over disagreements on the distribution of territories. Italian prime minister Vittorio Orlando's overtures to expand into the Balkans were refused by Wilson and his negotiators, a move that Kelley used to support his own agendas. In a chance meeting with Giuseppe Brambilla of the Italian delegation, in May 1919, Kelley convinced Brambilla that the way to undermine U.S. public support of Wilson was to settle the "Roman Question," the nearly seventy-year dispute between the Vatican and the Italian government. Sensing that Kelley had studied the issues, Brambilla arranged a meeting between Kelley and Orlando. Kelley reported, "I reminded Mr. Orlando that we were merely two gentlemen discussing a public question together and that nothing I would say had any more authority behind it than the simple opinion of an American Catholic."[26] Still, he understood the magnitude of this conversation with Italy's leader. He immediately departed for the Vatican to share news of his "discussion" with Cardinal Gasparri.

Archbishop Bonaventura Cerretti, Gasparri's deputy secretary of state, was assigned to accompany Kelley to Paris to begin secret negotiations with the Orlando government. Cerretti and Orlando reached an agreement in June 1919, but before it could be made public, Orlando returned to Italy to address domestic problems. By mid-July his government was toppled, and the regime that replaced it quickly showed its fascist tendencies. All progress that had been made on the Roman Question was lost. In the years that followed the issue was occasionally addressed, but the timing and the participating parties did not align until February 1929, when Cardinal Gasparri and Benito Mussolini signed the Lateran Pacts, which created the Vatican City State, established Catholicism as the official religion of Italy, and provided compensation to the church for property lost almost seven decades earlier. Kelley's role was revived in the months before the signing of the pact. The church did not want to appear to be in collaboration with the fascist government, so Gasparri and Cerretti set about documenting the origins of the negotiations prior to fascist control of Italy. Kelley was asked to report on his role in the activities. Eventually, the Associated Press reported that Kelley had been a principal actor in the settlement through his interactions with *Mrs.* Brambilla, an error that infuriated Kelley. "I do not like," he wrote to his successor at the Extension Society, "the implication that Vatican diplomacy is done through teas."[27] Kelley was angry that the Vatican did not acknowledge his role in the affair. In May 1929 he asked Cerretti if the Holy Father was offended by his actions, but Cerretti indicated that the pope was pleased.[28] Wondering about the Vatican's silence in regard to the AP story, Kelley wrote to Hugh Boyle, bishop of Pittsburgh, "Every time I do something good I expect to get licked for it." A month later, he lamented, "If I get out of it without awakening a flood of jealousies I shall be satisfied."[29] In 1930 the Italian government made Kelley a Knight of the Order of St. Maurice and St. Lazarus, acknowledging his role in settling the Roman Question. The Vatican never acknowledged or rewarded his efforts, formally or informally. Kelley's expansion of Catholic borderlands had finally reached a limit.

Kelley's efforts at diplomacy always started in logical places; as director of Catholic home missions in the United States, it seemed natural that he might be consulted in discussions of the German missions. But for him, the ends justified the means, leading him to exaggerate his own importance and legitimacy if it suited his purposes. Although his biographer characterized Kelley as an accidental diplomat, Kelley clearly understood how to elevate himself and the issues that concerned him, whether or not he was authorized to do so. Most curious is how much time Kelley spent abroad as president of the Catholic Church Extension Society of the United States of America, an organization with an explicitly domestic agenda. Kelley's adventures throughout Europe were enabled by his appointment as representative of the Mexican hierarchy in the United States. His time in Europe also provided essential groundwork and contacts for his most significant diplomatic project, the Mexican mission. Still, as seen in his correspondence with Mundelein, Mexicans in Chicago were not central to the Mexican mission, and they bore little influence on the American imperial project.

While the Extension Society was focusing its attention on the faith of Mexicans in Mexico, it had little regard for the spiritual needs of those Mexicans within its own reach in Chicago. Matthew Frye Jacobson and others have considered the paradox of "immigrants at home and savages abroad," but that was not the imperial dilemma Kelley faced with Mexicans in Chicago.[30] Mexican immigrants in the Southwest had a place in Catholic borderlands, but when they made their way north they seemingly blended into the "immigrant church" framework that Kelley was so committed to disrupting. This contradiction in the actions of the Catholic Church is a reflection of broader contradictions that existed in U.S.-Mexican relations during this period. Although the Revolution worked in part to remove the influence of U.S. capital and the Spanish Catholic Church from Mexico, it did not anticipate the ways that the U.S. Catholic Church would operate in the interests of both: one an imperial presence seeking to expand its reach across the hemisphere, the other a lingering colonial structure with a new face.

Kelley most often saw himself and his church as distinct from the U.S. government, but there are curious intersections of government, business, and religious leadership that raise questions about how imperial structures interact. Kelley reflected on a meeting he had with Andrew Carnegie about the Mexican situation in 1915. During this conversation, Kelley and Carnegie explored ways to bring peace to the continent. Carnegie posed the question of how peace could be brought about "with credit to these United States—by other means than intervention, of course." Kelley proposed a religion-based plan that would have cost $1.5 to $2 million, in which Carnegie was interested—except for the sectarianism. Kelley and Carnegie could not agree on a plan and parted company.[31]

Francis Kelley put the Mexican Revolution on the map of American Catholic political discourse. He challenged government officials to protect the rights of Catholics regardless of their citizenship. Kelley had close ties with members of the Mexican hierarchy, but he did not demonstrate the same concern for common Mexican Catholics who had been in Chicago since the mid-1910s. In the 1910s the Extension Society denied Mexican nationhood by attempting to intervene in Mexican internal affairs. Mexico's religious crisis became a symbol of the rise to power of the Catholic Church in Chicago, where Mexicans themselves were getting in the way. Catholic borderlands had limits, but only within the American empire.

# 5

## Crisis in the Catholic Borderlands

*The International Eucharistic Congress and the Cristero Rebellion*

On June 18, 1926, the *Chicago Tribune* warned that Mexican secret police would be patrolling the streets of Chicago in the coming days. From June 20 to June 24 the city played host to the International Eucharistic Congress, a gathering of Catholics from around the world. Chicago had not quite embraced the old-world pageantry of the nation's largest archdiocese prior to this time, but the arrival of cardinals, bishops, and pilgrims captured the attention and imagination of the City of Broad Shoulders. The Eucharistic Congress also captured the attention of President Plutarco Elías Calles of Mexico. "A force of secret police of the Mexican department of the interior accompanied the Mexican pilgrims to the Eucharistic Congress at Chicago," the *Tribune* reported, citing *El Sol*, a Mexican labor newspaper. "*El Sol* expresses the hope that no Mexican will expose himself to prosecution by intemperate remarks in Chicago."[1] On the opening day of the congress, the *Tribune* reported the thoughts of "a high churchman whose name must be withheld for reasons of church policy." Although the Mexican situation was not officially on the program, it was, according to the source, "the main topic of private discussion." The *Tribune* reminded the unnamed prelate that Mexican government sources reported the priests were in the United States to lobby for intervention. The prelate responded, "The exiled Mexican bishops living in the United States decided to leave the United States for Canada when it appeared some time ago that intervention was possible. This was their only method of protesting against intervention."[2] Catholic borderlands enable the bishops to not only transcended the line between the United States and Mexico, but that between the United States and Canada, as well.

The 1926 International Eucharistic Congress in Chicago and the 1929 settlement between church and state in Mexico, which was negotiated by Ambassador Dwight Morrow, marked the beginning and end of the Cristiada, or Cristero Rebellion, the three-year civil war that nearly destroyed Mexico in the 1920s. Catholicism in the shadow of American empire maneuvered across international boundaries in the guise of U.S. and Mexican prelates and statesmen, who pursued political and religious goals on both sides of the border. This chapter demonstrates that Mexican laypeople, prelates, and politicians attributed the role of savior to the U.S. government in the mid to late 1920s. They recognized that the United States would intervene in Mexico and raced to shape how that intervention occurred and direct what it would accomplish. The U.S. government needed a settlement in order to secure the post-revolutionary gains of U.S. business interests, while the Mexican Catholic hierarchy wanted to regain its central role in Mexico's social and spiritual life. Mexican Catholic activists sought guarantees that a Catholic political party could exist, and Francis Kelley wanted to shame President Calles into restoring the Catholic Church to its former position of prominence in Mexico. Each of these goals affirmed that U.S. and Mexican Catholicisms were inextricably intertwined in this era. As the United States was refining its role as a world leader and as Mexico was redefining itself post-Revolution, both nations kept a weary watch over the activities of the other. Likewise, and partially in response to official U.S. involvement with the Mexican government, U.S. and Mexican Catholicisms were developing in relation to each other. American Catholics actively supported religious freedom in Mexico, and Mexico's Catholic leadership firmed up its base in San Antonio, Texas, and explored ways to exploit a direct strike on the Calles government by the U.S. government without harming the Mexican Catholic Church. These entanglements are emblematic of Catholic borderlands: in spite of Catholicism being the organizing principle, like other Pan-American projects of the era, this one had the United States in the position of power.

### Calles's Rise to Power and Catholic Resistance

President Alvaro Obregón was succeeded in 1924 by his former second in command, Plutarco Elías Calles, who had removed Monsignor Ernesto Filippi from Mexico and was a well-known enemy of the church.[3] Calles was described as having been "jubilantly atheist" as a child. He reportedly once said, "When I was an altar boy as a child, I stole the alms to buy candy."[4] As governor of Sonora, his most significant work was in education reform—inaugurating a vast system of public schools funded by the state and by mining and other companies that employed large numbers of Mexicans—effectively eliminating the influence of the clergy on early education. Eventually, Calles "solved" the lingering problem of clerical influence by expelling all Catholic priests from the state. He ruled Sonora with an iron fist, also expelling or executing Industrial Workers of the World and other anarchist and syndicalist activists. At the same time, he confiscated unused land from U.S. mining interests. His motives were neither capitalist nor communist; he simply distrusted foreigners of any stripe. Calles was paradoxically drawn to European forms of government and spent time in Germany and France before returning to Mexico to become president.

Early on, Calles's primary concern as president was Mexico's financial stability. He made dramatic strides, nearly eliminating Mexico's deficit by the end of 1925. He implemented the Caja Raiffeissen system, an agricultural cooperative bank modeled after a German reform program, which, ironically, Catholic leaders had advocated a decade earlier.[5] Calles also worked strategically to maintain the governing alliance that he and Obregón had established, which became a model for future transitions of power. With Calles's support, the Chamber of Deputies introduced a constitutional amendment to allow the nonconsecutive reelection of former presidents, thereby clearing the way for Obregón's return to power in 1928.

Calles did not actively work against the Catholic Church in his first year in office, though local and state governments realized that he would not block their actions against the church. These ranged from cosmetic changes to violent altercations with priests and Mexican Catholics. Tabasco's governor enacted a law that forbade unmarried priests and imprisoned those who refused to marry. Those who were not jailed left, effectively eliminating church services throughout the state. In 1925, Calles received requests from Aguascalientes and Colima to intervene in local situations. Ricardo Villapando sought Calles's assistance in removing members of the Caballeros de Colón—the Knights of Columbus—from the Aguascalientes Chamber of Deputies, while General Teodoro Escalona in Colima informed the president of strife between the Caballeros and the local military.[6] Even in the years that Calles refrained from an open attack on the church, provincial officials kept up the pressure. U.S. officials likely would not have picked Calles for president, but they were grateful for the peaceful transition from Obregón to Calles.

Calles received a reminder that Catholicism transcended the nation in April 1925 when Serafín Cimino, the new apostolic delegate, arrived in Mexico. His placement had been negotiated by the Vatican with Calles's representatives. Cimino did not last long, because, in the words of William Montavon of the National Catholic Welfare Conference (NCWC), he "was not able to endure the climatic conditions and high altitude of Mexico and was obliged to visit the United States to recuperate his strength."[7] Mexican immigration officials denied Cimino reentry six weeks later, and he returned to Rome. This episode provided additional fuel for U.S. Catholics to challenge the claim that Calles was securing religious liberty.

Calles proved to Americans and others that religious liberty was allowed by indirectly supporting the Iglesia Católica Apostólica Mexicana, an independent Catholic church started by a few renegade priests. Luis Morones, Calles's secretary of economy and leader of the Confederación Regional de Obreros Mexicanos (CROM), the Mexican equivalent of the American Federation of Labor, supported the schism, as did the Board of Missions of the American Protestant Episcopal Church, but the breakaway church was not terribly successful. Catholics reacted violently to the attempt to take over their church and threaten their traditions. Calles underestimated Mexicans' allegiance to their local churches.[8] While Mexicans would go to extremes to protect their churches and even their local pastor, few were willing to give their lives for the bishop.

In response to the escalation of attacks on the church, a group of middle-class lay Catholics in Mexico City formed the Liga Nacional de Defensa Religiosa. The founders wrote a manifesto that declared: "We must unite, therefore, concerting all our forces, so that in due time, and as one, we can make an effort that is energetic, tenacious, supreme, and irresistible, which will uproot once and for all from the Constitution all its injustices of whatever kind and all its tyrannies whatever their origin."[9] The Liga worked across Mexico and around the world to generate support for its agenda of religious freedom in Mexico. Within two years there were International Unions of Friends of the League for the Defense of Religious Freedom in Mexico throughout Europe and Latin America.[10] The Friends of the League never caught on in the United States, despite the Liga's significant contact with the NCWC. The prior decade of involvement and communication between Mexican and U.S. bishops made a group like the Friends of the League less necessary in the United States.

The Liga provided updates to Friends of the League around the world. For many European and Latin American clergy, this was their main source for information on the situation in Mexico. There was occasional Liga correspondence with organizations in the United States, such as the Liga Católica Mexicana in Laredo, Texas, and the Sociedad Beneficencia Pro-México in Chicago. None of these groups was directly affiliated with the Liga, and the correspondence was short lived. They were also in conflict with each other over both U.S. and Mexican regional and political issues.[11] By the end of June 1925 the Liga reported thirty-six thousand members spread through all regions of Mexico except northwestern Sonora, where Calles had been governor, and Campeche and Quintana Roo, in the far southeast. The Liga established a strong presence in rural areas, particularly in the central-west states. Regional variation in response to all aspects of the Revolution as well as to matters of religion was significant.

Mexico was marked by a significant range of Catholic practices. U.S Catholics and the Mexican hierarchy saw Mexican clerical leadership as central to Catholic practice, but for the average Mexican this was not the case. Private spiritual practice and public celebrations of the faith continued without priests in Mexico. In spite of the cultural divide between Mexican and U.S. Catholicism, Mexican Catholics recognized that they were in the Catholic borderlands and looked north for a solution to their stalemate with their government.

The Mexican hierarchy struggled to find a way to coexist with the government without giving up land, churches, and control of their own administration. The hierarchy also struggled to control the increasingly violent Catholic responses in both rural and urban areas. By the fall of 1925 the hierarchy and laity were reporting widespread repression to the Vatican, and Liga representatives visited the pope to express their concerns. Calles was unhappy with the hit-or-miss fashion in which states responded to the constitutional articles concerning religion. In January 1926 he sought the power to amend the penal code to enforce these articles. States acted quickly to reduce the power of the church, closing seminaries and schools and limiting the number of priests.

On February 2, 1926, Pope Pius XI (1922–39) issued an apostolic letter, *Paterna Sane Sollicitudo*, addressing the Mexican situation. He indicted the Mexican government for its repression, but it was not a call to action. In fact, it was clear in limiting the clergy to spiritual matters. Further, the pope encouraged laity to work together in passive, rather than armed, resistance to the Mexican government. The pope urged an embrace of Acción Católica (Catholic Social Action) in the face of the persecution.[12] Two days later, in an unfortunate turn of events, a 1917 letter written by José Mora y del Río, the archbishop of Mexico, criticizing the Constitution of 1917 was reprinted in *El Universal*, setting off a series of events that disrupted Mexico for years to come. Calles immediately invoked Article 130 of the Constitution of 1917, which restricted foreign priests and professionals. The fears of the Mexican hierarchy were realized a decade after the passage of the Constitution of 1917. On February 10, 1926, Spanish priests were rounded up and sent to Veracruz for deportation. The Vatican continued to take a wait-and-see attitude, which created some discord among the Mexican hierarchy, many of whom wanted swift action to be taken. Across Mexico, violent confrontations erupted between lay Catholics and government agents.

On February 18, a three-hour riot took place between police and two thousand protesters in Mexico City. U.S. Catholics pushed Washington to intervene, but they were not alone. Religious concerns were never enough to force U.S. involvement, but they were a significant force alongside economic and political concerns. In March, at a CROM convention, Calles reaffirmed his resolve to enforce the Constitution of 1917. As in previous administrations, labor served as enforcers for the Calles government.

Archbishop George Caruana arrived in Mexico for his brief but eventful stay as apostolic delegate in March 1926. Caruana had served as bishop of Puerto Rico and was fluent in Spanish, so he likely served more than just a ceremonial role. In April the Mexican hierarchy released a pastoral letter calling for Catholics to use lawful means to resist the repression and to amend the Constitution of 1917. At the same time, the Liga sought the endorsement of the hierarchy. The clerics wisely supported the Liga, but publicly they kept their distance from the organization. Caruana suggested that the Liga Nacional de Defensa Religiosa be renamed the Liga Nacional Defensora de la Libertad Religiosa (National League for the Defense of Religious Freedom, or LNDLR). He seemed to anticipate the argument that could be made regarding religious freedom as a universal human right, and therefore one that ought to be supported by the United States and other powers. Within two years of his taking office, Calles's hostility to the church stimulated a powerful and multi-pronged international defense. Catholic borderlands loomed, and once again the U.S. Catholic Church took the lead in defending the church in Mexico.

## The U.S. Catholic Church Strikes

As early as April 1926, concerns about the impending International Eucharistic Congress in Chicago appeared in correspondence between Mexican government officials in the United States and Mexico. The Mexican consul, Lujual, regularly sent the Secretaría de Relaciones Exteriores (SRE, Ministry of Foreign Affairs) newspaper clippings about the event, including the expected participation of at least two hundred Mexicans.[13] In late May, consuls around the world were instructed to notify the Mexican ambassador in Washington, DC, "in case of attacks on the policies of the Mexican government." SRE officials were concerned that "the Catholic element" in the United States would "send a protest to Mexico."[14] It is unclear what kind of protest this might be, but Mexican officials feared the power of the U.S. Catholic Church to interfere in Mexican affairs in the Catholic borderlands.

By the time the Eucharistic Congress convened, Mexican officials were on high alert. Enrique Liekens, consul general at El Paso, Texas, wrote to his counterpart in Albuquerque, New Mexico, suggesting that, in light of the Eucharistic Congress, Mexican consuls along the border ought to be alert to "political-religious activities [that might] take place against Mexico, making an effort to bring an armed movement to the country."[15] Cardinal George Mundelein of Chicago, acting on urgent requests from Francis Kelley, now bishop of Oklahoma and a member of the presiding committee for the Eucharistic Congress, decided to showcase the Mexican situation at the congress. Mundelein invited the exiled apostolic delegate to Mexico, George Caruana, to be a celebrant at a stadium Mass and to offer services at the cathedral during Holy Hour, the period of Eucharistic adoration and height of Catholic celebration during the congress. "The fact that we thus place you in a prominent position during the Congress will make better known our united support of you at this time than any mere protest in words," Mundelein wrote. Caruana, in exile in Washington, DC, and under attack by Mexican consuls in the United States, declined the invitation to play a prominent role in the congress, but he did attend, and did so expressly as a representative of Mexico, rather than his home diocese.[16] With great caution, so as not to endanger any of the Mexican hierarchy, the planning committee succeeded in having Mexico present and represented at this gathering in the bosom of the Catholic borderlands.

Many in the Mexican delegation opted to stay behind, for fear that their parishes would suffer in their absence or that they would not be allowed to reenter Mexico. Archbishop José Gonzales of Durango reported to Mundelein that property was being confiscated and schools closed, making it impossible for "us to separate even for a moment from our herd, so closely followed around by so many hungry wolves."[17] Archbishop Francisco Orozco y Jiménez, a close friend of Kelley's, attended the Eucharistic Congress and managed to return to Mexico without being noticed by border officials. Unlike most of the Mexican hierarchy, Orozco y Jiménez frequently made this journey—often in disguise—always escaping the notice of immigration officials. Cardinal Secretary of State Gasparri, reinforcing the international pressure on Mexico, sent word to the Eucharistic Congress formally condemning the treatment of Archbishop Caruana and others by Mexican government officials. Cardinal Mundelein wanted to present a united Catholic front in solidarity with the Mexican hierarchy, drawing national as well as international focus to the Mexican situation. In the end, the Eucharistic Congress probably did more damage than good to the Catholic Church in Mexico. Attention by the U.S. Catholic leadership and public prompted a response in Mexico. Through Catholic borderlands, the U.S. and Mexican Catholic Churches had become intertwined during the previous decade; the border was so porous to Catholicism that even without the Mexican hierarchy, the Eucharistic Congress presented a threat to the Mexican government.

In response to the celebration of Mexican Catholicism in Chicago, Calles finalized his national plan for dealing with the clergy. On July 2, 1926, he published the so-called Calles Law, which outlined the new penal code regarding the church. Foreign priests were

Fig. 23. Cardinal John Bonzano and his attendants at Mundelein Seminary, outside Chicago, during the International Eucharistic Congress, June 1926.

prohibited, religious education was eliminated, the clergy were not allowed to comment on politics, religious newspapers could not comment on politics, political parties could not include any reference to religion, political meetings could not take place in churches, worship could only take place in churches and under the supervision of local government officials, priests could not wear their religious garb outside the church, and all church property became the property of the nation, under the control of local government officials. The Calles Law took effect at the end of the month. The international Catholic Church understood itself to be at war with the Mexican government. The U.S. Catholic Church had contributed its share to Mexico's new religious crisis.

## The Liga in the Catholic Borderlands

The Liga took on new importance with the absence of the clergy from Mexico. The national movement led in part by the Liga was

Fig. 24. Priests from around the world line up for a procession at the
International Eucharistic Congress, Chicago, June 1926, with onlookers
and photographers gathered to watch. The decorations throughout
the city included American flags.

social, political, and, perhaps more than anything, religious. The
Cristero Rebellion, which raged from 1926 to 1929, is often framed
as an anti-revolutionary or reactionary campaign, but Catholics did
not seek to undo the gains of the Revolution. The Liga and the Cristeros were as interested in Mexico's revolutionary goals and future as
Calles was. Catholics under Porfirio Díaz were active in the social
movements of the day. Through the 1910s they had fought for social
change alongside other revolutionaries, but their vision of Mexico's
future, like Father Hidalgo's independence movement a century
earlier, included the church as a central part of Mexican identity.

Working across Mexico and around the world, the Liga pressured
the Calles administration to incorporate religious liberty into the
constitution. The Liga was astute in asserting religious liberty in their
call for constitutional reforms, rather than arguing specifically for

Fig. 25. Sioux Indians with their missionary priest at the International Eucharistic Congress, Chicago, June 1926. The Sioux were mostly dressed in "civilized" clothes but had some native adornments as well.

the protection of Catholicism. "Dios y mi derecho" ("God and my right"), with which they closed correspondence, invoked that basic right in every letter or broadside they distributed. Miguel Palomar y Vizcarra, a member of the Liga's executive committee, attended the International Eucharistic Congress in Oxford, England, in 1925 to report on the religious repression in Mexico and network with European Catholics. The Liga assigned a permanent representative in Europe, a Spanish layman, to oversee the propaganda campaign and fund-raising on their behalf.[18]

The Liga recognized, however, that its most important support had to come from the United States. In 1925 they sent a letter to *Revista Católica*, based in El Paso, pledging support for the publication despite the fact that the Mexican government was not allowing *Revista Católica* to be delivered to subscribers in Mexico. The Liga tried to make the most of this slight to the American publication, announcing it had "sent to all the news publications in the country our most forceful protest for this most reprehensible and unjust fraudulent abuse which is victimizing you as well as your subscribers." The Liga offered its support for and defense of *Revista Católica*, but only "in an entirely disinterested manner."[19] The Liga, in trying to build support in the Catholic borderlands, was hardly disinterested. Public support from an American publication, even a Spanish language one, would have been invaluable to the Liga. In 1926, Liga leader René Capistrán Garza received a letter of introduction from the Mexican bishops to support his fund-raising efforts in the United States. Although his efforts largely fell on deaf ears, Capistrán Garza spent the better part of the next three years in exile in the United States.[20]

The Catholic hierarchy, with the Liga as its messenger, encouraged nonviolent resistance to the Calles Law.[21] National boycotts were organized, going a step further than the localized economic boycotts of the previous decade. The Liga instructed Catholics to remove their children from public schools and to conduct public displays, such as women wearing black to mourn the loss of the church, "to create a grave general situation paralyzing as much as possible the ECONOMIC AND SOCIAL LIFE of the country."[22] Still, violence erupted in many places throughout Mexico, despite calls by the bishops to remain calm in the face of religious persecution. A month after the Calles Law was enacted, the Liga collected five hundred thousand signatures on a petition calling for reforms to the Constitution of 1917 and had a significant impact on the economy in many areas.[23] In Mexico City movie houses were forced to close because of the boycott.[24] Liga leaders and young Catholics from the Asociación Católica de la Juventud Mexicana (ACJM, Catholic Association of Mexican Youth) were imprisoned for sedition, and women wore black to show their support of the boycott. Calles remained intransigent. On July 25, after secret talks with the Secretaría de Gobernación failed, the Mexican hierarchy released a pastoral letter announcing the suspension of Masses and other services on July 31, 1926.

In reaction to the Calles Law, violence erupted in many states, including Coahuila, Jalisco, and Guerrero, where a municipal president was stoned to death by Catholic women as he attempted to inventory the property in their church. On August 2, Ambassador James Rockwell Sheffield reported to Secretary of State Frank B. Kellogg that "the political situation here has reached the greatest crisis since the accession of President Calles to the Presidency."[25] At their national meeting in Philadelphia, the Knights of Columbus adopted a resolution condemning Calles and began fund-raising for a massive propaganda campaign. The $500,000 fund-raising goal raised fear on both sides of the border that the Knights were raising money to arms the Cristeros. It was widely rumored that some of this money went to the Cristeros, but this was never proven.

In late August, layman Eduardo Mestre succeeded in convincing Calles to meet with two representatives of the Mexican hierarchy. Archbishop Leopoldo Ruiz y Flores and Bishop Pascual Díaz met with Calles on August 21. Morrow wrote of his discussion with Mestre, "The President had treated them courteously, had let them preach their regular sermons to him, and has spoken to them quietly and reasonably." The hierarchy wrote a statement, which was reviewed by Calles and then appeared in the papers on August 22. The following day, an interview with Calles was published in which he reasserted that if the priests returned to the churches they would be subject to the full force of the Constitution of 1917. What the hierarchy saw as a settlement, Calles saw as a confirmation of what the limitations on priests would be. This misunderstanding significantly escalated the tension between the two groups and pushed them even further apart. News of the meeting stunned Vatican officials, who had not authorized the Mexican hierarchy to negotiate a settlement.[26]

Sporadic violence continued in the following months. In December the Liga, which until then had officially employed only nonviolent resistance, called for a rebellion to begin on January 1, 1927. Their stated goal was the overthrow of the government and the reform of the constitution. ACJM members burned railroad bridges, and miners rebelled against their employers, appropriating dynamite and other supplies for the Cristiada. Sustained rebellion proved impossible in most parts of the country, but the Cristeros in the states of Jalisco, Michoacán, Colima, and Guanajuato successfully continued the fight. Since federal forces were committed to putting down the unrelated Yaqui uprising in Calles's home state of Sonora, the president provided arms to *agraristas* (agrarian activists) battling Cristeros in parts of west-central Mexico. The Cristeros forced Calles to change his national strategy—he had spent several years trying to disarm the agraristas. In Catholic stronghold Jalisco, fearing agraristas might rebel and join the Cristeros, he distributed arms to urban workers as well.[27] The Cristero Rebellion, like the Revolution, was characterized by regional, class, political, and religious divisions.

On January 17, 1927, the Committee of Mexican Bishops, residing in Rome, wrote to Cardinal Dennis Dougherty of Philadelphia to request financial support from the U.S. bishops for the Liga. This was particularly troubling, since it came after the call for an armed movement in Mexico. Americans had historically expressed fears of Catholic leadership becoming involved in politics, a fear echoed in post-revolutionary Mexico. The Mexican bishops' appeal to the U.S. hierarchy from the Vatican affirmed recognition that U.S. forces ruled the Catholic borderlands, even in Mexican affairs. The committee wrote, "The Holy Father has set a noble example of generosity to the whole world by contributing, of his own accord, the sum of one million Lire, which has been transmitted to the Apostolic Delegate of the U.S. to the committee of Bishops in Mexico." Given the economic distress across Mexico, the bishops indicated, "The National League for the defense of religion stands therefore in urgent need of material help in order to meet the incumbent obligations of organization and propaganda."[28] One Liga broadside from 1927 read "Glory to Mexico! privileged nation which has formed with its noble sons, the vanguard of the armies of the King of Kings." The flier continued, in the spirit of the Revolution, embracing many sectors of Mexican society, "For whose cause and glory have they spilled their blood, the priest as well as the educated or the dark, humble Indian who has fallen like the others and has risen from earth to heaven with the same crown?" As always, the Liga concluded by reinvoking Jesus: "Christ conquers, Christ reigns, Christ rules, year of our lord, 1927."[29] The Catholic press experienced a resurgence due to the increased need to communicate religious concerns without the clergy or use of churches. The Liga also put out "war bulletins" from time to time to keep Cristeros updated on the movements and motivations of the opposing forces. This Catholic political machine, with its U.S. and Vatican components, was formidable.[30]

A decade earlier, Mexicans had had a much stronger voice in the United States through the hierarchy's official spokesman, Francis Kelley. This time they focused on Dwight Morrow, who was well connected with Catholics in Washington, DC, including the apostolic delegate to the United States. The Vatican was presumed to be central in negotiations between the church and the state in Mexico. In the end, however, U.S. bodies were more involved in the settlement, and in fact proceeded with the 1929 accord against the wishes of the Vatican, which traditionally believed the church could outlast local political unrest.

Bishop Pascual Díaz was expelled after being falsely accused of playing an active role in the January 1, 1927, rebellions. He eventually went to the United States, where he stayed in New York and Washington, DC, working with the apostolic delegate to the United States and with the U.S. Catholic hierarchy to pressure the Mexican government and the Cristeros to end the violence. There were semi-permanent communities of clergy and nuns in exile throughout the Catholic borderlands, including San Antonio, New Orleans, and Havana, working with local Mexican residents or exiles, waiting out the violence and repression with the hopes of returning to their flocks. Many Mexicans surely agreed with Calles that bishops who relocated to the United States were deserting their flocks to align themselves with Mexico's mortal enemy. Calles, like so many Mexican leaders, maintained conflicting public and private views of the United States, decrying U.S. interference while privately seeking to use U.S. influence to his advantage whenever possible. Arturo Elías,

Fig. 26. Local Catholics in Texas greeted a train whose passengers were mostly disguised nuns escaping religious repression in the Cristero era, September 1926.

Calles's half brother, was also based in the United States, working to subvert the church's agenda. He released several publications, in both English and Spanish, on the religion question and made many public appearances to speak on the issue.[31]

In March 1927, at secret meetings in Sonora, Obregón made it clear to a church representative that he wanted the religious conflict settled before he resumed the presidency. He assured the representative that if the bishops would agree to compromise, he would deliver Calles. Before the meeting with Calles could be arranged, violence escalated significantly, complicating the prospect of a settlement. In April, War Minister Joaquín Amaro gave state governments arms to distribute to local people to protect their lives and property. U.S. officials expressed concern that armed peasants would only lead to more deaths of noncombatants.[32] On April 19 the Cristeros stormed a train in Guadalajara, reportedly killing fifty passengers and soldiers on board. Ambassador Sheffield reported on a meeting between a member of his office and Manuel Sierra of the SRE. Sierra told U.S. officials that "the unfortunate political moves of the Government since the attack on the Guadalajara train were due solely to the fanaticism of President Calles against the church," confirming what many in the United States already believed. Sierra further stated his belief that "the President cannot be reasoned with in his attitude towards the church."[33] The escalation of Calles's anger toward Catholics led much of the Mexican hierarchy to flee again to the United States. Mexican officials, in an attempt to turn the Mexican people against the church, reported that the clergy had chosen to leave rather than face the consequences of their attack on the train.[34]

Sheffield contributed little to surmounting the challenges facing Mexico. In April he reported that three issues confronted Mexico: "the agrarian question, the policy of the Government towards labor, and the religious question." He identified "Mexican Indians" as central to solving each of these problems. Given their presumed inability to understand the issues, Sheffield assumed that "Indians" would not join the agrarian or urban labor movements. "On the question of religion, however, it is easy to appeal to the Indian, and it is for this reason that all revolutionary elements are employing this as a catch-word."[35] It is unlikely that the agraristas were claiming to defend religion, as they were most often fighting the Cristeros. It is also unclear exactly whom Sheffield meant by "Indians."[36] Notwithstanding his flawed understanding of the social, cultural, and racial divisions creating conflict in Mexico, he continued to exert influence, and therefore shaped U.S. officials' impressions of the religious crisis in Mexico.

The Liga claimed to have a national army of twenty-five thousand, but the first year of the Cristero Rebellion was marked by its local character, so the power or influence of national groups like the Liga was limited.[37] Recognizing the strength of the Cristeros in west-central Mexico, the Liga sent its strongest leaders there in August 1927. Jesus Degollado y Guízar and Enrique Gorostieta arrived on the scene to coordinate rebellions across the region. Of the two, Gorostieta was more successful in coordinating with local leadership to organize attacks on key sites. However, he was not a strict Catholic. He was more driven by the military challenge of the Cristero Rebellion than by its ideals. Maria Elena Negrete writes: "Rumors that he was not a true Catholic caused many of [the Cristeros] not to want to take orders from a military man who did not fight for religion nor for Christ the King." The Liga leadership explained that "Gorostieta had gone to war to lead and organize a group of free men, not fanatics. He was going to command an army, not a religious confraternity." By late in the year, the Cristeros had accepted his leadership and gathered enough momentum to launch successive attacks across the region.[38]

In preparation for the 1928 presidential elections, several military and other leaders declared their intentions to run. They assumed that Obregón would respect the Constitution of 1917, which did not allow for reelection. Calles clearly intended, however, to pass the presidency back to Obregón, and he worked with the Chamber of Deputies to clear Obregón's path with an amendment to allow for nonconsecutive reelection. In June, Obregón finally announced his intention to succeed Calles. Divisions within government ranks deepened, making successful management of the Cristeros significantly more difficult.

In August, Obregón sent his former minister of foreign affairs, Aarón Sáenz, to San Antonio, the heart of the Catholic borderlands, to negotiate with the exiled Mexican hierarchy. The fact that the hierarchy frequently retreated to the belly of the beast rankled Mexican officials. The power center for the Mexican Catholic hierarchy remained in the United States, now under the protection of Archbishop Arthur Drossaerts, whose San Antonio diocese was among those receiving the most Extension Society funding.[39] Once again, subtleties in interpretation prevented the two sides from agreeing on terms. The Liga, concerned that a settlement would be reached without assuring them a slice of power, bombarded the Vatican with protests against the hierarchy's negotiations with the government. This rift rested on basic differences in each group's approach to the revolutionary government. The hierarchy wanted priests to be permitted to return to their churches and serve their parishes. The Liga's goals were more overtly political. From their perspective, the Cristero movement would be a failure if Catholics were not guaranteed the right to form a political party in Mexico. Catholics in Mexico were divided by religious standing, geography, and ideology.

The Liga claimed a membership of 1.5 million Mexicans by late 1928, but it recognized the power of the U.S. government in Mexican affairs. Its leaders appealed to the Frank Kellogg when the prospect of a settlement between the church and the Mexican state seemed imminent. The Liga challenged the legitimacy of all Mexican presidents since the Constitution of 1917 and appealed to the democratic heartstrings of U.S. government officials. "There is no liberty for teaching, no liberty of association, no liberty to own or possess what has been honestly acquired. No liberty to say or print anything for the Press is absolutely gagged." Pandering to U.S. fears of socialism, the Liga warned that "time honoured professors have been thrown out of the University for not having red hot revolutionary ideas."[40] An earlier Liga report had asked whether the United States would choose the Catholic Church over bolshevism. José Tello, Liga secretary, suggested that people in the United States were "more afraid of white radicalism [Catholicism] than red [bolshevism], and if it were necessary to choose one of them, they would unhesitatingly prefer the red one."[41] The Liga dared the United States to choose the Catholic Church.

While it sought U.S. support, the Liga warned against U.S. involvement in Mexico. Even "with the powerful United States against us we shall keep the field until our wrongs are redressed. It must be fully understood that we are fighting for most elemental principles," the Liga continued, invoking democratic ideals deeply woven into U.S. history. "We are fighting for the same things you fought for in 1776, only that we are fighting a harder and crueler tyrant." The Liga's turn to the United States for support wisely played on U.S. patriotism. It sought not intervention by "an honest but misguided administration," but an end to the perceived support of an evil government. It asked for the recall of Morrow as ambassador due to his close alliance with Calles, which made him untrustworthy. Tello did not accuse Morrow of arming fighters against the Cristeros, but he stated that others believed Morrow provided "the help and money, arms, ammunition and poisonous gases" provided to Calles to fight his own people. "The Mexican people ardently desire Mr. Morrow to be recalled and that no means of wholesale killing [of] Mexicans shall be furnished to bad Mexicans by the Washington administration."[42] The message was clear: Morrow and the United States were on the wrong side. Neither side favored U.S. intervention, but neither would they cease their efforts to win favor from the U.S. government.

## Dwight Morrow's Mexican Mission

Until there is peace between the church and state in Mexico there will not be complete peace in Mexico, and there will not be an untroubled understanding between Mexico and the United States.

—Walter Lippman, 1927[43]

Ultimately the American empire prevailed in securing a settlement, one that required compromises by the Mexican government, the Mexican hierarchy, and the Vatican, but not the United States. In October 1927, Dwight Morrow had replaced James Sheffield as U.S. ambassador to Mexico. Morrow brought no diplomatic experience to the position, but he had been a fixture on Wall Street as a corporate lawyer. His appointment alarmed many in Mexico, who feared the ambassador from Wall Street had come to reclaim anything and everything for the North Americans. Morrow's priority was to bring stability to Mexico, but he knew that involvement in the religion question was inevitable and could cause trouble. He worked on the oil issue, which, as a foreign-policy question, was an appropriate way to initiate his relationship with Calles. Within a few weeks, he and Calles reached an accord whereby the Constitution of 1917 would not be applied retroactively to properties owned by U.S. citizens. This was important to safeguarding U.S. business interests, but social stability was critical for businesses to become profitable again.

In late November, Morrow had his first conversation with Calles about religious issues, and by December he was accompanying Calles on his private train taking trips around Mexico. His public closeness with the president drew the ire of many Catholics in Mexico and the United States, but Morrow redeemed himself with many Mexicans by bringing aviator Charles Lindbergh, his future son-in-law, to Mexico for two weeks at Christmas. Lindbergh played the prominent tourist, exploring Mexico City's important historical and cultural sites. Calles even presented him with the key to the city. The year ended with Morrow more certain of his standing in Mexico but still uncertain about the possibility of a religious settlement. In a December note to Undersecretary of State Robert Olds he pondered a possible role for a liberal Catholic, like Father John Burke of the NCWC. The NCWC was an arm of the U.S. Catholic hierarchy and thus might, he hoped, help with negotiations.[44] Although Kelley was not involved, he had laid the groundwork for this U.S. government and U.S. Catholic Church involvement a decade earlier. The American empire's own Catholic Church inserted itself in Mexico's future.

In January 1928 the Vatican, frustrated with the ongoing church strike and concerned with the hierarchy's lack of cohesion, began to explore the possibility that Morrow could negotiate a settlement. Cardinal Gasparri instructed the apostolic delegate to the United States, Pietro Fumasoni-Biondi, to contact Morrow. Before he left the United States in the fall, Morrow had met with Father Burke in an effort to gain as complete an understanding as possible of the religion question. Morrow had inquired who the important players were, and during a trip to Cuba he secretly asked Burke if he would consider becoming involved. Burke indicated that he would participate if Calles invited him. Knowing full well that Calles would never make such an overture toward any priest, especially an American, Morrow began an elaborate shell game that lasted for over a year. His goal was to get Calles to agree to an interview with Burke, at which point he would convince Burke to request an interview with Calles. Such "exchanges" were orchestrated by Morrow over agonizing months of taking two steps forward and one step back. Of course, the "discussion" was never limited to these three partners.

When Burke returned to the United States he met with Luis Bustos, a Caballero de Colón and representative of the Liga, and told him of his discussion with Morrow and the plans to negotiate a settlement. Bustos feared that a settlement negotiated by these parties would not allow for the existence of a Catholic political party. In Mexico, Morrow was approached by a group of lay Catholics, likely leaders from the Liga, who expressed concern that the emerging settlement would risk the future of Catholic Mexico. Lay Catholics argued that the only way to ensure long-term peace in Mexico was to guarantee that a strong Catholic party could exist. Morrow was quickly frustrated with the group and forced them to retreat. He scolded them for not trusting the Mexican hierarchy to make decisions in the best interests of Catholics.[45] When word of all of this was leaked to the press in the United States and Mexico, Calles canceled the proposed meeting with Burke. The Mexican hierarchy was divided on this issue, with some aligning themselves with Bustos and the Liga while others, like Morrow, sought a compromise if it would allow them to return to their dioceses. Mexican Catholic leaders were spread through the United States, Mexico, Cuba, and Europe, making the likelihood of coming to consensus on any issue small. Increasingly there was no Mexican Catholic Church; there were instead several different Catholic networks that included members living throughout the Catholic borderlands. Legions of Mexican Catholics continued their private spiritual practice and engaged in a holy war to preserve their faith as part of Mexico.

The battles in west-central Mexico continued to escalate. In February 1928, Cubilete, Guanajuato, became the focus of attention. It was home to a statue of Cristo Rey of great national significance, and local and federal officials decided to destroy the monument. Luella Herr, a U.S. citizen, described the situation for her family back home: "They ordered first one general, then a second, to destroy the statue and both refused and advised against it—knowing local conditions—but a third general from some other part of Mexico was sent to do the dirty work. . . . [T]he unrest will doubtless continue for a while but the so-called rebels are friends of all the countryside and merely have it in for those in authority, in which most of us sympathize with them."[46] Although she never mentions religion, Herr understood the symbolic importance of Cristo Rey of Cubilete, the geographic center of Mexico, a lesson the military was slower to learn. She also understood the local conditions that federal perspectives in both Mexico, DF, and Washington, DC, seemed to overlook. The government, in the form of military repression, was the enemy of the people in this instance. Americans "on the ground" in Mexico understood the religious tensions better than most U.S. officials.

In the midst of such chaos, Morrow sought to bring the Vatican and Mexico closer together. He suggested to the Holy See, through a fairly circuitous route, the appointment of a Mexican as apostolic delegate to Mexico. In the meantime, he continued to orchestrate communications between Burke and Calles and to collect information on the situation. During Holy Week, President Calles "vacationed" in Veracruz, accompanied by Morrow. They met Burke, who arrived with an indirect message from the Vatican hoping for peace. Burke took the additional step of separating himself and the Vatican from questionable practices of some in the Mexican hierarchy, who had been implicated in Liga activities. The usual arguments were exchanged, and it became clearer to Morrow that without a member of the Mexican hierarchy involved, little progress could be made. He continued to write and exchange letters between Burke—informed by his conversations with the Mexican bishops in the United States and by the apostolic delegate to the United States—and Calles. After the death of Archbishop José Mora y del Río, the senior Mexican prelate, Morrow sought the involvement of Archbishop Ruiz y Flores of Michoacán, who was considered more flexible than his predecessor. When agreement was reached on preliminary issues, Morrow telegraphed Robert Olds in the State Department, who was in contact with the apostolic delegate in Washington, DC. The apostolic delegate then telegraphed Cardinal Gasparri in Rome, who was in contact with Pope Pius XI. The pope responded to Morrow through the same circuitous network.

Surely some of the essence of the conversations between Calles and Ruiz y Flores was lost during the trip to the Vatican and back. When Ruiz y Flores was summoned to Rome, all anticipated an immediate settlement. The Liga stepped up efforts to undermine Ruiz y Flores's mission in Rome, with the support of some members of the hierarchy who were in Mexico. They criticized Ruiz y Flores for living in exile—in the United States of all places—and thus being out of touch with Mexican Catholics. On May 31, the day before Ruiz y Flores arrived in Rome, the Liga, the ACJM, and the Caballeros de Colón sent a telegram to the pope decrying the settlement. Upon arriving in Rome, Ruiz y Flores met with U.S. reporters and spoke openly about a settlement and the roles of Burke and Morrow in negotiations with Calles. Morrow, on vacation in the United States, refused comment, and Arturo Elías, Calles's half brother and consul general in New York, denied that any negotiations on the religion question had involved Calles. Even the NCWC retreated and insisted that Ruiz y Flores had been misunderstood or misquoted. The response of Vatican officials likewise was discouraging. Cardinal Gasparri reiterated that the Holy See wanted a settlement but said that, given the fact that Ruiz y Flores came "with no definite mandate, with no definite suggestions, and with no authority, his visit could lead to no result."[47] The Vatican wanted to see a show of contrition by the Mexican government for acts of the past and guarantees for the future before agreeing to a settlement. The Vatican, which often approached political issues with the conviction that it would outlast any president or regime, was willing to wait until Obregón became president, assuming he would make more concessions than Calles.

On July 1, 1928, Obregón was elected president. He was immediately in contact with Morrow, and both expressed optimism that an agreement would be reached in the near future. Like the Mexican people, Obregón understood the importance of allying with the American empire. Before any progress could be made, a Catholic fanatic assassinated Obregón, destroying the months of progress that had been made by Morrow and Calles. On September 1 Calles announced that he would not seek the presidency and that on November 30 he would inaugurate an interim president to serve while the nation prepared for elections in November 1929. Calles proposed the formation of the Partido Nacional Revolucionario (PNR, National Revolutionary Party) to maintain the goals of the

Revolution through institutionalized political structures. Emilio Portes Gil was named president by congress. The status of negotiations between Mexico City and the Vatican remained uncertain.

José Vasconcelos, minister of education under Obregón, returned from his self-imposed exile in the United States to announce his candidacy for president. He had been active in exile communities in the United States and now sought their support for his campaign. He also counted on support from the U.S. entities with which he had been affiliated, including the University of Chicago and Stanford University. In his autobiography, Vasconcelos wrote of his experience at the University of Chicago: "In spite of the pro-Calles conspiracy, the spirit of free discussion, the novelty of my attacks, or something or other, attracted considerable attention. The vigorous, enlightened people who dominated the Yankee universities were not grudging in their praise."[48] He counted on his good reputation with such institutions to provide a U.S. base of support, should he need one later. Vasconcelos understood the actual and metaphorical language of American empire and had established his credibility within that empire.

Vasconcelos believed that unseating Calles would make possible the return of Mexicans in exile. In his words, Mexicans "have been forced to seek in the United States a refuge from the political tyranny and economic disaster of a partisanism maintained solely by the activity, from one end of the country to the other, of a band carrying out summary executions."[49] Vasconcelos had fled the violence of CROM, the labor organization, and the danger created by Obregón's refusal to rein in Luis Morones, his minister of economy, in 1925. Vasconcelos accused Obregón of choosing U.S. recognition over national progress and cited that as his reason for leaving. Vasconcelos also blamed U.S. support for Obregón and Calles for the violence of the early 1920s. It is curious that Vasconcelos chose the belly of the beast for his home in exile. He estimated that two to three million Mexicans—the best and brightest—were in exile in the United States and believed their return was critical to Mexico's future. The split between the church and the revolutionary state had to be healed in order to bring home Mexico's future leaders.[50]

A vocal supporter of the Cristeros, Vasconcelos moderated his stance and sought a peaceful settlement. His economic program was clearly nationalist, mildly socialist, and oriented toward Latin America over the United States. He strongly supported the armed forces, though he was uncomfortable with having military officers in the highest levels of government. He supported unionization and training of workers but did not want the union to be controlled by the government, as was CROM. Vasconcelos was not entirely opposed to the Constitution of 1917, but he saw the selective application of several articles as problematic. The implementation of land reform was, he insisted, unfair: "While U.S. citizens controlled 51.7 percent of all the acreage in foreign hands and Spaniards controlled 19.7 percent, 53 percent of the land expropriated from foreigners had belonged to Spaniards and only 27 percent had belonged to North Americans."[51] He was also concerned about the enforcement of articles of the Constitution of 1917 against Catholics but not Protestants. Although—or perhaps *because*—Vasconcelos spent most of the mid-1920s in the United States, he was critical of the many ways Mexican structures imitated or affiliated with U.S. institutions. As a credentialed revolutionary, he wanted to see U.S. influence reduced. His lived contradictions are emblematic of the complex relationship between the two nations and between Mexican and U.S. nationals within the church. Vasconcelos made that case from the United States and used the cultural authority of U.S. educational institutions to gird his support from the American empire.

The Cristeros continued to fight in the west-central states. Vasconcelos was contacted by the Cristero leadership in January 1929. Each side quickly saw ways the other could help. Vasconcelos's legitimacy could draw more support to the Cristeros from urban areas. Armed supporters could be important to Vasconcelos should the election be fraudulent. By May, he and Enrique Gorostieta, who reportedly commanded twenty-five thousand Cristeros, had a verbal agreement to support each other. Although Gorostieta's religious credentials were suspect, Vasconcelos was not concerned. He, like the Liga leadership years before, was interested in Gorostieta's military talents.

Vasconcelos's platform was popular with a wide range of constituents: exiles of many stripes, students (most of whom were trained in schools he organized as minister of education under Obregón), Catholics, and intellectuals.

Calles was largely in control while Portes Gil was acting president, and his role as minister of war allowed Portes Gil to consider a religious settlement in a different light. Still, Calles continued his diatribes against the church. He reportedly told a group of soldiers he "would stamp out Catholicism and the Catholic Church if he had to tear unborn children from the wombs of their mothers." Morrow heard this from a disgusted Wilbur Bates of the Mexican People's Bureau of Public Information in the United States.[52]

Also in May 1929, Archbishop Ruiz y Flores was appointed apostolic delegate to Mexico—the first Mexican to serve in the position—and requested permission to reenter Mexico. He and Bishop Pascual Díaz traveled to Mexico on Morrow's private train and were met outside Mexico City by Georgetown University's vice president, Father Edmund Walsh. The prelates did not have contact with the Liga or with the Mexican bishops who opposed a settlement. They met with Portes Gil on two occasions, the first being filled with great optimism, the second once again undermined by doubts and mistrust. On June 15, Morrow again entered the negotiations, providing written statements to each side. When all the details had been settled, the Vatican was informed of the agreement and refused to approve it. Ruiz y Flores, seeing the necessity for the bishops to return to Mexico, feeling the pressure from the apostolic delegate to the United States and the U.S. ambassador, and perhaps knowing that the election was not likely to improve the chances of an amicable settlement, ignored the Vatican and agreed to the settlement. The following day the accord was signed and released to the press. Portes Gil agreed that the registration of priests was merely a statistical matter, not an attempt to select or approve priests. He also allowed for religious education to take place within churches. The hierarchy agreed to reopen the churches within the limits imposed by the Constitution of 1917. Ruiz y Flores ordered the Liga to cease and desist and to surrender to federal troops. While amnesty was granted to most involved in the rebellions, Portes Gil expelled several bishops and many leaders of the Liga. Several hundred Cristeros were shot when they surrendered to federal troops. The agreement did not change the Constitution of 1917, but it did allow church and state to coexist. In the words of one government official, "Let them violate the Constitution, but only a little. And let us look stupid, but also only a little."[53] Morrow had succeeded in intervening in the internal affairs of Mexico. Doing so had not required an army or the threat of military intervention; it was instead made possible by the transnational networks created within the Catholic Church, networks that stimulated debate and the possibility for compromise about the nature of a Catholic borderlands, largely controlled by the United States like other Pan-American projects of the era.

With the dispersal of the Cristeros, Vasconcelos lost his armed support. Gorostieta was killed when he surrendered, making his agreement with Vasconcelos worthless. The church-state settlement was timed to undermine Vasconcelos's campaign, though much of the Liga leadership campaigned relentlessly for him. Catholic antagonism toward Morrow was only reinforced when the settlement was reached. A November 1929 letter to President Herbert Hoover from the Liga warned that a new revolution was inevitable if Calles's candidate, Pascual Ortiz Rubio, won the election. If Vasconcelos did not win, the letter continued, "We are not going to let . . . American Ambassadors . . . rule Mexico and rule it through bloody bandits against the will of the Mexican people." If Morrow continued to cozy up to Mexican tyrants, "we will punish him if it is necessary with death."[54] The Liga recognized that Morrow was critical to the legitimacy of the settlement and therefore a great peril to a Catholic opposition party. It so feared his influence that it was willing to issue a threat that put any chance of U.S. support at risk. After months of courting American empire, with clear evidence that the empire had chosen the other side, the Liga responded with the only power it had left, the promise of violence.

Morrow was seen as a danger to the Catholic nation not because he was from the United States but because he was aligned with Calles. For many Mexican Catholics, Calles was antipatriotic. "In Defense of Citizenship," a broadside by "various Catholics" in Orizaba, Veracruz, accused him of destroying Mexico's citizenry with his anti-religious laws. "The thousands of children who will be sent to the United States to receive an education that is denied them here will only have one thing that is Mexican when they return—their names." By destroying Catholic education, these Catholics charged, the revolutionary government was denying *any* legitimately Mexican education. "And that foreign country, like a charitable woman, has adopted them, has educated them, has formed them, because it pleased the radicalism of the present government, THE MOST EFFECTIVE PROPAGANDISTS OF YANQUI IMPERIALISM."[55] Once again, the link between the United States and any Mexican body made that body un-Mexican. Here that meant both Calles and those Mexicans who would be educated in the United States if the church were forced to leave. The threat from the United States was greater than ever and more disheartening for Mexican Catholics because it was imposed on them by the Mexican government. In this particular moment, then, the Mexican government became an even greater menace than the United States. The alignment of the United States with the Catholic cause only confused this picture more. Although the U.S.-negotiated settlement guaranteed religious liberty on paper, it did not address the Liga's primary concern—the right to have a Catholic political party. As a result, the Liga moved from lobbying the U.S. government for an intervention of its own design to attacking U.S. involvement. From the Liga's perspective, Morrow, the Mexican bishops, and the Mexican president (Calles or Portes Gil) formed an unholy trinity. Calles and the bishops surrendered Mexican sovereignty to the empire. The United States was the only party that did not lose face in the settlement.

After nearly two decades of fending off the United States on the religion question, Mexico relented and opened the door not only to Washington but to the church as well. Mexican identity remained—

and remains to this day—tied to Catholicism, despite subsequent breakdowns between church and state. While Catholic nationalists were willing to fight the revolutionary state to the death—and many did—the government was so desperate to end the Cristero Rebellion that it welcomed U.S. intervention. The Catholic movement was severely divided by this time, but even in fragments it was able to outlast the government, as the Vatican had always assumed. The Vatican surely had not envisioned the church would come out broken, with lay groups and the hierarchy at odds.

A century after gaining independence from Spain, Mexico still struggled with the legacies of colonialism. The Catholic Church, racial hierarchies, and foreign influence promoted and sustained tremendous social inequality in Mexico. After the downfall of Díaz, Mexicans searched for ways to unify the nation and build a new Mexico. Mexican nationalist intellectuals embraced Mexico's mestizo past and attempted to build a new future on that foundation, celebrating *mestizaje* as a core and unique trait of Mexico. The role of the church, though criticized throughout the revolutionary period, could be reshaped, but it could not be removed. For many, being Mexican and being Catholic could not be separated.

Likewise, the economic and cultural presence of the United States was even more vexing than before. One million Mexicans made the United States their temporary or permanent home. Through remittances, visits, and return migration, U.S. culture and financial resources invaded Mexico more powerfully than ever. The question was not whether the United States would intervene in Mexico's crisis but rather how the United States would get involved. The Liga wanted some say in the matter and went to the source, the U.S. government, in an effort to achieve their desired ends. The Liga's goals, however, did not coincide with broader U.S. aims, and thus fell on deaf ears. In response the Liga adopted the rhetoric of anti-Americanism, a Mexican tradition revived with great efficacy during the Revolution, and the common recourse for those unable to lure the American empire to its side.

Portes Gil made another savvy move during this time: granting autonomy to the national university, thereby pacifying the students, who were another of Vasconcelos's bases of support. While many believe that Vasconcelos won the election in November, he lacked the institutional support necessary to challenge the presumed electoral fraud. The Mexican government managed to diffuse the religious tension with the support of the Vatican and the United States. On its own, it could not have stopped the Vasconcelos-Cristero alliance and likely would not have been able to rig the November elections such that Pascual Ortíz Rubio, Calles's candidate, emerged the official winner. Vasconcelos returned to exile. One opposition leader said of the elections, "Democracy has been assassinated; there were no elections."[56] The settlement was not a solution to Mexico's ills, but rather a temporary truce.

The three-year battle between church and state devastated Mexico. In addition to the tremendous loss of life—70,000 by most estimates—the conflict consumed half the federal budget and caused a substantial drop in agricultural production. The latter can be attributed to the migration to the cities of an estimated 200,000 and to the United States of another 450,000 to 1,000,000 Mexicans.[57] Equally important, the nation remained socially and ideologically divided. The Revolution's redistribution of land became less pressing because of the urban migration and the destruction of much of the infrastructure over the previous two decades. The role of the church was still ill defined, and its return signaled, for some, the failure of the revolutionary government.

Mexico reformulated its national identity and its social institutions, but the United States and the Vatican both worked to maintain and solidify their stakes in the Mexican national project. U.S. economic interests were often the overriding concern of the government and media, but those closest to the situation recognized that without the stability that a settlement of the religion question could bring, U.S. interests could not be safe. In his quest for stability, Morrow assisted Calles in the creation and maintenance of his political machine, the PNR.[58]

For those on either side of the religion question in Mexico, Morrow's involvement was a disgrace. Had Morrow provided a satisfactory resolution, it would have been worth the blow to national and religious pride. For Catholics, the settlement kept the church vulnerable to a crackdown by the government at any time, as was seen in another era of religious repression in the 1930s. For supporters of the Revolution, the Vatican and the United States undermined Mexican sovereignty and imposed the will of the United States on the Mexican people.[59] The Catholic Church and the United States, ideologically the two most significant external enemies of the Mexican Revolution, were the only ones that could solve the religion question and secure the institutionalization of revolutionary reforms. These two behemoths defied historical expectations by working together to regain their mutual presence in Mexico and ensure the presence of Catholicism and American empire in Mexico's future.

In 1964, René Capistrán Garza asserted that the Mexican Revolution and the Cristero Rebellion were inseparable events. Each movement had sought to redefine the nation in contrast to the other. They fought for the minds, the souls, and the pocketbooks of the citizens of the new Mexican nation. In addition, they wanted to define which institutions deserved a role in the new nation. Ironically, each movement also fought for the support of the Vatican and the United States in bringing its vision to fruition.

# 6

## Preaching *Mestizaje*

### *Catholicism and Race in the Catholic Borderlands*

In June 1926, while Mexican Catholicism was being celebrated in Chicago, *Eugenical News*, the official organ of the Eugenics Research Association, was reporting the dangers presented by Mexicans in California. A Mexican family was deemed responsible for a small-pox outbreak in one California town. "Recently two Mexican children had smallpox. The father," according to the report, "could not forgo his customary game of pool." He spent thirty days in jail for breaking quarantine, but ten others in the poolroom were subsequently infected with smallpox, presumably by the Mexican man, and five of them died. The report suggested that Mexicans often carried smallpox, but it identified this as a minor concern compared to Mexicans' effect on U.S. society as a whole. "With his numerous offspring [the Mexican] tends to dilute our old American blood. Thus he is giving us a new color problem." The Mexican problem had possessed the Southwest for generations. By the 1920s Mexicans were in the national discourse not only for religious repression in Mexico but also for the potential damage Mexican migrants would have on American racial stock.[1]

Writers in the United States were consumed with race betterment. Anti-immigrant and eugenicist sentiment and practice in the United States assigned characteristics of inferiority and impurity to Mexicans, among others. The 1924 National Origins Act sought to engineer the future racial composition of the United States by limiting immigration from racially suspect nations in southern and eastern Europe. Harry Laughlin of the Eugenic Records Office, who served the U.S. House of Representatives as an "Expert Eugenical Agent" in the 1920s and 1930s, advocated for restrictive immigration leg-islation and state sterilization laws. Mexican immigration was not numerically limited at this time. However, Mexicans crossing into the United States faced border inspections that included disinfection of their belongings and their very bodies to secure the racial hygiene of the United States.[2] Discussions of "good stock" and "bad stock" mapped a future for a super race, a master race, or other dominant genetic stock refined over generations, with other stock reproduc-ing itself into presumed infertility.[3] Positive and negative eugenics used coded language to characterize various movements, but each had the same goal: preserving "superior" Anglo stock in the United States to the exclusion—or extinction—of other stock. For many in the secular world, the racial future of the United States was clear: survival of the fittest—as defined by social conventions of the era.

Religious leaders from a variety of denominations expressed con-cern over humane treatment of those perceived as poor stock. Most leaders were willing to endorse so-called positive eugenics, through which "the fit may be induced to mate, and by combining their fit-ness in their offspring, to raise up each new generation, out of the flower of the old." "Better baby" and "fitter family" contests were the public face of positive eugenics. Religious leadership was less certain about negative eugenics, by which "the unfit will be restrained from mating and perpetuating their unfitness in the future."[4] Father John A. Ryan of the National Catholic Welfare Conference and Catho-lic University and Father John M. Cooper of Catholic University were involved with the clergy committee of the American Eugen-ics Society (AES) from the mid-1920s to 1931.[5] Ryan was active in a number of reform movements and saw eugenics as an outlet for social reform. Cooper, an anthropologist, was invested in the bet-terment of parents and families. Ryan and other Catholic leaders opposed negative eugenics, which clearly violated natural law in its focus on sterilization and contraception. But Ryan and Cooper embraced the "positive" euphemism of race betterment. As a Ryan protégé wrote, Catholics needed to be active in the eugenics move-ment to ensure that it would work "for good, and not for evil."[6] It is unlikely, however, that they envisioned *mestizaje* as an example of race betterment.

In the midst of this biological chaos, an unexpected take on racial mixing emerged. Bishop Francis Kelley's writing on Mexico culminated with his 1935 epic history, *Blood-Drenched Altars: Mexican Study and Comment*.[7] From his perspective, racial mixing could be justified, at least in the case of Mexico. Kelley's writings contradicted the Western imperial and racial ideologies of the time while reinforcing another imperial project, Spain's conquest of Mexico, which allowed Kelley to see racial mixing as positive. It was part of, and in fact evidence of, the success of the civilizing mission. Accordingly, the potential removal of the Catholic Church from Mexico in the revolutionary moment indeed meant the removal of civilization from this neighboring land. Kelley presented a challenge to the notion that racial mixing was negative. He did not, however, deny a racial hierarchy with Anglo-Saxons clearly above "Latins," as he termed them.

This unlikely mix of perspectives provides us with an opportunity to examine an unusual discourse on race and racial mixing in Mexico and the United States. The predominance of eugenics in the early-twentieth-century United States meant that Kelley was not alone in using both religion and race to claim intellectual and moral authority over racialized others. His writings capture deep ambiguities and contradictions in the rhetorics of race and religion that dominated Mexico and the United States in the 1920s and 1930s. Racial mixing or racial marking have been part of all imperial projects. While the United States struggled with assorted iterations of the color line in the early twentieth century, Kelley looked south to a seemingly painless racial amalgam created through evangelization. Whereas the Spanish colonial project included the *castas*, emphasizing racial purity and distinction, Kelley's "modern" take embraced *mestizaje* as a civilizing force in Mesoamerica.

This chapter considers a U.S. Catholic response to Mexican racial mixing through an examination of the xenophobic and racist rhetoric that dominated discussions of race in the United States in the 1910s and 1920s and the sacred-secular divide that captured discussions of eugenics. At the same time, during Mexico's post-revolutionary nation-building, both Manuel Gamio and José Vasconcelos imagined a future for Mexico that included the Catholic Church. Kelley's writing on Mexico both supports and deviates from those rhetorics. The U.S. Catholic defense of Mexican Catholicism produced a contradictory discourse on race, particularly racial mixing. Kelley's insights on *mestizaje* are surprising given the time in which he wrote. I suggest that Catholic borderlands, the discourse and activity Kelley had built over the previous two decades, allowed him to embrace *mestizaje* as evidence of the success of Spain's Catholic civilizing mission four hundred years earlier. In contrast to the eugenic and segregationist United States, Kelley preached *mestizaje*.[8]

### Mainstream Discourses on Eugenics

In the aftermath of World War I, U.S. national identity blossomed on a new world stage. Walter Benn Michaels theorizes a "nativist modernism" that focuses on a collective national identity based on language, nation, culture, and race. He sees the family as the fulcrum on which each of these identities balanced. Implicit in this formula are race and heredity. Citizenship changed from something that could be acquired by "immigrating, becoming 'civilized,' getting 'naturalized' . . . to a status that could better be understood as inherited."[9] In other words, increasingly, only Americans could produce Americans—or the best Americans, anyway. "The Super Race," wrote Scott Nearing, was "America's distinctive opportunity." Because of its newness as a nation, the United States could socially engineer its population through immigration policy and state-sanctioned eugenics.[10]

Eugenics discourse permeated many aspects of society in the first third of the twentieth century. Christina Cogdell suggests that eugenics was a factor influencing design. Streamline designers of the 1930s rounded the edges off buildings, toasters, and furniture to present what they imagined to be a cleaner, sleeker aesthetic. Like eugenicists, they "considered themselves agents of reform, tackling problems of mass (re)production, eliminating 'defectiveness,' and 'parasite drag' that were thought to be slowing forward evolutionary progress." Streamline design, accordingly, was the material expression of the ideology of eugenics—both were marked by efficiency, hygiene, and the ideal type.[11] Streamline design and eugenics sought to smooth the ragged edges of U.S. society, much as the Extension Society, since its founding, had smoothed the ragged edges of the expanding nation.

Eugenics was not just about sterilization and "better breeding." It encompassed an array of federal and local policies that marked who belonged in the United States and who did not. By the 1920s, eugenicists were aiming more of their pseudoscientific concern toward immigrants. The 1924 Johnson-Reed Act sharply reduced immigration from southern and eastern Europe—predominantly Catholics, Jews, and Orthodox—through the national origins formula. *Eugenical News* strongly encouraged readers to support the new immigration bill and protect "white America."[12] Johnson-Reed did not strictly limit migrants from the Western Hemisphere, but was shortly followed by the creation of the Border Patrol to monitor the boundaries of the nation and inspect those seeking access.[13] The presence of the Border Patrol and the policies it enacted on the border with Mexico sought to control, contain, and disinfect Mexicans through the use of permanent ink branding, quarantines, and chemical showers. These actions formalized the long-standing racialization of Mexicans as dirty, dysgenic, and unfit. Eugenicists sought to create "a new biopolitical order" by managing "racial, ethnic and class interactions and categories through marriage, sterilization and alien land laws."[14] These federal policies, as well as state and local laws, formed the basis of material eugenics—attempts by the state to limit the national and individual body. From language use to disease rates to intelligence testing, eugenicists marked the ways immigrants were not only a poor fit for American society but even a drag on the society, holding it back from a better, fitter, whiter future.[15]

Mexicans were legally white, but they were rarely afforded that status in their daily interactions. They were not well regarded in the broad category of foreign-born whites. *Eugenical News* reviewed a January 1922 census report, noting citizenship status of immigrant whites: "Wide differences in citizenship status appeared among those 21 years of age and over ranging from 74.4 per cent for the Welsh, to 5.5 per cent for the Mexicans." Little regard was given for the physical proximity of Mexico or the political situation creating the migration. "Among white races in the United States, regardless of nationality, racial assimilation follows rapidly the process of political naturalization, and the acquiring of the English language."[16] A subsequent census report suggested Mexicans were also a problem in terms of English-language acquisition. In Texas, New Mexico, and Arizona approximately 50 percent of the foreign-born whites were unable to speak English.[17] The following month it was noted that two-thirds of the foreign-born in these states were natives of Mexico.[18] "In no other state was the percentage so high as 20 per cent, and in only two other states . . . was it higher than 14 per cent." Language acquisition was considered an important factor in "racial fortunes," as it dictated the range of "personal acquaintances and consequently of mate-selection."[19] Although Mexicans were framed as white, they were consistently marked as outliers in that category, and as immigrants they were framed as a drag on their local communities and the nation.

Mexicans were also compared to American Indians. In September 1922, an article in *Eugenical News* titled "An Investigation of the Intelligence of Mexican and Full and Mixed Blood Indian Children" attempted to map out the consequences of racial mixing. In the article, Thomas Garth of the University of Texas showed that racial germ plasm had a direct bearing on the intelligence of individuals, with mixed-bloods topping the intelligence list, full-bloods bottoming out the list, and Mexicans falling in between. Garth and others sough to categorize Mexicans further, as they became a lasting part of the American racial landscape.[20] Alexandra Minna Stern documents the divergent racializing forces for Mexicans: eugenicists, who asserted that Mexicans should be excluded as a mongrel race, versus growers, who "contended that this same biological composition endowed Mexican laborers with remarkable 'stooping abilities' and the capacity to work long hours in the fields."[21] The portrayal of Mexicans as laborers also elicited comparisons to blacks. A 1928 report by the AES warned: "Our great Southwest is rapidly creating for itself a new racial problem, as our old South did when it imported slave labor from Africa." Fearing the power of growers to continue importing Mexican labor, the report continued, "This is not a question of pocketbook, or of the 'need of labor' or of economics. It is a question of character of future races. It is eugenics, not economics."[22] This danger was increased by a high Mexican birthrate.

The 1924 immigration and border legislation and the 1927 U.S. Supreme Court sterilization case *Buck v. Bell* illustrate a two-pronged attack by eugenicists to shape U.S. society from the outside, through immigration restrictions, and from the inside, via sterilization. The Court declared, "It is better for all the world, if instead of waiting to execute degenerate offspring for crime or to let them starve for their imbecility, society can prevent those who are manifestly unfit from continuing their kind," affirming the normative view that the germ plasm of those considered substandard posed a danger to all.[23] By 1927, Mexicans and other Latin Americans were considered more dangerous than ever. In an open letter to the president and Congress, the leaders of the Eugenic Record Association wrote, "We urge the extension of the quota system to all countries of North and South America from which we have substantial immigration and in which the population is not predominantly of the white race." They deemed the current legislation inadequate and noted it would be "increasingly so in the near future." The letter, perhaps attempting to preempt the labor issue, suggested that Mexicans were bringing down the standard of living for American workers because they were accustomed to a lower standard of living in Mexico.[24]

Religious leaders believed they played a special role in eugenics. Better breeding was an important *moral* imperative, and leaders of all denominations saw themselves as the guardians of morality in the United States. In 1926 the AES, desperate to extend its reach, sponsored its first sermon contest. The theme, "Religion and Eugenics:

Does the Church Have Any Responsibility for Improving the Human Stock?," encouraged religious leaders to invoke their moral claim on the American mind. Sermons were submitted from pastors of every Christian denomination as well as from rabbis, and from every part of the country. The AES formed a Committee on Cooperation with Clergymen to help manage the religious perspective on eugenics.

Catholic leaders were often conflicted about eugenics. They appreciated the goals of eugenics but were not always comfortable with the means. Father John Ryan of the NCWC and Father John Cooper were both active in the AES.[25] Reform-minded Ryan saw eugenics as part of broader societal shifts that had benefited average working Catholics. Recent Catholic immigrants were often considered part of the mass of unfit in the United States, but Cooper and others insisted that science could help improve society. One Catholic doctor, Lawrence Flick, saw Catholics as central to the eugenic project, noting that "There is no power on earth except religion which can maintain the essential conditions for eugenics in the human family." Eugenics was often used to interfere with God's plan for families, but for a time, some Catholics were able to overlook that.[26]

The sacred-secular divide was reflected in the tension between moral eugenics and material eugenics. The ultimate condemnation of material eugenics came from Pope Pius XI in his 1930 encyclical *Casti Connubii*, which one *Chicago Tribune* writer called "the most important document in the field of pure morals since Gregory VII enforced celibacy on the clergy in the eleventh century."[27] Pius XI emphasized the urgency of natural law over governments: "In order, therefore, to restore due order in this matter of marriage, it is necessary that all should bear in mind what is the divine plan and strive to conform to it."[28] Marriage, in other words, existed for the explicit purpose of procreation. "Those who [interfere with God and nature] are at fault in losing sight of the fact that the family is more sacred than the State and that men are begotten not for the earth and for time, but for Heaven and eternity."[29] From the Catholic perspective, then, eugenics was interfering not only with life on earth but with the life of the soul. *Casti Connubii* was reprinted in numerous Catholic publications and debated in secular newspapers and magazines. Several months later, the AES issued its response, *Organized Eugenics*, a pamphlet that promoted birth control and sterilization and advocated for more options for divorce. In the aftermath of *Casti Connubii*, Cooper and Ryan both resigned from the AES.

Mexico was also reflecting on it racial makeup in this era. Mexican intellectuals, in the aftermath of the Mexican Revolution in 1910, were rewriting their nation's history to acknowledge and embrace the indigenous and mestizo past. Increasingly, intellectuals and artists embraced this past in ways that centered them in Mexico's history and celebrated them—at least in theory and imagery—in Mexico's present.

### *Mestizaje* and Catholicism in Mexican Nation-Building

We inherit the indigenous nationality of the Aztecs, and in full enjoyment of it we recognize no foreign sovereigns, no judges and no arbiters.

—Benito Juarez, 1867[30]

*Mestizaje*, or racial mixing, was the central challenge *and* triumph of Mexican revolutionary nationalist discourse. The recognition and embrace of Mexico's indigenous and mixed populations was a pivotal change in the intellectual direction of Mexico. The nationalist project sought equality by promoting and embracing racial mixing—an anticolonial swipe at Spain's purity-based social castes, and perhaps a reaction to the U.S. past, marked by slavery, or its present, in which eugenics, segregation, and anti-immigrant sentiments prevailed. Although the Revolution sought, and in many ways achieved, sweeping changes, the church and the United States remained integral parts of Mexico's present and future.

Mexican intellectuals understood that Mexico's Catholic traditions would remain, even at times when anticlericalism raged. Mexican nationalism was also constructed with an understanding that the United States would always be present. Through technology, the economy, migration, and return migration, the United States remained in Mexico despite the nationalization of property and industry. The shadow of American empire lurked in Mexican intellectuals who were trained and educated in the United States, as well as in the estimated one million Mexicans who migrated north for survival during the Revolution. Whether or not they returned to Mexico, their remittances and family ties connected the new Mexican nation indelibly to the United States. The rise of race-focused nationalist discourses in Mexico was shaped by Catholicism and by the United States during the revolutionary period. Mexican nationalism was not anti-Catholic, and Catholics were active in the revolutionary reshaping of the nation. Mexico's nationalist project runs counter to our understanding of modern nationalism as secular in nature. In addition, despite the battle cry "Mexico for the Mexicans," the U.S. presence in Mexico's future was understood.

The Catholic Church and the United States were—and are— longtime residents in Mexican national debates. The tensions between church and state in Mexico have existed since the arrival of the Spanish in what is now Mexico. In the late nineteenth century the relationship between the two changed, and an important precedent was set by President Benito Juárez, who led Mexico off and on from 1858 to 1872. Juárez wisely struck a deal for the church and state to agree to disagree—to accept each other with a wink and a nod, despite a constitution that curtailed the powers of the church. Mexican national identity also blossomed under Juárez, even with the increasing economic presence of the United States in Mexico.

The mid-nineteenth-century reform era showed mixed results in terms of modernization, land reform, and church control. Nonetheless, Juárez rose to mythical status by surviving and eventually defeating the French invasion. In the words of Claudio Lomnitz, "It was not until 1867, after the French departed and Maximilian was shot, that Mexico finally earned its 'right' to exist as a nation. Until that time, no strong central state had existed, and the country's sovereignty was severely limited."[31] Despite the economic hardship that continued after the defeat of the French, Mexican pride and nationalism bloomed under Juárez's post-Maximilian leadership.

In 1876, Porfirio Díaz began his thirty-five-year rule. The Porfiriato was marked by tremendous growth in infrastructure and foreign investment. Mining, petroleum, and textile industries grew, and fifteen thousand miles of railroad tracks were laid by 1910. Policies regarding the church were relaxed, and Catholic property holdings and power returned to near pre-Juárez levels. Well into the Porfiriato, halfway around the world, the Vatican responded to changes worldwide by issuing *Rerum Novarum* in 1891. Pope Leo XIII (1878–1903) was concerned about the alienation of workers from the church and the growing tensions between classes in light of the Industrial Revolution. "This order," he indicated, "is to bring together Catholics of all social classes . . . to deal with common central doctrine, propaganda and social organization."[32] In the decades that followed, organizations of Catholic workers, Catholic youth, and Catholic men and women formed around the world, dedicated to the broad mission of Acción Católica (Catholic Social Action).

The changes that Leo XIII sensed and that Acción Católica addressed were noted by others in Mexico as well. The best-known challengers to the Porfiriato were Jesús, Ricardo, and Enrique Flores Magón. In 1900, Jesús and Ricardo founded *Regeneración*, which published critiques of the Mexican government. In 1901 the brothers and other supporters of the cause formed the Partido Liberal Mexicano (PLM, Mexican Liberal Party), which was active in a number of states. The PLM, drawing on Juárez liberalism, wanted to change the basic structure of Mexican society—especially limiting the powers of the church and the military. They were nationalistic and influenced by contemporary socialist thought.[33] After considerable repression of *Regeneración* and other Magonista activity, leaders of the PLM fled to the United States, where they increasingly were influenced by anarchist philosophy and working-class issues.[34] However, their program drew on the Mexican liberal past, emphasizing education, legitimate elections, and the decentering of the church and the military.

The foreign presence in Mexico increased during the Porfiriato, particularly in the guise of modernization. Mexican nationalism grew significantly among those opposed to Díaz. Workers were suffering at the hands of foreign and Mexican landowners, and families struggled due to long working hours, low wages, and lack of protection for workers. Both Catholics, inspired by Acción Católica, and radicals, working through the PLM and other groups in the United States and Mexico, sought ways to reshape Mexico's future. They imagined a new and different nation: both Catholics and revolutionaries imagined Mexico for the Mexicans—free from U.S. influence and presence—but Catholic narratives in post-revolutionary Mexico show that the narrative of the United States in Mexico is linked with Catholicism. The U.S. Catholic Church conspired with the American empire to intervene in the building of the Mexican nation, as the Spanish Catholic Church had done centuries earlier in the building of New Spain.

### An Idealized Past and a Politicized Future for Mexico

The soul of Mexican culture is Indian, and its political body is destined to be ruled by mestizos against the Europeanizing project of the lackeys of foreign imperialism.

—Claudio Lomnitz-Adler, 1992[35]

Since the nineteenth century, Mexico, like much of Latin America, has struggled with the tension between preservation of national culture and modernization, or the past and the future. Struggles between nationalism and modernization were also struggles between the homeland and the United States, between the underdog and the empire. Most often, the United States represented the modern possibilities for Mexico, while Mexico's own countryside captured the weighted, primitive past. Religion continued to "haunt modernity," but not necessarily in the ways we would expect.[36] In the case of post-revolutionary Mexico, this picture was muddied by the migration of tens of thousands of Mexicans to the United States. Mexican anthropologist Guillermo Bonfil Batalla distinguishes between *México imaginario* and *México profundo*. *México imaginario* refers to that Mexico which strives to imitate the West, while *México profundo* embraces an indigenous past.[37] Claudio Lomnitz calls the relationship between nationalism and modernization Mexico's chronic crisis.[38] Mexico's crisis, like all of Latin America's, was also shaped in significant ways by the United States. Immigration history of the era portrayed that "the most energetic and enterprising members of the community" were the ones who left—this applied to the "average" Mexican migrant, not just well-known political and intellectual exiles like the Flores Magón brothers, Manuel Gamio, and José Vasconcelos. Many anxiously awaited the return of Mexico's most industrious citizens to build a new, modern Mexico using the skills and knowledge they garnered in the United States.[39]

This conflict between nationalism and modernism can also be expressed in terms of race, as Andrés Molina Enríquez did: "Over time, the anvil of Indian blood will always prevail over the hammer of Spanish blood."[40] A pro-mestizo nationalist, Molina Enríquez was considered part of the ideological drive behind the Mexican Revolution. Drawing on the masculine European invasion and the feminine Indian defense, the pro-mestizo nationalists glorified the racialized and sexualized combination that was simultaneously modernizing and protectionist.[41] As Molina Enríquez's metaphor indicates, however, the modernizing and protectionist roles were far from equal. Their gauging of these roles depended on which aspect of Mexican society was being examined. The intellectual leaders of the 1910 Revolution and the movements that followed recognized the need for a nationalist agenda—an Imagined Mexico, modern and unified. In Mexico, the modern context reasserted the presence of the invasive West—the United States—and its stranglehold on Mexican national culture and identity.

Anthropologist Manuel Gamio was one of the elites who made revolutionary nationalism synonymous with modernity. Gamio was a respected intellectual in various national movements and is considered the father of Mexican anthropology. He was the founding director of the Bureau of Anthropology under the Secretariat of Agriculture and Development (1917), served as undersecretary of education in 1924 and 1925, and led the Instituto Indigenista Interamericano from 1942 until his death in 1960.[42] Mexico's indigenous majority was central to Gamio's vision of nationalism. He was clearly an elite himself, having studied at Columbia University in New York, but his focus was on the masses. His 1916 book *Forjando patria pro-nacionalismo* attempted to create a roadmap for the national identity of Mexicans.

In an effort to understand Mexico's challenges, Gamio noted three similarities in "defined and integrated" nationalities around the world: racial or ethnic uniformity, common language, and—despite class, intellectual, or other differences—basic political, religious, and moral agreement. For Gamio, "the memory of the past, with all its victories and tears, is treasured in our hearts. The national tradition . . . is alive and well in the men, women and children, the knowledgeable and the ignorant, in the children of the simple and the refined, in the finest of art and the simplest of rhapsodies."[43] Perhaps this is the horizontal comradeship of which Anderson speaks. However, as Lomnitz argues, the comradeship is more vertical than horizontal, with elements of loyalty connecting members to each other and to the national body. Servant and master do not share a fraternal relationship, but they may share loyalty to the nation. Women and children, for instance, are not "represented" in the body of the nation but may still identify with and be cast in roles in the national sentiment or agenda. The horizontal comradeships Anderson imagined were indeed fraternal—made up of male citizens, only. Others were not allowed to be agents in nation-building.[44]

For Gamio, women were an integral part of the nation-building campaign, but in very specific, gendered roles. He identified three types of women: serving women, feminist women, and feminine women. The last drew on the best characteristics of the other two. "This is the ideal woman, generally preferred because she constitutes the primary factor to produce harmonious development and the spiritual and intellectual wellbeing of the individual and the species."[45] The idea of propagating the species certainly reduced women to a biological, sexualized identity. However, Gamio did recognize their contributions to the nationalist agenda. Mexican unity and character were tied to the transmission of Mexico's miraculous tradition. Surely, much of this transmission of culture was in the hands of women—the protectors of the *race*, if not the *nation*. Women and indigenous Mexicans were the protectors of the national spirit.[46] Still, as Gamio described in a 1926 lecture, the ramifications of the conquest's negativity remained embodied in the female indigenous body: "The offspring of these inharmonious and forced unions had none of the advantages of a normal origin. Moreover, the mestizo, or half-breed, born under these circumstances was educated by the mother, since the father abandoned the woman sooner or later, and he in turn increased in body and spirit the indigenous masses— passive enemies of the white colonists."[47] From this description, one hardly guesses that Gamio sees the mestizo as Mexico's saving grace. While white colonists were natural (foreign) enemies and Indians were backward and passive, mestizos—resisters of foreign or pure blood—were heroes! The challenge was to modernize the indigenous without giving up indigenous culture—to eliminate the indigenous through mixing, while embracing their history.

Gamio succeeded in putting the indigenous in the past, even though they were—and are—alive and well and living in Mexico. Gamio was torn by his commitments to the nation as timeless space and his commitment to endless progress.[48] Unfortunately, for Gamio, progress was not a natural phenomenon and, like interbreeding, had to be monitored. He expressed concern that the intermixing of the Spanish and the indigenous people was "done on the spur of the moment and defectively, from the colonial period to date. The ethnic fusion continues, producing an undesirable interbreeding under conditions unfavorable to the effective development of the Indian." For Gamio, when physical mixture took place without "amalgamation with abstract cultural concepts," the result was unacceptable. As an example, he indicated that simply giving an Indian a sewing machine does not modernize him or her. "An understanding of their mental attitudes, their hopes and aspirations, is essential to an effective substitution of the instruments and institutions of modern civilization, or to a fusion of the modern and the primitive."[49] Without the fusion of cultural structures as well as physical beings, then, we cannot forge *patria*, in Gamio's eyes. Ironically, he does not mention the role of the United States in modernization. Although he notes the foreign presence at times, Gamio does not explicitly discuss the role of the United States in Mexico. U.S. corporations and individuals built Mexican railroads, drilled for Mexican oil, and mined Mexican ore, all in the name of modernizing Mexico during the Porfiriato. The exchange, since Mexico was cash poor, was land grants to these U.S. entities. This physical and financial presence of foreigners in Mexico was one of the major reasons the Revolution was fought—to recover Mexico for the Mexicans. For all his desire for modernization and his concern about the foreign influence it might bring, the United States is virtually absent from Gamio's analysis.[50]

It is intriguing that although Gamio is a U.S.-educated anthropologist, his revolutionary nationalist credentials appeared to be untarnished. One could argue that his imagination was colonized through his experience living in the belly of the beast.[51] Throughout his life he maintained strong relationships with U.S. academics. In addition to bringing his Columbia University mentor, Franz Boas, to Mexico often, Gamio introduced University of Chicago anthropologist Robert Redfield to Tepoztlán, which became the preferred ethnographic site for U.S. anthropologists in Mexico throughout much of the twentieth century. Gamio sought further cooperation between Mexican and U.S. archaeologists and anthropologists on the study of Mexico.[52] Despite his discourse on national pride and identity, Gamio was well integrated in the American empire and helped smooth its access into Mexico's social and cultural fabric.

Later anthropologists may frame Gamio's imagination as "colonized," but his solution for Mexico's divisions, *indigenismo*, was a vital part of Mexico's nation-building ideology. Drawing on the work of Boas, Gamio believed that all races were equal and all cultures had something to contribute. Gamio reported that Boas had proven that differences in intellectual aptitude were "the result of causes of a historical, biological, geographic . . . nature: that is, causes brought about by education and milieu," and that by varying that milieu, inferiority could be made to disappear.[53] Herein lies one of many contradictions in Gamio's sweeping project: he professed cultural relativism, yet he believed Mexico's indigenous were inferior and had to be blended into the nation through modernization. Gamio thought that by providing a different environment for Indians, they could be modernized and integrated into Mexican society. This was the responsibility of the Revolution, "for the Indian, because of his cultural inferiority, has the right to expect the white to understand his peculiar ways of thinking, since he cannot be expected to ascend mentally, rapidly, miraculously, to the plane of the difficult ideological and material mechanism which characterizes the modern civilization of the white minorities."[54] Whether Gamio was calling mestizos white or embracing the presence of the empire is not clear, but whoever the whites were, it was their responsibility in his schema to elevate the indigenous. As always, an examination of the role of the United States in this picture is critical. Modernization under Díaz was funded almost entirely by U.S. corporations. However, in the wake of the Revolution, with the massive migration of Mexicans to the United States, the role of the United States in Mexico's modernization was more complicated. Many Mexicans, including Gamio, hoped for the return of the tens of thousands of compatriots from the United States. The nationalist agenda often saw a special role for returning migrants. During their time in the United States, emigrants experienced modern factories and agricultural techniques. Mexico's modern future was dependent on the skills and experience of these migrants. The U.S. presence in these national bodies cannot be denied. Yet Gamio and others chose to forgive the transgressions of emigrants by embracing their enhanced contribution to the national project.[55]

The fundamental element of Gamio's plan was always race. Throughout *Forjando patria*, he was consumed with mixture: "Fusion of races, convergences and fusion of cultural manifestations, linguistic unification and economic equilibrium of the social elements . . .

*ought to characterize the Mexican people so that they will constitute and incarnate a powerful fatherland and a coherent and defined nationality.*"[56] The Revolution of 1910, Gamio believed, was the last in a long line of revolutions that sought to unify Mexico. "It is now the turn of the Mexican revolutionaries to grip the mallet and wear the apron of the forger so that from the miraculous anvil the new nation made of fused iron and bronze will emerge," he wrote. For the first time, the hammer was in the hands of Mexicans. "Behold the iron. . . . Behold the bronze. . . . Mix them up, brothers!"[57] Gamio seemed to believe that once everyone had been mixed—or forged—much of the economic and social inequality of Mexico would disappear. For centuries, "gestating furnaces . . . burned with noble nationalistic impulses except the Pizarros and Avilas tried to chisel incomplete nations then, since they only counted the steel of the Latin race, setting aside the strong indigenous bronze in the refuse."[58] The Revolution of 1910, however, had learned from these mistakes, Gamio wrote, and recognized the value of the indigenous bronze in the amalgamation that would be modern Mexico. Racism in Mexico, according to the plan, was a thing of the past.

To Gamio's mind, Catholicism was well integrated into Mexico's national identity. In the beginning it was used to soften the blow of the bloody conquest, but eventually the "attractive modalities of Catholicism" were incorporated into the indigenous mythologies to create a workable situation for the nation.[59] Gamio identified three types of Catholics in twentieth-century Mexico: pagan-Catholics, true Catholics, and utilitarian Catholics. "Pagan-Catholics are not to be blamed for their ignorance; they need understanding and help. It is necessary to educate them in civil and religious matters. True Catholics are worthy of all consideration and respect." In contrast, "utilitarian Catholics deserve that the church and the country throw them out."[60] Gamio's description of pagan-Catholics illustrates his belief that indigenous Mexico was in need of not just religious education but civic education as well. In order to contribute to the Mexican national agenda, indigenous Mexico needed guidance. True Catholics were sincere in their beliefs, but they must "admit science is science and religion is religion." They embrace two central themes: "to Caesar what is Caesar's" and "my reign is not of this earth."[61] Gamio embraced true Catholics as long as they recognized the appropriate role of the church. He reserved his condemnation for the utilitarian Catholics—largely the clergy. His critique was placed in both a Mexican and Christian context. "For the sake of fanaticism, they would bring back the Holy Office," he wrote, referring to the body that instituted the Spanish Inquisition. "For the sake of avarice," he continued, "they would sell Christ again, except that it would be for more money than Judas did; because of cowardice, they would deny Christ, so many times that the roosters of the world would not be able to crow enough for them."[62] While Gamio recognized the strong Catholic presence in Mexico, he identified precisely that Catholic element which was problematic for the revolutionary nationalist agenda. True Catholics, and even pagan-Catholics, could participate in the national project, but utilitarian Catholics were detractors from Mexico's future. Gamio may not have trusted the clergy, but he clearly was not anti-Catholic.

Catholic activists saw their faith as central to the revolutionary agenda. While Anderson viewed nationalism as a substitute for a religiously constituted community, for Mexican lay and clerical leadership, nation and religion could not be separated.[63] For the revolutionary left, Catholicism—embodied by Gamio's utilitarian Catholics or the clergy—was the major factor holding back the indigenous masses, and therefore the nation. In contrast, Gamio's true Catholics were working to build a better Mexico, with Catholicism as a defining theme.

In the spirit of Gamio's true Catholics, the Partido Católico Nacional (PCN, National Catholic Party) was established in 1911. The clergy informally supported the party, but Archbishop José Mora y del Río dutifully indicated in a pastoral letter that the church was not involved in, and should not be confused with, the political party.[64] In December 1911, *Restauración Social* presented the "Theoretical and Practical Guide of the Partido Católico Nacional." The PCN pledged to "work tirelessly to see to it that democratic and republican institutions, especially that of effective suffrage, become real in the whole country. To this end, it accepts the principle of no reelection in its broadest sense, as it refers to executive, federal and state powers."[65] In June 1912 the PCN started publishing its own daily newspaper, *La Nación*, which promoted "God, Country and Freedom" on its masthead. *Restauración Social* and other monthly publications supported the PCN, but the party likely saw the need for a daily publication to prepare for the 1912 elections. One issue of *La Nación* was dedicated to the role of the clergy in Mexican independence. An open letter asked that a list of priests involved in independence movements be published "so that the Mexican Nation can see who the Catholic Clergy are and that we owe our independence to them."[66] PCN members refused to let anticlerical politicians write the church out of Mexican history. One editorial challenged the liberal attack on Catholics: "What have those liberal gentlemen who accuse us done in half a century of domination? Promise, promise, promise . . . and not accomplish anything. Even now, are the rich not with them, the big landowners and the powerful industrialists? Who, then, are the 'conservatives' and who are the 'progressives?'"[67] These defensive efforts were all aimed at the elections, where PCN candidates sought to gain significant representation in the Chamber of Deputies. The PCN reminded anticlerical elements of the Revolution that the church's role in building and sustaining Mexico could not be denied.

*La Nación* instructed Mexican Catholics to rally around their candidates in local elections as well. Mexicans were urged to vote their conscience "so that the elections will be successful and those who can initiate and carry out the prodigious social restoration, which all patriotic Mexicans wish for, are elevated to positions of power."[68] The PCN was very conscious about linking Catholicism to patriotism, given the rhetoric of the revolutionary left. Catholics were successful in electing a number of representatives to the Chamber of Deputies, mostly from the states of Jalisco, Michoacán, México, Querétaro, and Zacatecas. The certification of a number of PCN deputies was challenged, but the PCN sent thirty representatives to the Chamber of Deputies.[69] *La Nación* declared, "The chamber of deputies is divided into four blocks. 'The luminous triangle' is transformed into the 'mysterious quadrangle.'"[70] The PCN saw itself as an equal partner in building Mexico's future—it was staking its claim to the Mexican national future.

In Jalisco, the PCN also controlled the state government. Catholic leaders moved quickly on a revolutionary agenda, legalizing labor unions and licensing cooperatives and mutual-aid societies. A land-reform program was also implemented, though it required families to own land outright before guaranteeing inheritance rights. As such, few families benefited from this program. Revolutionary troops passed through Guadalajara, Jalisco, in mid-1914, destroying most of the gains made by the PCN in the state.[71] Still, as the Jalisco case suggests, Catholics, like other revolutionary nationalists, imagined Mexico with less social inequality, better relations between owners and workers, and ownership that reflected Mexican rather than foreign concerns. Like other Mexicans, PCN members wanted out from under the American empire.

In the fall of 1913 the PCN began preparing for fall elections with a party convention. Again, links were made between patriotism and Catholicism: "This candidacy is a guarantee of our national salvation. . . . Above the party, the interests of the country."[72] Reportedly, six thousand workers in Orizaba, Veracruz, were committed to the PCN presidential candidate, Federico Gamboa, demonstrating the wide regional and class appeal of the party.[73]

The PCN envisioned religiously oriented solutions to the same social ills that revolutionary leadership was working to solve: "Let our enemies say what they will, there is only one solution: the Christian solution; love for the people, the true social and economic improvement for the people."[74] Recognizing the gains being made by socialists and other leftists, the PCN was deliberate in addressing economic and social issues. Quoting Pope Leo XIII, the editorial continued, "To procure common well being is to give religion the preeminent honor it deserves, it is to open the core of its intimate virtue and communicate it abundantly with saving effectiveness to social, domestic and economic life."[75] In addition to the types of programs implemented in Jalisco, the PCN supported the organization of various Catholic groups throughout the country—students, laborers, farmers, artisans, and women. The PCN tried to formulate a national agenda for rebuilding Mexico, and, much like Gamio, Catholic nationalists saw a role for everyone.

In September 1912, *La Nación* highlighted a new Catholic women's organization, the Obolo Católico (Catholic Mite), organized by the Círculo Nacional Católico, a lay Catholic organization, and the PCN. This move signaled recognition of the unique role women could play in the national Catholic movement. An editorial in *La Nación* read: "The Catholic woman is throughout the country; she is the center of every home; she exerts her influence both sweet and effective over all members of society." Her role in society and the family was central to the role she could play in religious matters. "She takes matters of religion more seriously, and being more patient and self-denying, better knows how to obtain by means which appear more modest, the greatest triumphs of our faith, due to these and many other qualities she possesses."[76] The PCN's agenda placed Mexican women in a limited, gendered role. As in Gamio's scheme, women were clearly an important, if troubling, part of the Mexican national body, in contrast to Anderson's fraternal imagined community.

Part of the agenda for any nation-building project in Mexico since at least the 1830s has been defining the nation in contrast to, if not explicitly against, the United States. This sentiment increased exponentially in the late nineteenth century as American business interests penetrated the Mexican nation-space. In 1913 an editorial in the newspaper *Nueva Era* invoked the ultimate insult against the PCN. The editors referred to the PCN, rather than "the threat from the North," as the "verdadero fantasma"—the true threat. Editors of *La Nación* defended the patriotism and honor of the PCN and accused *Nueva Era* of slander and lies. "Why does the columnist of the *Nueva Era*, who recalls the Empire often, not recall for us that if the Latin Alliance which was thrust upon us was repelled, it was not through our own effort, but by Anglo help which was set us up at the discretion of our neighbors to the North?"[77] The accusation that *Nueva Era* was soft on anti-Americanism was implied in the Catholic response. As the PCN described it, Mexico was increasingly "facing" north, rather than south, and that was the work of the revolutionary nationalists, not the Catholics. In the struggle for national purity, Catholics had an edge in distinguishing themselves from the Protestant United States. In this case, the lurking U.S. presence was obvious; more often it was shrouded in the discourses of modernization and foreign influence during this period.

This tension regarding the empire, or the North, was certainly not new, but defining Mexico in contrast to the North was critical to revolutionary nationalism. As Deborah Baldwin and others have noted, the connection to the United States delegitimized Mexican nationalist credentials.[78] Efforts at modernization and removing the foreign presence in Mexico included embraces and rejections, respectively, of the United States. Although the Mexican Revolution was implicitly anti-foreign, the U.S. presence could not be removed from Mexico's present or future. The United States and Mexico were inextricably tied—not just economically or politically, but in the minds and bodies of some of Mexico's greatest revolutionaries and intellectuals, along with a million of its average citizens who spent time in the United States during the Revolution, shaping Mexico for generations to come.

For the previous one hundred years, Mexico's national identity had been defined in part in relationship to the United States, Mexico's closest neighbor and the occupant of half of Mexico's former territory. In the 1910s, Mexico was more dependent than ever on U.S. approval. Recognition, investment, aid, and arms all had to come from the United States in order for Mexico to continue its revolutionary and nationalist agendas. The roles of the United States and the Catholic Church often brought about conflicting emotions and contradictory actions for the Mexican national agenda. As Lomnitz notes, "Although early Mexican patriotism was identified with a superior loyalty to the Catholic faith, and Mexican nationalists vehemently excluded other faiths from the national order, both the

British and the Americans coincide in their interests in propagating freedom of religion."[79] This description of the religion question post-independence demonstrates Mexico's staunch affirmation of Catholicism as part of its national identity in the early nineteenth century. A century later, efforts to limit the power and reach of the Catholic Church were often framed as attempts to provide religious liberty by decentering the Catholic Church. Over time, the roles of the church and the indigenous in Mexican political thought were transformed.

Although Gamio centered the indigenous in his discourse on nationalism, a significant contradiction was central to his thinking. He embraced the indigenous past, but he sought its amalgamation into a mestizo future. María Josefina Saldaña-Portillo writes "Revolutionary nationalism was born more out of a desire to suture the indigenous populations into the fabric of a new, modern nation than out of an appreciation for ancestral, or living, Indian culture."[80] He valued the bronze indigenous masses, but only for how they could temper the Spanish iron. In the decade following the start of the Revolution, there were many attempts to identify a platform that would unite Mexico—*sufragio efectivo/no reelección, tierra y libertad, justicia y caridad, indigenismo*, and so on.[81] Due to regional struggles and instability in the capital, none of these ideas was enough to formulate a Mexican nationalist agenda. Madero, "the apostle of democracy," was ousted by the Constitutionalists, who were challenged by the Conventionalists; and each struggled with parallel Catholic movements and the presence and interference of the United States. It was not until the national stability established by Alvaro Obregón and the work of José Vasconcelos in promoting a national past that Mexican national identity became a significant effect of the Revolution. One of the central goals of 1920s revolutionary Mexico was not only the creation of a national past but the training of Mexican citizens to invest in that "new" history. The anticlerical leadership provided by Plutarco Elías Calles, both as Secretario de Gobernación under Obregón and during his own term as president, solidified a Mexican *Catholic* identity as well. Each imagined Mexico out from under the shadow of American empire.

Professions of Faith and Citizenship in 1920s Revolutionary Mexico

All revolutions degenerate into governments.

—Mexican proverb

Mexican labor, religious, and other movements in resistance to the Porfiriato were building in the years before 1910. Claims that revolutionary nationalism started in 1910 disregard this period of resistance and coalition building. Partha Chatterjee argues that counter-nationalisms form long before independence movements take place. Established regimes have clear control of what he terms the "material" aspects of society; meanwhile, anticolonial or anti-imperial movements solidify their control over the "spiritual" elements of society. The material domain is dominated by technology and modernization; the spiritual embraces the distinct culture of the occupied land. Nationalist histories often cite an event, such as independence, or in the case of India the formation of the Indian National Congress, as the beginning of nationalist thought. This ignores the developments that preceded such prominent markers of national change. In the case of Mexico, while revolutionary nationalism became a more organized ideology in the decade following 1910, it was not until 1920, under Alvaro Obregón, that Mexico used that ideology not only to create and embrace an indigenous national past but also to promote the idea of Mexican national citizenship. In keeping with the nationalist fervor that swept Mexico, Catholics increasingly linked religion and nation.

Alvaro Obregón provided economic and social stability for Mexico from 1920 to 1924, in part due to the elimination of many of his rivals, but also to his willingness to turn a blind eye to most church activity. Emiliano Zapata had been killed, Francisco "Pancho" Villa had been pacified, and in spite of the Constitution of 1917, many clergy returned to their former positions in churches and communities throughout Mexico.

As early as 1912, Mexican states took education out of the hands of the church. The Constitution of 1917 made this a national requirement. In some areas, literacy increased substantially; in other areas, without church support, educational opportunities diminished. Vasconcelos made it his mission to create a Mexican citizenry. The ideal Mexican citizen was mestizo, embracing the best of both Spanish and indigenous qualities. While the essence of U.S. identity was drawn from the virgin feminine landscape and the male fantasy of conquering it, the essence of Mexican identity, for Vasconcelos, was built on the mixing of races. David Noble suggests that the great "American" novel was the key to creating ideal citizens in the United States. In Mexico, embracing the Revolution and the indigenous past, with all their contradictions, was central to the new Mexican citizen. The national body was first imagined through this shaping of citizens—national education without the church. Vasconcelos was not anti-church; in fact, he was a practicing Catholic for most of his life. Like Gamio, though, he believed the church should know its proper place.

Vasconcelos's new curriculum proclaimed *la raza cósmica* as a victorious, liberated, and liberal people.[82] His idea of *la raza cósmica* was related to Gamio's *indigenismo* but was much more aesthetically pleasing. Vasconcelos envisioned the "four races" of the world—black, white, red, and yellow—mixing to form a fifth race, a perfect race that would take the best of the others and create a new, better human species—*la raza cósmica*. He did not claim Mexicans as the cosmic race, as has often been assumed decades later, but he did believe *la raza cósmica* would develop in the tropics. "The Indian is a good bridge for racial mixing. Besides, the warm climate is propitious for the interaction and gathering of all peoples." Vasconcelos, like Gamio, believed the people produced from Spanish and Indian mixing in colonial Mexico were problematic. However, Vasconcelos could see a future where the mixing would occur for positive reasons, and thereby produce positive results. "In the future," he wrote, "as social conditions keep improving, the mixture of bloods will become gradually more spontaneous, to the point that interbreeding will no longer be the result of simple necessity but of personal taste or, at least, of curiosity. Spiritual motivation, in this manner, will increasingly superimpose itself upon the contingencies of the merely physical."[83] For Vasconcelos, the spiritual—expressed in his very metaphor, *la raza cósmica*—was much more important to the story than in Gamio's industrial imagery of forging *mestizaje* from assorted metals.

In 1921, Vasconcelos created the shield for the national university: a map of Latin America with the motto "Por mi raza hablará el epíritu"—"The spirit shall speak through my race." Although he was a practicing Catholic, the spiritual nature of *la raza cósmica* seemed to emerge from a different source. In 1948, *La raza cósmica* was reissued, with a prologue by Vasconcelos that incorporated the church where it had not been explicitly two decades earlier. "Even the most contradictory racial mixtures can have beneficial results, as long as the spiritual factor contributes to raise them. . . . A religion such as Christianity made the American Indians advance, in a few centuries, from cannibalism to a relative degree of civilization."[84] Vasconcelos had always recognized the superiority of the white race in his original work, though he had not attributed the "progress" of the Indian to the church. Rather, he saw that *mestizaje* was the key to bringing Indians into the present and the future.[85] Vasconcelos, like José Martí, was consistent in his desire for Mexico to turn to Latin America, rather than the United States, for examples of leadership, nationalism, and independence. Despite this frequently claimed goal, when Mexico was no longer welcoming to Vasconcelos he fled to the United States. Unlike José Martí, who made a career out of studying the United States from inside the belly of the beast, Vasconcelos rarely reflected on this contradiction between his nationalist project and his own actions.

The battle of Latinism versus Anglo-Saxonism was central to Vasconcelos's theory. For him, the Latin American independence movements only solidified Anglo superiority in the region. "The founders of our new nationalism were, without knowing it, the best allies of the Anglo-Saxons, our rivals in the possession of the continent."[86] By breaking up into many independent nations, Latin America allowed the United States to be the dominant force in the Americas. Anglos annihilated the indigenous and excluded Africans, thereby solidifying a white-supremacist ideal. "The so-called Latin peoples, because they have been more faithful to their divine mission in America, are the ones called upon to consummate this mission. Such fidelity to the occult design is the guarantee of our triumph." While Vasconcelos is often maligned in the present for his racialist notions, in 1925 his remarks on race in the United States were most insightful. In contrast to the "spontaneous mixing" that took place in Latin America, the United States displayed "the inflexible line that separates the Blacks from the Whites . . . and the laws, each time more rigorous, for the exclusion of the Japanese and Chinese from California."[87] Vasconcelos believed that this racial segregation would be the downfall of the United States and that *la raza cósmica* would thrive in the future. In an ironic turn on the thinking of the era, he wrote, "We belong to tomorrow, while the Anglo-Saxons are gradually becoming more a part of yesterday. The Yanquis will end up building the last great empire of a single race, the final empire of White supremacy." It was the emergence of the fifth race that would defeat the great "White Empire."[88] Vasconcelos drew on José Martí's "Nuestra América," which was opposed to Anglo North America— the United States. Although Latin American nationalist movements had forsaken state solidarity against the United States, racial solidarity and, more importantly, racial mixing could conquer Anglo separatism, in Vasconcelos's eyes. After a falling out with Obregón and Calles, Vasconcelos left the government and spent much of the mid to late 1920s in exile in Chicago. Ironically, he and Francis Kelley never seem to have crossed paths, though their interests were very much the same.

## Civilizing the Mestizo

In 1519 Spain and the Roman Catholic Church affixed themselves to Mexico's throat and were with extreme difficulty detached from it only after three hundred years. . . . [T]he metaphorical expression "he could not call his soul his own" was true of the inhabitants in its baldest, its most literal sense.

—Charles Macomb Flandrau, 1950[89]

In the November 1914 edition of *Extension Magazine*, Francis Kelley announced to U.S. Catholics that Mexico was in need: "Mexico has been transformed from a land of hope to a land of grim and black despair. If Mexico has sinned it has paid a horrible penalty; but can we afford to pay our share of it?"[90] With such fire-and-brimstone rhetoric, Kelley embarked on a decades-long journey to defend the honor of Catholic Mexico. He raised funds to transport exiled religious to the United States, and he operated a seminary in exile in Texas for the exclusive training of Mexican priests to serve Mexico. Kelley's most significant contribution to this effort, by far, was his writing. Through *Extension Magazine*, *The New World*, and numerous Catholic and secular publications, Kelley bombarded the public with messages of the peril and bloodlust besetting neighboring Mexico. In the process of educating laypersons about Mexico, Kelley both transcended and reinforced the American empire. Catholicism circulated relatively freely between the United States and Mexico, crossing in either direction, asserting U.S. Catholic needs and concerns over the Mexican Catholic Church and the Mexican government. Catholic borderlands theorizes the role that the church has played not only in the colonial relationship between Spain and Mexico but also in the imperial relationship between the United State and Mexico. Particularly in their missionary manifestations, Eurocentric churches had continued to work to "civilize" peoples of color throughout the world. Protestant missionaries often represented "American" values in foreign lands. In the case of Mexico during and after the Mexican Revolution, the U.S. *Catholic* presence became more significant. This presence, however, was not in Mexico itself. It was in the public and political discussions in the United States. The United States, through the constant agitating of Kelley, worked to defend Catholicism in Mexico.

Much of the early contact between the United States and Mexico was chronicled by men who fancied themselves historians, particularly Hubert Howe Bancroft and Frank J. Dobie. Bancroft, a book and stationery seller, became interested in documenting the history of California, and in the 1870s he collected *testimonios* from the Californios—those who owned land in California during the Spanish and Mexican periods and "lost" their land shortly after the United States occupied northern Mexico. While many of the original *testimonios*, as documented by the Californios themselves or by employees of Bancroft, still exist in their entirety, Bancroft selectively used this and other information to produce a history of California that glorified the role of the United States in maximizing the use of the state's storied resources. He painted a picture of Mexicans as quaint, simple people who did not really know what to do with the land they occupied. Similarly, Frank Dobie, in the first half of the twentieth century, wrote histories of Texas that vilified the Mexican government and people for their mistreatment of U.S. citizens encroaching on Mexican territory in the 1840s. Bancroft and Dobie both wrote histories that illustrated the superiority of Anglo-Americans and painted U.S. imperialist expansion with the brush of the white man's burden.[91]

For many in the United States during the 1930s and 1940s, notions of cross-national collaboration were framed by the ideas of Pan-Americanism rooted in the Monroe Doctrine. Issued in 1823 by President James Monroe, the doctrine declared further expansion of European nations into the Western Hemisphere off-limits. Monroe offered up the United States as protector of independent nations in the hemisphere and affirmed that the United States would not intervene in European affairs. Although largely regarded as a ploy to affect the upcoming presidential elections in the United States, the Monroe Doctrine, perhaps more than any other pronouncement, shaped U.S. policy and public opinion regarding Latin America. Eighty years later, President Theodore Roosevelt amended the Monroe Doctrine to justify U.S. intervention throughout the Western Hemisphere. In "advancing" U.S. policy toward Latin America in 1904, Roosevelt envisioned a more integrated, though hardly egalitarian, hemispheric body.

In light of Roosevelt's corollary to the Monroe Doctrine, much U.S. thinking turned toward ideas of Pan-Americanism in the decades that followed. In his 1932 presidential address to the American Historical Association, Herbert Bolton spoke of "The Epic of Greater America." Unlike many of his colleagues, Bolton not only did not see the United States as exceptional; he also saw that U.S. history was incomplete and even inaccurate without studying the history of other American nations and understanding their inter-actions with the United States. Moving beyond the Frontier Thesis of his mentor, Frederick Jackson Turner, Bolton saw the signifi-cance of borders as much as the frontier. "Besides being the crux of international relations," he wrote, "border zones were areas of cul-tural influence, quite as significant as that of the isolated frontier."[92] Much of Bolton's career concentrated on bringing U.S. history into focus as part of a hemispheric history, "from the North Pole to the South Pole and from Columbus to Now."[93] He believed that stu-dents should study the history of the Western Hemisphere before narrowing their focus to the national level.

Throughout the first half of the twentieth century, various forms of Pan-Americanism emerged, exploring ways for nations in the Western Hemisphere to cooperate. In 1915 the Pan-American Finan-cial Congress, with business representatives appointed by each gov-ernment, was established "to outline plans for the development and regulation of the hemisphere's commerce."[94] Business and political leaders were not the only ones forging Pan-American alliances. The U.S. Catholic Church, like many Protestant denominations, was also attempting to make inroads in Latin America, particularly in Mexico. In this context, we might expect Francis Kelley to have been attentive to the work of Bolton or other U.S. historians, but that does not appear to have been the case.

Kelley's writing on Mexico revealed his belief in "Anglo" superior-ity. Kelly characterized the Spanish invasion of Mexico as a benign conquest. Cortés, beloved by the Indians, desired to preserve, Chris-tianize, and civilize the Indians.[95] Kelley did not bring the same civilizing agenda to his work in Europe. In those instances he was working to maintain or restore Catholicism in a Catholic border-land, but civilization was never in doubt. In Mexico, however, the challenges for the church were greater, due in large part to racial difference. For Kelley, as for many a historian or anthropologist, Mexico's people were an intriguing bunch. As he wrote in *Blood-Drenched Altars*, "No one knows much about Mexican racial origins, but these origins contribute mightily to the fantastic character of the story." Kelley viewed the *mestizaje* of Mexico's people as an accomplishment rather than the result of a brutal invasion: "What took centuries for others to do Mexico actually accomplished in decades; and for a very great part by herself. There is a touch of the marvelous as well as the admirable in such a people."[96] His view of Mexicans as exotic was a significant departure from the eugenic discourses that saw Mexicans as dysgenic and a threat to American germ plasm.

Race was not based on just the physical. Social factors such as assimilation, language use, and social class shaped the identities of colonial subjects.[97] The concern of colonial governments with mixed-race subjects is paralleled by the concern of historians of race, as demonstrated by "the disproportionate concern of the field of comparative race relations with the incidence and treatment of mulattoes," Barbara Fields notes, "as though race became problematic only when the appearance of the people concerned was problematic."[98] Mestizos did not fit neatly into the categories that are used to talk about colonialism and race—they are at times simultaneously both and neither, the colonizer and the colonized. Robert Young, in his work on historical writing about hybridity, similarly finds that the idea of mixed-race people poses special challenges to both scholars and colonial institutions: "The idea of race here shows itself to be profoundly dialectical: it only works when defined against potential intermixture, which also threatens to undo its calculation altogether."[99] The threat Young identifies to racial purity is the same threat Mexico and Mexicans posed to the racial order and separation of the United States.

Kelley and Wilson's representative to Mexico, John Lind, shared a fascination with Mexico's racial homogeneity. Although they were politically quite opposed to each other, both believed that Mexicans were inferior to people from the United States. "Mexicans, and Latin Americans generally, are so different from us racially and psychologically that we have no common ethical standards," Lind wrote. "I have become firmly convinced that the differences [between us] . . . can be overcome under conditions of social and industrial enlightenment."[100] Echoes of the Monroe Doctrine, the Roosevelt Corollary, and American empire reverberate in Lind's words. He was committed to the promise of technology in defeating backwardness. In terms of policy and religious affiliation, Lind and Kelley were polar opposites, but their thinking on race, shaped by U.S. relations with Mexico over nearly a century, was almost identical.

Kelley cited Mexican independence as the fall from grace of this admirable people. El Grito de Dolores, the 1811 uprising led by Father Miguel Hidalgo, was a "throwback to savagery, blood-lust, and the red altar. It was not a mob urged on by hunger. It was a *jealous* mob, an embodiment of blind hate, with no grievance beyond the thought that others had something it wanted."[101] It was another ten years before Mexico's first independent government, led by Agustín Iturbide, ousted the Spanish crown. Shortly thereafter, the United States interfered, in Kelley's eyes, by recognizing Iturbide's government, reinforcing the rule of Mexicans in their own affairs.

For Kelley, this rupture of colonial ties with Spain was also a rupture of ties to the Catholic Church. Even under Spanish rule, however, the powers of the church were seriously curbed. In 1767 the Jesuits, who had been particularly active in educating the elite of New Spain, were expelled from all Spanish territories for suspected conspiratorial activities in Spain. The 1804 Act of Consolidation appropriated church assets to pay for Spanish debts in Europe and less successful colonial ventures in other parts of the world. With the onset of Mexican independence, the role of the church became less certain, as a series of unstable governments worked to find a combination of colonial and new structures that functioned to preserve power for the criollo elite while granting enough rights to the mestizo and indigenous masses to ensure their cooperation.

According to Kelley, the Mexican Revolution was a continuation of the mob attack that led to Mexico's independence. Mexico became adept at using the U.S. government and public to accomplish its goals. "The American Front," as Kelley dubbed it, was a well-orchestrated propaganda army designed to invade "parlor pinks, uplift societies, clubs, anybody or anything that can be impressed by sentiment and shallow talk."[102] Mexicans were not equipped, however, to go toe to toe with "Americans." "Mexico uses very few Mexicans on its American front line," he wrote, "and for a wise reason: apart from the universal power of the bribe they are worthless in the United States. They have not the approach. They cannot learn it. Their mental processes are radically different from those of Americans. They have the 'Latin' rather than the 'Saxon Mind.'"[103] Despite the bumbling of Mexican officials, they seemed able to dupe Protestants fairly easily, including the U.S. government. The Mexican revolutionary governments succeeded in getting the United States to provide arms only for governmental armies, thus reducing the likelihood of uprisings among the people.

On the Mexican front, Protestant missionaries were easily drawn into the Mexican revolutionary agenda of persecution. "We have had a chance to observe the work of these distinguished graduates of [Protestant] missionary schools in the cause of Christianity and are not enthused," Kelley wrote. Protestants embraced the revolutionary agenda because they believed "that the program of the revolution represented what these churches had been preaching through the years and that the triumph of the revolution meant the triumph of the Gospel." Indeed, Kelley continued, "the revolution did triumph. It waded through blood to its goal. So many of those delightful graduates of the [Protestant] mission schools are in their graves. No Protestant American minister or teacher may officiate in Mexico today."[104] With the help of Protestant missionaries in Mexico and the Protestant U.S. government, Mexico was able to successfully defeat the Catholic Church, as Kelley told it. For him, the maintenance of colonial ties with Spain would have prevented the following century of ruin of an otherwise admirable people.

During the course of the Revolution, pressure was brought to bear on Catholic Church officials regarding the power and resources the church had amassed over the course of several centuries. In *The Book of Red and Yellow* and *Blood-Drenched Altars*, Kelley described in excruciating detail the experiences of Mexican clergy and the actions taken by various revolutionary governments in Mexico.

The revolutionary anticlerical movement enforced laws first passed in 1857, as part of Benito Juarez's reforms, and later built into the Constitution of 1917. Many priests fled Mexico for San Antonio, Texas, where Oblate Father Henry Constantineau housed them. In need of assistance and support, he sought out the archbishop of Chicago, "who promptly sent [Kelley] to the border with orders to go to Vera Cruz or anywhere else [he] was needed."[105] The exiled priests reported to Kelley their efforts to avoid imprisonment or death, or the sacrifice of their parishioners. Kelley accepted the mission of educating the American public, particularly Catholics, about "the Mexican situation." He reported on the journeys of priests across the border to seek refuge from the violence, the coercion, and the "kidnappings." Kelley wrote, describing the capture of priests, "The more this victim had endeared himself to the people, the more valuable he was to the robbers." Priests were then "tried" and sentenced to pay fines. When a priest could not pay the charge, he was made to go door to door trying to extract his ransom from his parishioners. Kelley charged Protestants in Mexico and the United States with aligning with anti-Catholic forces to defeat the church. "It may seem strange," he wrote, "but yet it is quite true, that many of the most outrageous stories told by lying Protestants—I use the adjective advisedly—were actually believed by Catholics in America, even by members of the clergy."[106] He started an all-out effort to draw church and public attention to the plight of the exiled priests and nuns. In *The Book of Red and Yellow*, Kelley drew on affidavits by priests and nuns to illustrate the horrors brought upon Catholics in Mexico. However, throughout most of his work on Mexico the voices of Mexican Catholics themselves were surprisingly absent, even when exiled Mexican archbishops lived with him in Chicago or Oklahoma City. With the benefit of American empire, a Canadian Catholic priest based in the United States could in fact assume this role. Kelley represented the Mexican hierarchy, with or without their approval, because from the base of Catholic borderlands, he could.

Kelley's publicity schemes did not go unnoticed by Mexican government officials. In 1926, Arturo M. Elías, consul general of Mexico, wrote a letter "to the American people" denouncing Kelley and his stand on Protestants in Mexico. Bishop Kelley "charges that Protestant missions have made no friends for the United States in Mexico but have raised up resentment against this country," Elias wrote. "The 'resentment' that has been raised up has been by the efforts of the Catholic Hierarchy who resent the presence of any clergyman in Mexico but those of their own faith." Emphasizing the damage he believed Kelley was doing to Mexico's reputation in the United States, Elías continued, "the real sentiments of the Church Hierarchy should be known to those who are being appealed to for help in the fight the Hierarchy is making against the Mexican Government for the special privileges that it has enjoyed for so many centuries which it has so sadly abused."[107] Kelley engaged in wars of words with a number of Mexican officials in U.S. publications throughout the Revolution. He saw himself as morally and racially superior to his Mexican combatants in these exchanges, embodying the mantle of American empire.

Kelley's view of the U.S. government changed over the course of Mexico's history, perhaps because eventually he was in a position to influence the government, especially in its interaction with Mexico. He astutely recognized Mexico as the "upturned diplomatic tack in the American Presidential chair." Kelley asked President Taft, as he prepared to leave office in 1912, what his intentions were toward Mexico. Reportedly, Taft was pleased to pass that challenge on to his successor. Although rumors persisted that Taft had suggested to Mexican dictator Porfirio Díaz that his reign must end, neither Taft nor Díaz ever confirmed this conversation. In Kelley's words, "Taft never mentioned it and Díaz possessed the Indian gift of stolid silence."[108] Kelley reveled in his access to the men behind the curtain, suggesting that he had full membership in the American empire, even as a Catholic priest.

Kelley and the Extension Society were very active with the exiled priests in the United States. Kelley saw himself and the United States as saviors for priests from this troubled land. His goal, like that of earlier missionaries, was "to round up . . . the world between the center of Christianity and its lost periphery in order to bring it back into the confines of the flock guarded by the Divine Shepherd."[109] In this case, the center of Christianity was the United States; Mexico was the Catholic borderlands' lost periphery.

Kelley characterized the Mexican bishops as clownlike and childlike: "Few had saved more than the clothes they wore—and what clothes! My first job was to go to a wholesale clothing house and arrange for something more decent."[110] The bishops were in exile, thousands of miles from their war-ravaged homes. Perhaps this was a reflection on the difference in national and class status, though Kelley seems oblivious to that. He also portrayed the bishops as infantile, much as indigenous people were described by invading Europeans. Referring to Archbishop Francisco Orozco y Jiménez of Guadalajara, Kelley wrote, "His best friends were some children who lived across the street. . . . When I heard a noise downstairs I knew it was the 'Byrnes kids' after the Archbishop."[111] Years later, Kelley wrote of Orozco y Jiménez, "He never seemed to mind fingers that were sticky, perhaps because he himself had supplied the candy that made them so."[112] Orozco y Jiménez spent months with Kelley, but he is hardly recognized in Kelley's extensive writings for his leadership among the Mexican bishops or his efforts to support his countrymen in Chicago. Orozco y Jiménez's compassion for his flock in Guadalajara drove his risky travel to Mexico during times of intense border inspections for Catholics. Even in Kelley's "strain on memories" he recalled the archbishop as more of a caricature than a dignified prelate, even though Orozco y Jiménez significantly outranked him.

Kelley thrived on his role as savior to Mexican Catholics—in Mexico. By virtue of the fact that he was an American prelate, with economic power and political access, he was able to intervene on behalf of Mexican Catholicism in both the United States and Mexico. Kelley brought together two highly racialized national dramas: the anti-immigrant, nativist, and eugenicist U.S. rhetoric of the early twentieth century and the *mestizaje* of post-conquest Mexico. Like many historians and anthropologists of the time, Kelley relegated Mexicans to history. Rather than addressing the powerful pro-mestizo nationalist ideology that was rising in Mexico, he focused on the past heroics of Spain's civilizing mission in the New World. Kelley used time to create distance between himself and the subject of his study. In the words of Johannes Fabian, *"geopolitics* has its ideological foundations in *chronopolitics."* Citing the role of anthropologists in colonialist-imperialist expansion and the rise of global capitalism, Fabian describes a one-way history in which "progress, development and modernity" meet "stagnation, underdevelopment and tradition."[113] Kelley used such time travel to distance himself from both Mexican and American contemporaries who shared some of his ideals and goals. He remained more wedded to the Spanish Catholic past than the Mexican Catholic present or future. Kelley was able to merge these histories into one that promoted U.S. Catholics as an active part of the American empire seeking to sustain Catholic histories and identities wherever they encountered them, in response to the U.S. secular and Protestant efforts to the contrary.

# Conclusion

## *Religion in the Borderlands*

---

In the early twentieth century, Catholics were slowly establishing themselves in the social and political fabric of the United States. For generations they had been represented as impoverished, superstitious, and hopelessly primitive. By the 1920s they were representing themselves in numerous Catholic publications and increasingly in the mainstream press and broader civic debates. Francis Kelley did not shy away from these national debates; in fact, he sought out these opportunities to create, and represent, a consummate American Catholic ethos. Kelley saw Catholics as transcending political boundaries; he imagined Catholics as cosmic citizens, not limited to a role in the United States. As the United States expanded its reach in the Western Hemisphere, so too should the Catholic Church—under Kelley's supervision—extend its scope and reach. The expansion of American empire provided American Catholics an opportunity to access more territory; American Catholics, led in part by Kelley and the Extension Society, used that opportunity to counter American protestantization projects. They did this by supporting evangelization, building schools and churches, staffing and supplying missions, and rewriting American history to recognize and embrace the Spanish Catholic presence in U.S. territories and Mexico.

By adopting an imperialist stance, Kelley made Catholics supremely American. Through him Catholics were no longer peripheral to the nation: they were part of the imperial legacy in the New World. Kelley invoked Spain's conquest of Mexico: Spain tamed Mexico—freed it from the devil—in 1521. Now, the United States must do the same—rescue Mexico from the devil as revolution, with Kelley as the spiritual guide.

Kelley embodied an array of contradictions. He was, among other things, a Canadian priest with an American sense of entitlement, an American defender of Mexico's Catholic Church, a Chicago priest representing the Mexican Catholic hierarchy, and a worshipper of the Spanish Catholic past in revolutionary Mexico. There were more powerful men in the Catholic hierarchy in the United States, but few had a stronger voice than Kelley did as president of the Extension Society from 1905 to 1924. His framing of Mexico remained forceful through the International Eucharistic Congress in 1926, but after that his light dimmed. His legacy, however, was already established: American Catholics believed in their mission in the Catholic borderlands, both at home and beyond the continental United States.

In the years following his elevation to bishop of Oklahoma City and Tulsa, Kelley worked to build the far-flung reaches of his diocese, a massive missionary field. He felt the strain of isolation from his friends and colleagues in the East and the day-to-day goings-on of the Extension Society and the Archdiocese of Chicago. He may have outgrown his post at the Extension Society, but not the lifestyle it allowed him: editorial control of *Extension Magazine* and access, as the society's president, to the editorial pages of Catholic publications across the country. The Archdiocese of Chicago was a destination for Catholic leadership from across the country and around the world. In Oklahoma City, Kelley felt he had been sentenced to a life of silence and irrelevance. The glory days of the International Eucharistic Congress and his tête-à-têtes with Mexican, U.S., and other business and political leaders were behind him, for the most part.

In 1935, with the explosion anew of religious repression in Mexico, the Mexican hierarchy sought to revive an interdiocesan seminary in exile. They once again turned to the U.S. hierarchy for assistance, and in November of that year the U.S. bishops responded, establishing a committee to explore the feasibility of the project. Archbishop Michael Curley of Baltimore, Archbishop Arthur Drossaerts of San

Antonio, and Kelley were assigned the task of reporting back to the U.S. hierarchy the costs, challenges, and possibilities of reviving a Mexican seminary in the United States. Kelley took this assignment as a mandate and began raising money for the seminary immediately. With the permission of Curley and Drossaerts, he asked for and received the approval of Pope Pius XI, and two thousand dollars from the Vatican for the seminary. Kelley established a commission to collect the funds and hired a prominent Philadelphia layman to lead the charge. He convinced a former governor of New York to provide rent-free space in the Empire State Building for the commission, and set up a lay advisory committee. When the hierarchy and the apostolic delegate discovered Kelley's unauthorized activities, he was told to disband the commission and close the New York office. He was also forbidden to mention the pope's approval and contribution.

Despite this inauspicious start, the Committee of Bishops on the Mexican Seminary was organized and met with the Mexican hierarchy in early 1936. Recalling his frustrations with San Felipe de Neri Seminary, Kelley pushed for a ten- to fifteen-year commitment to the project. This was agreed to, as was the curriculum of philosophy and theology. The goal was to house four hundred to five hundred students at any one time. The facility would be owned by the U.S. hierarchy but managed by the Mexican hierarchy. Mexican dioceses would pay one-half to two-thirds of the tuition, with the U.S. hierarchy providing the rest. The plan was approved by the U.S. bishops, and in September 1936, "Mexican Seminary Sunday" attracted contributions of nearly $385,000—40 percent more than the largest national collections at the time, which were for Catholic University of America and the American Board of Catholic Missions, which oversaw the work of the Extension Society.[1] U.S. Catholics understood that Catholicism was under fire again in the borderlands, and it was up to them to protect it. Kelley's campaigns decades earlier had trained a generation of American Catholics to understand the significance of Catholicism in Mexico and to embrace, again, their responsibility to sustain the faith there.

In May 1937 the U.S. hierarchy purchased eight hundred acres in the foothills of the Sangre de Cristo Mountains near Las Vegas, New Mexico. The Mexican hierarchy desired a location near the border to ease transportation, and perhaps to minimize cultural adjustment issues for the seminarians as well. Four months later, the National Pontifical Seminary of Our Lady of Guadalupe, more commonly known as Montezuma Seminary, welcomed its first class.[2] The repairs and upgrades necessary to maintain the seminary quickly devoured the funds raised during Mexican Seminary Sunday. In the late 1930s, Kelley, treasurer of the Committee of Bishops on the Mexican Seminary, hired Joseph Quinn to photograph Montezuma extensively and write an accompanying narrative for a glossy, over-sized magazine aimed at soliciting funds. Kelley named the publication *Montezuma: The American Douai*, drawing on the history of sixteenth-century English Catholics who trained for the priesthood in exile in France. Although Quinn is credited as author, the writing shows Kelley's influence. Quinn wrote, "Just as the Gallinas river that runs by Montezuma is fed by crystal springs up in the snow-tipped Sangre de Christo [*sic*] hills and sweeps southward toward the open sea, so these Vocations are nurtured from pure fonts in the mountains of New Mexico and, flowing with divine grace, one day will turn southward, drawn longingly toward the land of blood-drenched altars."[3] A decade earlier, Mexican Catholics had expressed a fear of Mexican children being educated in U.S.-run Protestant schools in Mexico. Now they were sending their own young men to the American-run seminary in the U.S. Southwest, strengthening the linkages within the Catholic borderlands.

Still, as in most Pan-American projects of the day, it was an opportunity for the United States to express its superiority over Latin America by lending a helping hand but refusing to see how the United States could benefit from what Latin America, in this case, Mexico, had to offer. A wider Pan-American approach would have "upset the most cherished national narratives of the United States."[4] In March 1943, Solomon Rahaim, a Jesuit professor of cosmology, psychology, economics, and ethics at Montezuma, proposed a plan for Montezuma men to serve Mexican immigrants in the United States. They should be carefully selected, Rahaim warned, since "otherwise there is the danger that the remedy will be worse than the evil itself."[5] He advised that if the U.S. hierarchy was interested, Montezuma was producing men for the job. Many seminarians were already doing work among the "Spanish Americans" in New Mexico, and though some were asked by local communities to stay on, they all returned to Mexico. The U.S. hierarchy failed to recognize the value of Montezuma's graduates for use in the United States.

It is not clear if Kelley saw Rahaim's report, but a month later, Kelley wrote to Bishop Joseph Schlarman of Peoria, another member of the Committee of Bishops on the Mexican Seminary. Kelley's concern was framed differently, but it also raised the question of contact between Montezuma men and U.S. Catholics. "My visit [to the seminary] seems like a trip to Mexico," he wrote. "I am disappointed that the students are not getting much knowledge of this country, its language and what culture we have. . . . Mexico needs a body of well-educated priests understanding the Church in America and speaking English." Kelley wanted to train the future leaders of the Mexican Church to have a greater appreciation of the empire. Kelley continued, "your idea of getting the senior students around teaching catechism is excellent." Schlarman and Kelley also imagined deeper connections between the Mexican seminarians and U.S. Catholics.

Kelley's concern was not just for the Pan-American cultural exchange between Mexican priests and U.S. Catholics but also for the survival of Montezuma. He wanted the seminary to have a good reputation in Mexico, but he did not see that happening if its graduates were not spreading "the good word" about American empire as well as the gospel. He also suggested the possibility of having U.S. dioceses in the Southwest send Anglo-American students to Montezuma to prepare them for interacting with Mexican-origin parishioners in the United States. "Texas is full of proselytizers," Kelley explained to Schlarman, "and they are accomplishing more than we give them credit for. The reason is simple. The bishops have to either send them Mexican pastors who are certainly no brilliant lights, or Americans who speak little or no Spanish." American-trained Mexican priests could perhaps offer the best of both worlds: American empire could polish these crusty gems from Mexico and make them presentable. As it was three decades earlier, Kelley had to not only save the Mexican Church from a hostile government but also to save the individual clerics, who had the faith but were still mere caricatures shaped in part by the Black Legend, which Kelley so strongly resisted.

Kelley had doubts about Mexican clerics, but he also saw that U.S. priests were not equipped for working with Mexicans and Mexican Americans in the United States. "Montezuma might be a great help in training American students to tackle the proselytizing situation intelligently," he wrote Schlarman.[6] While Kelley's view of Mexicans was still condescending, he was at last seeking ways to embrace those Mexicans who were in the United States. No longer just looking for a way to save Catholicism in Mexico, he realized that he must address the role of saving Mexicans in the United States.

Apparently, Rahaim's and Kelley's suggestions went unheard. More than a decade later, after Kelley's death, Montezuma rector Father Pablo López de Lara suggested an even more collaborative use for the seminary. The minutes of a March 1955 meeting record that "Montezuma Seminary would be pleased to give a Spanish course during the summer for the benefit of American seminarians who as future priests will have to work with Spanish speaking people."[7] López de Lara's plan included a buddy system whereby a Mexican priest would take a U.S. priest under his wing and assist him with reading and speaking in Spanish. A series of lectures in Spanish could be offered on religious art, Mexican folklore, and teaching catechism to Mexicans. His one note of caution was to send only those who "have a sincere desire to know and understand the Mexican people and to seek their spiritual welfare." As he reported, "prejudices against Mexicans would be a handicap."[8] As rector, López de Lara saw ways the seminary could move beyond its original mission to be of service to the U.S. as well as the Mexican hierarchy, and most importantly, serve Mexican immigrants in need in the United States.

There is no evidence that this plan was ever carried out, either. It seems that Rahaim, Kelley, and López de Lara, despite problematic attitudes toward Mexicans, were all on the verge of a significant realization. Kelley did come to understand that whether or not the religion question and other issues were settled in Mexico, Mexican immigrants were a significant presence in the United States and needed to be reached. Rahaim and López de Lara made this same realization based on their time at Montezuma. The Mexican presence in the United States, regardless of the religious question in Mexico, was not going to disappear, and the Catholic Church needed to find ways to address that population. One obvious way to do that involved Montezuma Seminary, whether that meant training U.S. priests to work with Mexicans or asking for the services of Mexican priests trained at Montezuma to do this work. It appears that all of these appeals were ignored, and Montezuma continued to work solely with Mexicans and to train them for work in their native land. Catholic leadership in the United States was committed to helping Mexican Catholics but not to working with them to strengthen their training or to train U.S. priests to work with Mexicans. The U.S. hierarchy was willing to bail out the Mexican hierarchy—to extend religious Monroeism to them—but did not envision a Catholic borderlands in which Mexicans could be of use to Americans.

Montezuma existed into the 1970s, but it was unable to move beyond being a seminary in exile. It never had the cross-cultural, Pan-American existence that Kelley, Rahaim, and López de Lara had imagined. While Kelley never called his work Pan-American, he was clearly riding the Pan-American wave that existed in the United States at the time. He sought to protect and guide Mexican Catholics during their time of trouble. Due to its proximity and the unrest of the Revolution, Mexico was the most obvious target for those who sought to demonstrate hemispheric power and presence. Because the U.S. hierarchy would not give Mexicans equal footing with U.S. Catholics, Montezuma was not able to change with the times. It was successful in its own right and trained hundreds of

Mexican priests, but it was not able to bridge the gap between the United States and Mexico to serve those Mexicans who left the land of blood-drenched altars and settled in the United States. Empire had its limits: it looked outward, not inward. Kelley had imagined the U.S. Catholic Church shepherding Catholics not only in the United States but around the world. Mexicans entered Kelley's purview as subjects in need of guidance. In his decades of working with Mexican Catholics, as editor, diplomat, and even writer, Kelley did not see ways they could contribute to creating their own solutions. However, in his final years he imagined how Mexican Catholics might help U.S. Catholics with the challenges they faced in the American empire in the mid-twentieth century.

More than a century after Kelley, the penniless priest, conducted his cross-country begging circuit, the Catholic Church Extension Society still thrives on the contributions of American Catholics across the country, supporting their less fortunate brethren in the still-ragged fissures of the national landscape: rural areas and those dominated by communities of color throughout the country. The demographics of Catholic borderlands have shifted significantly; the future of the U.S. Catholic Church is, indeed, Latino. One might argue after the elevation of Cardinal Jorge Mario Bergoglio of Argentina to pope in 2013, the future of the Roman Catholic Church is Latin American.

Catholic borderlands was not a redemptive space; this was not a space of retreat or protection for Mexicans, Mexican Americans, mestizos, or others. Rather, it was a space where multiple imperial projects—Spanish, U.S., and a twentieth-century U.S. Catholic empire—redefined the geopolitical landscape of U.S. territorial, social, cultural, and political reach.

# Notes

## Abbreviations

ACARC: Archdiocese of Chicago Joseph Cardinal Bernardin Archives and Records Center, Chicago, Illinois

CUA: Catholic University of America, Archives and Manuscript Collections, Washington DC

INAH: Instituto Nacional de Antropología e Historia, Mexico City

LUC: Loyola University of Chicago, Archives and Special Collections, Chicago, Illinois

SRE: Secretaria de Relaciones Exteriores, Archivo Histórico Genaro Estrada, Mexico City

## Introduction

1. Kelley, *The Story of Extension*, 190–91. I use the term "American empire" to refer to the continental expansion of the United States, the acquisition of additional territories through the Spanish-American War, and the growth of the United States as an economic and political powerhouse in the first decades of the twentieth century, as evidenced by U.S. interventions in Mexican affairs during and after the Mexican Revolution.

2. Bender, *Rethinking American History*, vii.

3. Bolton, *Wider Horizons of American History*, 3. Also see Bannon, *Bolton and the Spanish Borderlands*; and Magnaghi, *Herbert E. Bolton*. On cultural contact and conflict, see White, *The Middle Ground*; and Mary Louise Pratt, "Arts of the Contact Zone," *Profession* 91 (1991): 33–40. On religion in the American West see Guarneri and Alvarez, *Religion and Society in the American West*, especially articles by Eldon G. Ernst, "American Religious History from a Pacific Coast Perspective" (3–39), and Jeffrey M. Burns, "The Mexican American Catholic Community in California, 1850–1980" (255–73); and D. Michael Quinn, "Religion in the American West," in Cronon, Miles, and Gitlin, *Under an Open Sky*, 145–66.

4. David J. Weber advocates a U.S. history that expands beyond the nation in his foreword to Truett and Young, *Continental Crossroads*, ix. Charles Bright and Michael Geyer advocate a turn to neglected aspects of U.S. history in their chapter, "Where in the World Is America? The History of the United States in the Global Age," in Bender, *Rethinking American History*, 64. See also Truett and Young, *Continental Crossroads*; Schmidt-Nowara and Nieto-Phillips, *Interpreting Spanish Colonialism*; Cañizares Esguerra, *Puritan Conquistadors*; Cañizares Esguerra, *How to Write the History of the New World*; and E. H. Gould, "Entangled Histories, Entangled Worlds."

5. Cañizares Esguerra, *Puritan Conquistadors*, 219.

6. Paredes, *A Texas-Mexican Cancionero*, xiv. Paredes executes this in *With His Pistol in His Hand*. He transcended the border between the United States and Mexico in his studies of the *corridos* and folklore of south Texas, as well as his creative writing. He laid the groundwork for Mexican American and Chicana/o studies scholars for generations to come.

7. Lugo, "Theorizing Border Inspections," 355. See also Lugo, *Fragmented Lives, Assembled Parts*; and Anzaldúa, *Borderlands/La Frontera*. Also see Michaelson and Johnson, *Border Theory*; Rushdie, *Step across This Line*; J. D. Saldívar, "Américo Paredes and Decolonization"; J. D. Saldívar, *Border Matters*; J. D. Saldívar, *The Dialectics of Our America*; R. Saldívar, *The Borderlands of Culture*, especially chapter 6, for a keen analysis of Paredes's river poems; Truett and Young, *Continental Crossroads*; Vila, *Crossing Borders*.

8. See, for example, Ruiz, *From Out of the Shadows*, especially chapter 2.

9. Matthew A. Redinger notes that "Kelley's work accomplished far more for Mexican Catholics than did the best efforts of a more powerful and respected prelate, Archbishop [William H.] O'Connell of Boston." Redinger, *American Catholics*, 55. Paredes also crossed disciplinary boundaries. His 1958 study, *With His Pistol in His Hand*, "contested the nationalist and chauvinistic new interdisciplinary project of American Studies." Paredes resisted the consensus-based discipline of American studies to show that there were multiple American cultures, many formed in response to dominant cultural forms. In the half century since *Pistol*, American studies has been transformed from a strictly patriotic endeavor to a more hybrid and critical discourse that considers social struggle not only within the United States but between the United States and other nations and peoples. J. D. Saldívar, "Américo Paredes and Decolonization," 295. See also Noble, *Death of a Nation*, especially chapter 7.

10. See Amy Kaplan, "'Left Alone with America': The Absence of Empire in the Study of American Culture," in Kaplan and Pease, *Cultures of United States Imperialism*, 15; E. H. Gould, "Entangled Histories, Entangled Worlds," 784; J. D. Saldívar, "Américo Paredes and Decolonization"; and J. D. Saldívar, *Bor-*

*der Matters*. See also Streeby, *American Sensations*; and R. Saldívar, *The Border-lands of Culture*.

11. Kagan, "Prescott's Paradigm." On Prescott, see Costeloe, "Prescott's *History of the Conquest*." See also Franchot, *Roads to Rome*, especially chapter 3; and Rivera, *A Violent Evangelism*. Dipesh Chakrabarty shows that narratives of "modernity" are linked to European imperialisms and the centering of northern Europe as preeminently "modern." Chakrabarty, "Postcoloniality and the Artifice of History"; Chakrabarty, *Provincializing Europe*; and Rafael, *Contracting Colonialism*.

12. Bolton, "Mission as a Frontier Institution."

13. Johannes Fabian argues that time is used to create a one-way history in which progress, development and modernity are the flipside of stagnation, underdevelopment, and tradition. Fabian, *Time and the Other*, 144. Also see Wallis, "Chronopolitics."

14. Pike, *Hispanismo*.

15. Bokovoy, *The San Diego World's Fairs*, 225. Kagan documents the reproductions of the Giralda, originally part of a mosque in Seville and later a tower attached to a Gothic cathedral, across the United States. Kagan, "The Spanish Craze in the United States." See Rosaldo, "Imperialist Nostalgia," for a look at the mourning for the pasts destroyed by imperial activity. In his earlier work, Bolton focused on the lingering colonial structures and habits of the Spanish past. He was committed to documenting and understanding the Spanish presence in the United States. The language, culture, and laws of Spain and Mexico persisted in parts of the U.S. Southwest, shaping "American" culture, at least locally. See especially Bolton, "Mission as a Frontier Institution"; and Bolton, *The Spanish Borderlands*. See also Kropp, *California Vieja*; Deverell, *Whitewashed Adobe*; and on New Mexico, C. Wilson, *The Myth of Santa Fe*. Activist and historian Carey McWilliams also pursues the "fantasy" Spanish heritage of southern Californians in his seminal book, *North from Mexico*.

16. Bokovoy notes the late-twentieth-century response of Californians to the impending sainthood of Junípero Serra by Pope John Paul II, which produced a revival of the Black Legend. Bokovoy, *The San Diego World's Fairs*, 222.

17. Truett and Young note that, historiographically, the mid-nineteenth century represents a "spatial and narrative rupture." However, for those who lived along the shifting border "it marked the beginning of years of negotiation between colonial, national, regional, and global coordinates that were—despite the U.S. annexation of land and people—anything but fixed." Truett and Young, *Continental Crossroads*, 6.

18. In January 1899, Pope Leo XIII issued an apostolic letter to Cardinal James Gibbons, leader of the U.S. hierarchy. *Testem Benevolentiae Nostrae* cautioned that "Americanism," the presumed "modern" form of Catholicism feared

to be developing in the United States, was a danger to the faith and its followers. Catholic leadership and writers furthered this narrative in their writing in this era, avoiding the language of acculturation and remaining faithful Catholics, as outlined by Gibbons. For more on Americanism, see McGreevy, *Catholicism and American Freedom*; O'Toole, *The Faithful*; and F. Michael Perko, *Catholic and American: A Popular History* (Huntington IN: Our Sunday Visitor Publishing, 1989). See Gibbons, *Faith of Our Fathers. Faith of Our Fathers* was originally published in 1876 and was also published in the United Kingdom. Also see *The Columbiad*, the official publication of the Knights of Columbus, and the Jesuit publication, *America*. For more on Gibbons, see Boucher and Tehan, *Prince of Democracy*. On space and place in American religion, see Tweed, *Crossing and Dwelling*; and Tweed, *Our Lady of the Exile*. On triumphalist Americanism, see Tweed, *America's Church*. The Knights of Columbus, a Catholic fraternal organization, also drew on the historical Catholicity of the hemisphere. See Kauffman, *Faith and Fraternalism*; and Kauffman, *Patriotism and Fraternalism*. On the conquest of the West, see Limerick, *Legacy of Conquest*.

19. Fairbank, "Assignment for the '70s," 877.

20. LaFeber, *The New Empire*, 72.

21. Strong, *Our Country*, 46–59. Strong also labeled immigrants a peril; from the mid-nineteenth century to 1920 the Catholic Church is framed as the immigrant church in the historiography, making this an even greater peril. Szasz notes that Catholics were the largest denomination in many western states. Szasz, *Religion in the Modern American West*, 4–5.

22. On Catholic missionaries, see Dries, *The Missionary Movement*. The Extension Society funded Catholic missionaries from all over the world who were assigned to U.S. territories. For example, in this era, many of the priests in the New Mexico Territory were from France.

23. On the immigrant church, see Dolan, *The Immigrant Church*; Dolan, *The American Catholic Experience*; Fisher, *Communion of Immigrants*; and O'Toole, *The Faithful*. On specific immigrant groups, see Díaz-Stevens, *Oxcart Catholicism on Fifth Avenue*; Dolan and Hinojosa, *Mexican Americans and the Catholic Church*; Matovina, *Guadalupe and Her Faithful*; Matovina, *Latino Catholicism*; Orsi, *The Madonna of 115th Street*; Orsi, *Thank You, St. Jude* (on European immigrant women); and Cummings, *New Women of the Old Faith*, on Irish American women. On rural Catholics see Yohn, *A Contest of Faiths*; and Marlett, *Saving the Heartland*. In the last couple of decades, a number of scholars have explored how race, religion, and migration have interacted in the United States. See McGreevy, *Parish Boundaries*; Hayashi, *"For the Sake of Our Japanese Brethren"*; Jacobson, *Special Sorrows*; Orsi, "The Religious Boundaries of an Inbetween People"; and Yazbeck Haddad, Smith, and Esposito, *Religion and Immigration*.

24. See, for example, Boucher and Tehan, *Prince of Democracy*; Patrick Carey, "Recent America Catholic Historiography: New Directions in Religious History," in Stout and Hart, *New Directions in American Religious History*, 445–61; Cummings, *New Women of the Old Faith*; Charles R. Morris, *American Catholic: The Saints and Sinners Who Built America's Most Powerful Church* (New York: Vintage, 1998); and Reher, *Catholic Intellectual Life in America*.

25. *Extension Magazine* was first issued in June 1906 as a quarterly publication. It became a monthly the following year. Circulation figures for selected monthlies in 1910 show the size of Kelley's audience compared to other sacred and secular publications: *American Messenger* (Evangelical), 45,000; *Baptist Home Mission Monthly*, 21,095; *National Geographic*, 49,900; *Atlantic Monthly*, 25,000; *Extension Magazine*, 78,444. *N. W. Ayer and Son's American Newspaper Annual and Directory*, 601–2, 111, 362, 158. Tweed shows that donating became a crucial form of religious participation for Catholics in the early twentieth century. Tweed, *America's Church*, 245. On the development of a Catholic middle class, see Moloney, *American Catholic Lay Groups*.

26. See, for example, J. A. Meyer, *La Cristiada*; J. A. Meyer, *The Cristero Rebellion*; J. A. Meyer, *Las naciones frente al conflict religioso en México*; Aguirre Cristiani, *¿Una Historia Compartida?*; Butler, *Popular Piety*; and Wright-Rios, *Revolutions in Mexican Catholicism*; among many others. From the U.S. perspective, see Redinger, *American Catholics*; and Slawson, "The National Catholic Welfare Conference."

27. On Latino evangelicals, see Felipe Hinojosa, *Latino Mennonites: Civil Rights, Faith, and Evangelical Culture* (Baltimore: Johns Hopkins University Press, 2014); L. Leon, *La Llorona's Children*; Sánchez-Walsh, *Latino Pentecostal Identity*. For a fine overview of Latino theologies, see Isasi-Díaz and Segovia, *Hispanic/Latino Theology*. On women's theologies of liberation, see Isasi-Díaz and Tarango, *Hispanic Women*; and Medina, *Las Hermanas*. On Mexican American theology, see Elizondo, *The Future Is Mestizo*; Elizondo, *Galilean Journey*; Elizondo, *Guadalupe*; and Matovina, *Beyond Borders*.

28. Peter D'Agostino's *Rome in America* broke significant ground by placing the story of American Catholics in a broader, transnational framework. This comprehensive study shows how U.S. Catholics embraced the myths and symbols of old-school Catholicism while painting themselves as progressive and therefore American. His transnational scope grounds American Catholicism in a broader framework, as I do, but D'Agostino centers the Vatican. On transnational religious communities, see Chesnut, *Devoted to Death*; Ana María Díaz-Stephens, *Oxcart Catholicism on Fifth Avenue: The Impact of the Puerto Rican Migration Upon the Archdiocese of New York* (Notre Dame: University of Notre Dame Press, 1993; Maloney, *American Catholic Lay Groups*; Tweed, *Retelling U.S. Religious History*; R. S. Warner and Wittner, *Gatherings in Diaspora*.

29. For a fine overview of Catholic historiography and the absence of Latinos in it, see Matovina, "Remapping American Catholicism." For a sweeping history of Latino Catholics, see Matovina and Poyo, *¡Presente!* Mario García has led the way in creating a space for Catholic history within Chicano history. His *Católicos* features case studies of Catholic communities and leaders around the Southwest from the 1930s to the 1970s. See also Espinosa and García, *Mexican American Religions*; Matovina and Riebe-Estrella, *Horizons of the Sacred*; and Szasz and Etulain, *Religion in Modern New Mexico*. There are a number of fine studies of Mexican American Catholics in particular locations. See, for example, Matovina, *Guadalupe and Her Faithful*; Nabhan-Warren, *The Virgin of El Barrio*; and Treviño, *The Church in the Barrio*. On specific Latino Catholic organizations, see Carroll, *The Penitente Brotherhood*; Richard Edward Martínez, *Padres: The National Chicano Priest Movement* (Austin: University of Texas Press, 2005); and Medina, *Las Hermanas*. For specific devotions, see Carroll, *The Penitente Brotherhood*; Chesnut, *Devoted to Death*; and J. Rodríguez, *Our Lady of Guadalupe*.

30. On Mexican liberalism, see Charles A. Hale, *The Transformation of Liberalism in Late Nineteenth-Century Mexico* (Princeton: Princeton University Press, 1989). Also see Pablo Piccato, *The Tyranny of Opinion: Honor in the Contruction of the Mexican Public-Sphere* (Durham: Duke University Press, 2010); Schoonover, *Dollars over Dominion*; and Kathryn Sloan, *Runaway Daughters: Seduction, Elopement, and honor in Nineteenth-Century Mexico* (Albuquerque: University of New Mexico Press, 2008).

31. Lowe and Lloyd, *The Politics of Culture*, 5.

32. See, for example, Steven B. Bunker, *Creating Mexican Consumer Culture in the Age of Porfirio Díaz* (Albuquerque: University of New Mexico Press, 2012); Emilio Kourí, *A Pueblo Divided: Business, Property, and Community in Papantla, Mexico* (Stanford: Stanford University Press, 2004); Tenorio-Trillo, *Mexico at the World's Fairs*; and Elliott Young, "Imagining Alternative Modernities: Ignacio Martínez's Travel Narratives," in Truett and Young, *Continental Crossroads*, 151–79.

33. To encapsulate the Mexican Revolution in a few pages is impossible. As Thomas Benjamin titled his chapter on 1911–13 Mexico, "every event's name is itself an interpretation," a phrase he borrows from Joseph Brodsky. Benjamin, *La Revolución*. There are countless books on the Mexican Revolution, many of which contradict each other on major turning points, important leaders, regional conflicts, and so on. I am not attempting to get involved in those debates, but with the Revolution as the backdrop for this project, a basic outline of the conflicts and characters is necessary. I emphasize the significant ideas introduced into the revolutionary discourse, the involvement of the United States, and religion-related events and people. For a brief history of the Revolution, see M. C. Meyer,

Sherman, and Deeds, *The Course of Mexican History*, chapters 30–39. For a more thorough, class-based analysis of the Revolution, see Hart, *Revolutionary Mexico*. Benjamin's *La Revolución* provides an analysis of the collective memory that was created by *los voceros de la Revolución*—the journalists, intellectuals, and politicians. For a people's history of the Porfiriato, see Frank, *Posada's Broadsheets*. There are several notable biographies of Mexican revolutionary leaders. See Katz, *Life and Times of Pancho Villa*; Hall, *Álvaro Obregón*; and Womack, *Zapata and the Mexican Revolution*. On the anarchists at work prior to 1910, see Albro, *Always a Rebel*; and Albro, *To Die on Your Feet*. On religion see Aguirre Cristiani, *¿Una Historial Compartida?*; Baldwin, *Protestants and the Mexican Revolution*; and Quirk, *The Mexican Revolution*. On U.S. involvement see Hart, *Empire and Revolution*.

34. Religious violence in Mexico resumed in the 1930s, but the United States was never involved in the same way after the Great Depression. Kelley (then bishop of Oklahoma) and the Extension Service again worked together, this time with the backing of the U.S. Catholic bishops, to train Mexican priests at Montezuma Seminary in New Mexico, as I discuss in the conclusion to this book. See Martínez, "'From the Halls of Montezuma.'"

35. See Akira Iriye, "Internationalizing International History," in Bender, *Rethinking American History*, 47–62. Brenda Gayle Plummer's work also challenges the traditional frameworks of diplomatic history. See Plummer, *Rising Wind*.

36. On religion in U.S. foreign relations, see Andrew Preston, "Bridging the Gap between the Sacred and the Secular in the History of American Foreign Relations," *Diplomatic History* 30, no. 5 (November 2006): 783–812. Leo Ribuffo has written extensively on religion in U.S. foreign relations. See, for example, "Religion and American Foreign Policy: The Story of a Complex Relationship," *The National Interest* 52 (Summer 1998): 36–51.

37. Brack, *Mexico Views Manifest Destiny*, 170. The title of Brack's book is misleading. Although Brack examines Mexican public opinion on the United States, his language, attitudes, and conclusions are still very reflective of his U.S. perspective. See also Frahm, "The Cross and the Compass"; Malone, *Historians and the American West*; Fuller, *The Movement for the Acquisition of All Mexico*; and Weinberg, *Manifest Destiny*. Decades after the war with Mexico, Ulysses S. Grant characterized it as "a wicked war." See Greenberg, *A Wicked War*. On popular literature during the Mexican-American War, see Streeby, *American Sensations*. On Catholicism in this era, see Franchot, *Roads to Rome*. On the tensions between annexation and immigration, see Jacobson, *Barbarian Virtues*; and Noble, *Death of the Nation*.

38. Cited in McEniry, "American Catholics," 4–6. This chilling description is eerily similar to the anti-Catholic "outrages" that occurred in Mexico seventy years later.

39. Attacks against "Papists" continued well into the twentieth century. Throughout this era there were also concerns that the government was falling under the spell of the pope. See especially Fulton, *Washington in the Lap of Rome*. Fulton provides some wonderful illustrations, the most striking of which shows a serpent with the head of the pope circling and topping the Capitol. The snake metaphor was an enduring one. In Kensington forty years earlier, anti-Catholics had used a dead serpent to represent "the power of the Roman Church, now extinct." See also Higham, *Strangers in the Land*; and McEniry, "American Catholics," 5. See also Pinheiro, "'Extending the Light.'" The Batallón de San Patricio was a unit of the Mexican army largely made up of deserters from the U.S. Army—mostly Catholic, many Irish—who defected and fought on the Mexican side in five major battles. On the San Patricios, see McEniry, "American Catholics"; and R. R. Miller, *Shamrock and Sword*. For the role of Catholics in the war, see McEniry, "American Catholics," which focuses special attention on the Catholic press at the time, which, unlike many other media, was hesitant to condemn the war for any reason.

40. Brack, *Mexico Views Manifest Destiny*, 2, 170.

41. On the acquisition of brown bodies after the Mexican-American War, see Laura E. Gómez, *Manifest Destinies: The Making of the Mexican American Race* (New York: New York University Press, 2007); Guadalupe T. Luna, "Gold, Souls, and Wandering Clerics: California Missions, Native Californians, and LatCrit Theory," *U.C. Davis Law Review* 33, no. 4 (2000): 921–54; Guadalupe T. Luna, "On the Complexities of Race: The Treaty of Guadalupe Hidalgo and *Dred Scott v. Sanford*," *University of Miami Law Review* 53, no. 4 (July 1999): 691–716; and the extensive LatCrit literature on the Treaty of Guadalupe Hidalgo.

42. Walt Whitman, "The Foreign Press on the American President," *Brooklyn Daily Eagle*, February 8, 1947, reprinted in Cleveland Rodgers and John Black, eds., *The Gathering of the Forces: Editorials, Essays, Literary and Dramatic Reviews and Other Material Written by Walk Whitman as Editor of the Brooklyn Daily Eagle, in 1846 and 1847* (New York: Putnam, 1920), 33. On popular literature see Streeby, *American Sensations*; and Gretchen Murphy, *Hemispheric Imaginings: The Monroe Doctrine and Narratives of U.S. Empire* (Durham: Duke University Press, 2005). See also Robert W. Johannsen, *To the Halls of Montezuma: The Mexican War in the American Imagination* (New York: Oxford University Press, 1985); Merk, *Manifest Destiny and Mission*; and David M. Pletcher, *The Diplomacy of Annexation: Texas, Oregon and the Mexican War* (Columbia: University of Missouri Press, 1973).

43. Streeby, *American Sensations*, 11.

44. Kramer, "Empires, Exceptions, and Anglo-Saxons," 1332. Also see Kramer, *The Blood of Government*; Jacobson, *Barbarian Virtues*; Streeby, *American Sensations*; W. Anderson, *Colonial Pathologies*; McCoy, *Policing America's Empire*; Raul

Pertierra, *Religion, Politics, and Rationality in a Philippine Community* Honolulu: University of Hawaii Press, 1988), and K. Wilson, *The Island Race*.

45. See W. Wilson, *A History of the American People*, volume 5.

46. Arthur Link is Wilson's most renowned biographer. His works on Wilson include *Woodrow Wilson: A Brief Biography*; *Wilson* (5 vols.); *The Higher Realism of Woodrow Wilson*; and *Woodrow Wilson and the Progressive Era*. On the religious basis of Wilsonian diplomacy, see Bell, *Righteous Conquest*; Benbow, *Leading Them to the Promised Land*; Link, "Woodrow Wilson"; and Magee, *What the World Should Be*. See also Brands, *What America Owes the World*; and Levin, *Woodrow Wilson and World Politics*.

47. Young, *Colonial Desire*, 19.

## 1. An American Catholic Borderlands

1. Richard Aumerle [Richard Aumerle Maher, O.S.A.], "Juanita," *Extension Magazine*, September 1907, 18. Aumerle wrote extensively on the efforts on Protestants in Cuba, in addition to fictional works.

2. Aumerle, "Juanita," 19.

3. I use the term "extension priest" to refer to priests who, regardless of order or diocesan affiliation, wrote pieces in *Extension Magazine* or received funds from the Extension Society to support their mission work.

4. Aumerle, "Juanita," 19.

5. Genevieve R. Cooney, "Ponwaka," *Extension Magazine*, May 1907, 11.

6. See Tweed, "Narrating U.S. Religious History," in Tweed, *Retelling U.S. Religious History*, 1–24.

7. See, for example, Yohn, *A Contest of Faiths*; and Marlett, *Saving the Heartland*. Marlett's study focuses on agrarian projects such as the Catholic Rural Life Conference in areas of the Midwest and South. On women's roles in the civilizing of the West, including their role in Protestant home mission work, see Pascoe, *Relations of Rescue*.

8. Catholic Church Extension Society, *Family Appointment Calendar*, 2002.

9. Peter J. Muldoon, "Immigration to and the Immigrants in the United States," in *Report of the Second American Catholic Missionary Congress* (Chicago: J. S. Hyland & Company), 133.

10. For more on U.S. Catholic missions see Dries, *The Missionary Movement*.

11. Most Reverend Francis C. Kelley, Chicago, to Benedict XV, Rome, October 18, 1918, Madaj Collection, ACARC, 1–2.

12. The 2002 Catholic Church Extension Society's *Family Appointment Calendar* testified to Kelley's legacy. The back of the calendar read, in part, "In America, some of the first ripples of 'this new evangelization' [referring to missionary work as described by Pope John Paul II] began nearly a hundred years ago, when a pen-

niless priest embarked on a cross-country begging circuit. . . . He found he wasn't the only pastor stationed at a church described as a 'dry goods box with a cross.'"

13. *Extension Magazine*'s first issue appeared in June 1906. *N. W. Ayer and Son's American Newspaper Annual and Directory*, 111, 158, 362. The Knights of Columbus member publication was the only Catholic publication that surpassed *Extension*'s circulation.

14. See, for example, Joseph T. Roche, "A Practical Solution to the Immigrant Problem," *Extension Magazine*, May 1907, on ethnic diversity and harmony in Torrington, Connecticut.

15. Kelley published fiction under the pseudonym Myles Murdoch, including one novel, *Charred Wood* (Chicago: Extension Press, 1918), and numerous short stories, including some in *Extension Magazine*.

16. Mary J. Lupton, "Lost in the Western Mountains," *Extension Magazine*, May 1907, 6. Lupton was also city editor of *New World*, the official organ of the Archdiocese of Chicago.

17. Lupton, "Lost in the Western Mountains," 6.

18. Limerick, *Legacy of Conquest*, 12. McGreevy demonstrates that the national parish system reinforced the racial and ethnic segregation so pervasive in many northern cities. McGreevy, *Parish Boundaries*.

19. Pitaval first used this phrase, which was repeated by others throughout the Congress. In some sources, his name is spelled John Baptist Pitival.

20. Lamentations 4:4: "the little ones have asked for bread, and there was none to break it unto them." *Holy Bible*, Catholic ed. (Cleveland: World Publishing, 1954), 782.

21. John Baptist Pitaval, untitled address in *Report of the Second American Missionary Congress*, 246, my emphasis.

22. McWilliams, *North from Mexico*, 20. Pitaval represented one of the few cities in the West that was still discernibly Catholic, but for the purposes of his presentation the "wild and wooly west" was a better representation of his archdiocese. On Santa Fe, see Sheehan, *Four Hundred Years of Faith*; and C. Wilson, *The Myth of Santa Fe*.

23. Deloria, *Indians in Unexpected Places*, 7. On earlier mission work among Indians in what is now the United States, see Shea, *History of the Catholic Missions*.

24. Robert Michaelsen rightly notes that religious histories have generally failed to acknowledge American Indian religions in the portrait of the American landscape. Religious conflict is framed as Catholic and Protestant battles for the souls of American Indians. Kelley also used this narrative throughout his coverage of Indians. Michaelsen, "Red Man's Religion/White Man's Religious History." See also Wenger, *We Have a Religion*.

25. Genevieve R. Cooney, "Ponwaka," *Extension Magazine*, May 1907, 11.

26. Martin Marty writes: "Out of sight, [Indians] seemed to be out of mind as coreligionists. Instead they remained a problem for missionaries who would convert and civilize them on reservations." Marty, *Modern American Religion*, 1:95. Kelley was not content to have Indians be out of sight. Several editions of *Extension Magazine* included photo layouts of American Indian and Eskimo converts. See, for example, a May 1908 spread on Crow Indians and a September 1914 piece on Eskimos.

27. Rev. F. Bormann, "Schools and the Children of the Missions," *Extension Magazine*, February 1916, 13.

28. Rev. Aloysius Vrebosh [Vrebosch], S.J., "A Missionary among the Indians," *Extension Magazine*, May 1908, 12. See also Raymond DeMallie and William Sturtevant, eds., *Handbook of American Indians*, vol. 13, *Plains* (Washington DC: Government Printing Office, 2001), 94. Vrebosch and other Jesuit missionaries subsequently wrote English-Crow dictionaries and Crow grammar books. The Edward E. Ayer Manuscript Collection at the Newberry Library includes correspondence of Vrebosch and Crimont. Vrebosch reported an enrollment of sixty students at the mission school in 1908, but by 1921 the school had closed for lack of enrollment. See St. Francis Xavier Mission Records, 1887–2006, Foley Center Library Special Collections, Gonzaga University. On Indian boarding schools, see Brenda Child, *Boarding School Seasons: American Indian Families, 1900–1940* (Lincoln: University of Nebraska Press, 2000).

29. Vrebosh, "A Missionary among the Indians," 12. There was some federal funding for religious schools in Indian territories. See Bennison, "Americanizing the West."

30. Laurence S. Highstone, "An American Oberramergau," *The Columbiad*, January 1905, 4–5. An Ojibwe reenactment of Longfellow's interpretation of Hiawatha's life raises many questions about performance and authenticity. Also see Alan Trachtenberg, *Shades of Hiawatha: Staging Indians, Making Americans, 1880–1930* (New York: Hill & Wang, 2004).

31. Deloria, *Indians in Unexpected Places*, 225.

32. J. R. Crimont, S.J., Prefect Apostolic of Alaska, "A Little Corner of the Alaskan Field," *Extension Magazine*, May 1909, 15. Joseph Raphael Crimont was born and educated in France. He was assigned as a missionary to the Crow Indians in 1890 and to Alaska in 1904 after a stint as president of Gonzaga University in Spokane. Despite the constant requests for funding and staff, the King Island mission was not established until 1929. Louis L. Renner, "The History of the Missionary Diocese of Fairbanks, Part I: Its Pre-History: 1847–1962," *Alaskan Shepherd* 50, no. 2 (March–April 2012): 7.

33. In October 2012, Pope Benedict XVI described Kateri Tekakwitha, a seventeenth-century Mohawk-Algonquin convert, as impressive "by the action of

grace in her life in spite of the absence of eternal help and by the courage of her vocation, so unusual in her culture. In her, faith and culture enrich each other!" Pope Benedict XVI, "*Capella Papale*, For the Canonization of the Blesseds," October 21, 2012. A century before Kateri's elevation to saint, and more than two centuries after her death, Catholic missionaries continued to draw on this framework of culture and faith as an important contrast to the work of "whites." Bennison argues that Catholic and Protestant missionaries on the Rosebud Reservation affirmed their American identities through this work. Bennison, "Americanizing the West."

34. Gisleen Haelterman, "Missionary Life in New Mexico," *Extension Magazine*, February 1909, 11.

35. Rev. Charles Van Hulse, "Ten Years of Missionary Work," *Extension Magazine*, April 1909, 9. Van Hulse mentions a church built in Tulsa, Oklahoma, with funds from Drexel, apparently for an American Indian parish. Drexel paid for schools in Montana as well. See Vrebosch, "A Missionary among the Indians," 12. See also Theophile Cuadron, "A Mission Field of Five Thousand Square Miles," *Extension Magazine*, February 1916, 7–8. Cuadron describes a church in Boley, Oklahoma, built for blacks with funds from Mother Katherine Drexel. Drexel founded the Sisters of the Blessed Sacrament for Indians and Colored People in 1891.

36. Rev. M. Van Eyck, "My Missions in the South," *Extension Magazine*, November 1909, 5.

37. Francis Kelley, "Negro Mission," *Extension Magazine*, October 1909, 15.

38. On black Catholics see Cyprian Davis, *The History of Black Catholics in the United States* (New York: Crossroad, 2004). On early Catholic missionaries in the South, see Michael Pasquier, "'Though Their Skin Remains Brown, I Hope Their Souls Will Soon Be White': Slavery, French Missionaries and the Roman Catholic Priesthood in the American South, 1789–1865," *Church History* 77, no. 2 (June 2008): 337–70.

39. Rev. H. A. Spengler, "A Romance of Rodney," *Extension Magazine*, March 1908, 11.

40. Rev. John J. Albert, S.S.J., "The Command to Teach All Nations," *Extension Magazine*, May 1917, 5.

41. Ralston J. Markoe, "Can We Save the Negroes of the South?" *Extension Magazine*, May 1909, 4. Markoe wrote *Impressions of a Layman*, a guide of sorts for priest about how their parishioners saw every aspect of Catholic life: finances, sermons, and even the Spanish Inquisition.

42. Spengler, "A Romance of Rodney," 21.

43. Spengler, "A Romance of Rodney," 5. See also McNally, *Catholicism in South Florida*.

44. Rev. G. J. Buissink, "A Missionary Priest in the Far South," *Extension Magazine*, June 1917, 6.

45. Van Eyck, "My Missions in the South," 5.

46. Rev. Lucian Johnston, "Bigotry in the South," *Extension Magazine*, April 1911, 19. For more anti-Catholicism see Edward Cuddy, "The Irish Question and the Revival of Anti-Catholicism in the 1920s," *Catholic Historical Review* 67, no. 2 (April 1981): 236–55.

47. Francis Clement Kelley, "How a Catholic Feels about It," *Extension Magazine*, February 1924, 5–6. On Protestants and the Klan see Baker, *Gospel According to the Klan*; R. M. Miller, "Protestant Churches and the Revived Klan"; Jacobs, "Co-Opting Christian Chorales"; and Neal, "Christianizing the Klan." Charles C. Alexander notes the Klan that was active in the Southwest but was less anti-Catholic there than in the East and Midwest. Alexander, *The Ku Klux Klan in the Southwest*, 25.

48. E. de Anta, OMI, "Missionary Work in the Diocese of Galveston," *Extension Magazine*, August 1913, 6. The Missionary Oblates of Mary Immaculate (OMI), a French order that arrived in San Antonio in the late nineteenth century, managed the chapel car "St. Peter" for the Extension Society.

49. Emmanuel Ledvina, "The Motor Chapel Car at Work in the Field," *Extension Magazine*, August 1913, 9. The Extension Society had three motor chapels that served the South and West and made occasional visits to the Midwest and Northeast, largely for fund-raising purposes. For more on motor and railroad chapels, see Taylor, *Gospel Tracks through Texas*. Taylor's emphasis is Protestant missionary work in Texas.

50. Francis C. Kelley, "An Appeal to All Good Extensionists," *Extension Magazine*, September 1913, 3, Application no. 46. Kelley provided sample appeals from a wide range of applications for Extension Society funds.

51. Francis Clement Kelley, "The Second Catholic Missionary Congress," *Extension Magazine*, September 1913, 24. A number of speakers at the congress addressed immigration, but the *Official Report of the Second American Catholic Missionary Congress* (1914) does not list Archbishop Eulogio Gillow y Zavalza or other representation from Mexico on the roster of participants.

52. Muldoon, "Immigration to . . . the United States," 132.

53. Muldoon, "Immigration to . . . the United States," 144.

54. A Passionist Missionary, "A Glimpse of Missionary Conditions in Texas," *Extension Magazine*, October 1915, 9.

55. Leo Sweeney, C.M., "A Mississippi Missionary and His Work," *Extension Magazine*, September 1915, 5.

56. M. A. Dombrowski, "On the Texas Plains," *Extension Magazine*, April 1916, 6.

57. Arthur Drossaerts, "Between Friends: A Missionary Chat by the Vice President, The Bishop Speaks," *Extension Magazine*, September 1919, 6. In 1926, Drossaerts, a Dutch priest who came to the United States after his ordination in 1889, became one of the U.S. Catholic leaders of the movement in support of the exiled Mexican clergy during the Cristero Rebellion. For more see chapter 5.

58. Blacks and Indians were treated much like Mexicans in the pages of *Extension Magazine*.

59. Drossaerts, "Between Friends," 6, emphasis added.

60. Emile Barrat, "An Experiment in Parish Work," *Extension Magazine*, March 1908, 1.

61. Barrat, "An Experiment in Parish Work," 1. "Mass Intentions" refers to the practice of offering a Mass for a particular individual or cause.

62. Barrat was one of more than one hundred French priests assigned to the New Mexico Territory in the early twentieth century. In 1916 he was assigned to a parish in Costilla, New Mexico, where he fought for land and water rights for members of his congregation. On Mexican labor migration in this region, see Acuña, *Corridors of Migration*.

63. A Passionist Missionary, "A Glimpse of Missionary Conditions in Texas," *Extension Magazine*, October 1915, 9.

64. Isidore Dwyer, "Missionary Work on the Motor Chapel 'St. Joseph,'" *Extension Magazine*, October 1915, 17.

65. Dwyer, "Missionary Work," 18.

66. Dwyer, "Missionary Work," 41.

67. Ledvina, "The Motor Chapel Car," 9.

68. The "Black Legend" of Spanish failure in the Americas originated in 1914 when Spanish bureaucrat Julián Juderías y Loyot published a series of essays that later became *La leyenda negra: Estudios acerca del concepto de España en el extranjero.* The negative perception of Spanish involvement in the New World dates to the sixteenth century. Kagan calls this Prescott's Paradigm, after William Hickling Prescott's work. See Kagan, "Prescott's Paradigm"; and Griffin, "From Ethos to Ethnos." Also see a series of articles in *Hispanic American Historical Review*: Keen, "The Black Legend Revisited"; Hanke, "A Modest Proposal"; and Keen, "The White Legend Revisited."

69. Tweed has shown that donations to Catholic causes were an important form of participation for American Catholics in the early twentieth century. Tweed, *America's Church*, 245.

70. John Nieto-Phillips, "Echoes of Colonialism: Peninsulares, Wholesome Hispanics, Steamy Latins," in Schmidt-Nowara and Nieto-Phillips, *Interpreting Spanish Colonialism*, 250.

71. Thomas A. O'Shaughnessy, "Some Notable Catholic Landmarks," *Extension Magazine*, May 1907, 14. O'Shaughnessy, a practicing Catholic, later created a series of stained-glass windows in Old St. Patrick's Church in Chicago that are considered the best-known examples of Celtic Revival Art. See http://www.encyclopedia.chicagohistory.org/pages/652.html.

72. O'Shaughnessy, "Some Notable Catholic Landmarks," 14.

73. American Protestants had little interest in the decaying missions, but they did desire a Spanish architectural inheritance. See Bokovoy, *The San Diego World's Fairs*; Deverell, *Whitewashed Adobe*; Kropp, *California Vieja*; and C. Wilson, *The Myth of Santa Fe*.

74. A California Missionary, "In the Footsteps of Junipero," *Extension Magazine*, April 1922, 9.

75. See Pike, *Hispanismo*. *Hispanismo* served two roles: defending the Spanish trans-nation, as well as working to unify it by addressing tensions between *peninsulares* and Creoles. The Spanish cultivation of its deep roots in the New World hardly begins in 1898, as Jorge Cañizares Esguerra demonstrates. This patriotic project has antecedents in the eighteenth century. Cañizares Esguerra, *How to Write the History of the New World*. See also Schmidt-Nowara and Nieto-Phillips, *Interpreting Spanish Colonialism*.

76. Schmidt-Nowara and Nieto-Phillips, *Interpreting Spanish Colonialism*, 2.

77. See, for example, Carrera, *Imagining Identity in New Spain*.

78. Brother Lawrence, T.S.A., "One Mission School That Needs Help," *Extension Magazine*, February 1916, 20.

79. Lawrence, "One Mission School," 20.

80. Rev. A. Estvelt, "Where Danger Threatens," *Extension Magazine*, February 1917, 5.

81. Rev. Isidore Dwyer, C.P., "Missionary Work on the Motor Chapel 'St. Joseph,'" *Extension Magazine*, December 1915, 17.

82. Dwyer, "Missionary Work," 18.

83. Byrkit, *Charles Lummis*, xi. For Lummis's reports to newspapers of his travels, see Lummis, *Some Strange Corners of Our Country*; and Lummis, *A Tramp across the Continent*. See also Lummis Fiske and Lummis, *Charles F. Lummis*.

84. O'Shaughnessy, "Some Notable Catholic Landmarks," 14.

85. Ledvina, "The Motor Chapel Car," 9.

## 2. The Devil Is Having a Great Time

1. Francis C. Kelley, "The Call from Porto Rico," *Extension Magazine*, August 1909, n.p. This special four-page insert appeared between pages 16 and 17.

2. LeRoy, "Race Prejudice in the Philippines," 110.

3. LeRoy, *Philippine Life*, 117; and LeRoy, "Our Spanish Inheritance," 341. See also Kramer, *Blood of Government*. The Taft Commission, or Second Philippine Commission, governed the Philippines from 1900 to 1916.

4. LeRoy, "Our Spanish Inheritance," 342.

5. Kramer, "Empires, Exceptions, and Anglo-Saxons," 1331. Also see Beveridge, *The Meaning of the Times*. On the paradox of immigration and expansion, see Jacobson, *Barbarian Virtues*.

6. *Columbiad* had a circulation of 216,292, while *Extension Magazine*'s was 78,444. See *N. W. Ayer and Son's American Newspaper Annual and Directory*.

7. William D. O'Brien described Extension Society work in Puerto Rico, the Philippines, and Mexico in "Special Work of the Society," *Extension Magazine*, December 1915, 8. Kelley frequently used the phrase "special work of the society" in reference to work with Mexicans through the 1910s and 1920s.

8. Kramer, "Race, Empire, and Transnational History," 200.

9. Williams, *The Tragedy of American Diplomacy*, 55. Williams focuses on China, drawing on President Theodore Roosevelt's concern. See Barg, *Missionaries, Chinese, and Diplomats*; Blum, *Reforging the White Republic*, especially chapter 7; Breslin, *China*; and Laracy, "Maine, Massachusetts, and the Marists."

10. Roosevelt, "State of the Union."

11. Editorial, "Pan-Americanism," *Extension Magazine*, February 1916, 3.

12. Editorial, "Told You So," *Extension Magazine*, April, 1916, 3.

13. The See of Puerto Rico was actually established in 1504.

14. Domingo Miro, "To Save an Historic Ruin," *Extension Magazine*, November 1917, 12.

15. Francis Kelley, "The Society's Porto Rico Missionaries Depart for Their Field of Labor," *Extension Magazine*, October 1909, 3.

16. Kelley, "The Call from Porto Rico," 16d. Kelley does not provide the date or edition of *The Christian Missionary*.

17. "Between Friends, Missionary Chats by the President: The Isle of Mañana," *Extension Magazine*, June 1919, 5.

18. Kelley, "The Call from Porto Rico," 6.

19. "Isla of Mañana," 5.

20. Frederic E. J. Lloyd, "The Truth about the Philippines as Told by Archbishop Harty," *Extension Magazine*, June 1907, 13. Harty, appointed in 1903, was the first American archbishop of Manila. Hoganson shows that some U.S. politicians were explicit in making the case that Filipinos were Christians and thus should not be subject to atrocities by the U.S. military. "All the people we are fighting are members of the Catholic Church," one senator reported, while another reminded his colleagues the University of Manila existed long before universities in the United States, echoing U.S. Catholic claims to the American

continent. Hoganson, *Fighting for American Manhood*, 185. Also see W. Anderson, *Colonial Pathologies*; L. L. Gould, *The Spanish-American War*; Hofstadter, "Manifest Destiny and the Philippines"; McCoy, *Policing America's Empire*; S. C. Miller, *Benevolent Assimilation*; Weston, *Racism in U.S. Imperialism*; and Williams, *The Tragedy of American Diplomacy*, especially chapter 3. On Catholic concerns regarding U.S. expansion into the Philippine Islands, see Dye, "Irish-American Ambivalence." Despite Catholic ambivalence toward the war, 250 Catholic sisters served as nurses during the war. Graf, "Band of Angels." Kenton Clymer reports that Protestant missionaries were divided on whether it was appropriate to proselytize among Roman Catholics. Clymer, *Protestant Missionaries in the Philippines*, 94. Also see Hill, *The World Their Household*; Hutchison: *Errand to the World*; MacKenzie, *The Robe and the Sword*. There were American-based missionaries elsewhere in the Pacific. See Laracy, "Main, Massachusetts, and the Marists."

21. Rev. W. D. O'Brien, "Special Work of the Society," *Extension Magazine*, December 1915, 8.

22. J. A. Zandvliet, "Our Island Missions," *Extension Magazine*, August 1915, 18. Philip M. Finnegan (spelled Finegan in some sources) was a Jesuit from New York who was assigned to Manila.

23. Joseph Grimal, "A Cry of Distress from the Spanish Jesuits in the Philippines," *Extension Magazine*, September 1915, 6. The American schools also executed sanitation programs and a "health index" to measure the civilization of young Filipinos. See W. Anderson, *Colonial Pathologies*, 117.

24. William Finnemann, "Preaching the Gospel under Difficulties," *Extension Magazine*, March 1916, 9.

25. Thomas Mair, "Following the Flag—Religion or Infidelity?" (Manila, ca. 1912). Archbishop Harty sent this pamphlet with his endorsement to the Extension Society in March 1912. For the editorial Mair cited, see *America Magazine* editorial, January 13, 1912. Jacobson emphasizes the tension between immigration and expansion in *Barbarian Virtues*. For more on the Philippine Constabulary, see Hurley, *Jungle Patrol*.

26. G. Verbrugge, October 22, 1912, in "Letters from Missionaries That Need No Comment," *Extension Magazine*, April 1913, 6. This is likely Julius Verbrugge of St. Joseph's Missionary Society, commonly referred to as Mill Hill Missionaries, who was assigned to the Philippines in 1906.

27. Foreman, *The Philippine Islands*, 607. See also Ambrose Coleman, "The Inside of the Aglipayan Church," *American Catholic Quarterly Review* 30 (April 1905): 368–81. The Aglipayans are now affiliated with the Episcopal Church of the United States and known formally as the Philippine Independent Church. See *The Catholic Encyclopedia*; Willis, *Our Philippine Problem*; and Peter-Ben

Smit, *Old Catholic and Philippine Independent Ecclesiologies in History: The Catholic Church in Every Place* (Leiden: Brill, 2011). McCoy notes government surveillance of the Aglipayans as a result of Aglipay's close alliance with labor activist Isabelo de lose Reyes. See McCoy, *Policing America's Empire*, 106–9.

28. D. J. Dougherty, "Church Conditions in the Philippines," *Extension Magazine*, July 1913, 5–6.

29. Dougherty, "Church Conditions in the Philippines," 6.

30. *The Awful Disclosures of Maria Monk, as Exhibited in a Narrative of Her Sufferings During a Residence of Five Years as a Novice and Two Years as a Black Nun, in the Hotel Dieu Nunnery in Montreal* (1836), told the story of a Canadian nun who had been sexually exploited by priests. Monk's work has been widely discredited. See, for example, Ray Allen Billington, "Maria Monk and Her Influence," *Catholic Historical Review* 22, no. 3 (October 1936): 283–96. Also see Gibbons, *Faith of Our Fathers*.

31. Dougherty, "Church Conditions in the Philippines," 6.

32. Lawrence Rogan, "Where Catholic Schools Are Needed," *Extension Magazine*, July 1913, 8. The threat from godless schools was repeated in 1917 by Rev. Celso Hervas. Hervas, "An Urgent Plea," *Extension Magazine*, November 1917, 12. American Catholic support continued through the decade. A 1917 article listed churches that had been repaired with funds for American Catholics before asking for additional funds for schools. Rev. A. Brocken, M.S.C., "A Deplorable Condition," *Extension Magazine*, November 1917, 12.

33. "Let Them Talk?" *Extension Magazine*, April 1916, 4. The Jones Law, passed in August 1916, established a semi-autonomous government in the Philippines in preparation for independence in the future.

34. Kelley, *The Book of Red and Yellow*. It is not clear how Kelley measured this.

35. Kelley, *The Story of Extension*, 180. Emmanuel Ledvina, Chicago, to Archbishop George William Mundelein, Chicago, March 21, 1919, and A. E. Burke to President Wilson, March 4, 1919, Madaj Collection, ACARC.

36. Undated statement from Extension Society to the U.S. bishops, Kelley Papers, Archdiocese of Oklahoma City.

37. See W. Nugent, *Habits of Empire*.

38. "Where the Gates of Hell Are Open," *Extension Magazine*, November 1914, 3.

39. Undated statement, Kelley Papers, 7.

40. Robertson introduced Kelley to Daniel Guggenheim of American Smelting & Refining, giving Guggenheim all assurances that Kelley was working for peace in Mexico. See Joseph Andrew Robertson to Daniel Guggenheim, New York City, December 14 and December 21, 1914, Kelley Papers. Robertson was general manager of the Monterrey and Mexican Gulf Railroad. Barker, *A History of Texas and Texans*, 1190.

41. Francis Kelley to John Cardinal Farley, New York, February 28, 1916. See also "The Echo of the Cry for Help," *Extension Magazine*, April 1916, 27.

42. Francis Kelley, "A Voice Out of Mexico," *Extension Magazine*, December 1917, 3.

43. See, for example, Francis Kelley, "The Rule of the People," *Extension Magazine*, January 1918, 4; and Francis Kelley, "Mr. Shaw on Democracy," *Extension Magazine*, February, 1918, 3.

44. See Francis Kelley, San Antonio, to John Bonzano, D.D., Apostolic Delegate, Washington DC, October 18, 1914, and Francis Kelley, San Antonio, to Father Richard Tierney, October 19, 1914, Kelley Papers. Tierney edited *America Magazine*, a national Jesuit publication.

45. Francis Kelley, "The Seminary," *Extension Magazine*, June 1918, 4. Also see Kelley, "The Exiled Mexican Brothers of Mary," *Extension Magazine*, June 1915, 1.

46. Francis Kelley, "Archbishop Quigley: A Personal Tribute to Our First Chancellor," *Extension Magazine*, August 1915, 5.

47. Francis Kelley, "Mexico Again," *Extension Magazine*, January 1916, 3–5.

48. See Francis Kelley, "Carranza," *Extension Magazine*, February 1916, 3; and Kelley, "The Echo of the Cry for Help," *Extension Magazine*, April 1916, 27. See also Kelley, "Reputable?" *Extension Magazine*, June 1916, 3. For more on Kelley's political maneuverings, see chapter 4.

49. The leveling off of subscribers mid-decade might have been related to the 1913–14 recession in the United States.

50. Francis Kelley, "Humanity," *Extension Magazine*, September 1919, 3.

51. See Baldwin, *Protestants and the Mexican Revolution*.

52. Kelley, "The Tactics of Traducer," *Extension Magazine*, April 1917, 4–13.

53. Eber Cole Byam, "What the Church Has Done in Mexico," *Extension Magazine*, May 1917, 9–10. Byam did much of the research for Kelley's *Blood-Drenched Altars*.

54. Francis Kelley, "A Word about Mexico," *Extension Magazine*, October 1919, 4.

### 3. Religious Monroeism

*Title*: Andrés Barquín y Ruíz and Miguel Palomar y Vizcarra, Cristero activists, coined the phrase "religious Monroeism" in their article "La influencia de los Estados Unidos sobre Mexico en material religiosa," 36.

1. Gilbert O. Nations, Free Press Defense League, Washington DC, to President Woodrow Wilson, Washington DC, n.d., received at the White House on April 11, 1916. This likely was not the first time Nations had made this sort of claim. See Nations, *Constitution or Pope*; and Nations, *Papal Sovereignty*. Nations also edited a series of nativist publications: *The Menace, The Protestant, The Peril* and others. For more on anti-Catholic publications, see Nordstrom, *Danger on the Doorstep*.

2. H. M. Andrews to Secretary Joseph Tumulty, Columbus, Ohio, November 1, 1916, Records of the Department of State Relating to the Internal Affairs of Mexico, 1910–1929, Record Group 59, National Archives and Records Administration [hereafter Internal Affairs of Mexico]. Robert Mitchell of Detroit, Florence Griswold of San Antonio, and J. Webb Saffold of Cleveland sent similar correspondence, tattling on local Catholics. See Robert Mitchell to Frank B. Kellogg, Detroit, August 30, 1926, Florence J. Griwsold to Secretary of State, San Antonio, May 16, 1928, and J. Webb Safford to Everett Sanders, Cleveland, May 28, 1929, all in Internal Affairs of Mexico.

3. According to the Smithsonian Institution, Byam, a U.S. citizen, grew up on his family's rubber plantation in Chiapas, Mexico, and they lost their land after the Revolution. Byam spent the rest of his life campaigning against anticlerical revolutionaries in Mexico. National Anthropological Archives, National Museum of Natural History, Smithsonian Institution. Byam himself reported to Congress that he worked in Mexico from 1895 to 1907, including working on a lumber camp, the railroads, and a rubber plantation in Chiapas. He was in Chicago as early as 1920. Subcommittee of Committee on Foreign Relations, 66th Cong., S. Res. 106, Investigation of Mexican Affairs (testimony of Eber Cole Byam), 2684. Byam did research for Kelley's *Blood-Drenched Altars* (1935) and died in 1937.

4. Calvert, *The Mexican Revolution*, 10.

5. On the role of business in Wilson's foreign-policy decisions concerning Mexico, see Bell, *Righteous Conquest*. On oil, see Hall, *Oil, Banks, and Politics*; and Ansell, *Oil Baron of the Southwest*.

6. Andrés Barquín y Ruíz and Miguel Palomar y Vizcarra, Cristero activists, coined the phrase "religious Monroeism" in their article "La influencia de los Estados Unidos sobre Mexico en material religiosa," 36.

7. Arthur J. Drossaerts quoted in *San Antonio Express* articles enclosed in Florence J. Griswold to Secretary of State, San Antonio, May 16, 1928, Internal Affairs of Mexico.

8. Monsignor Antonio J. Paredes, January 1915 statement included in Silliman to Secretary of State, Eagle Pass, Texas, August 8, 1916, Internal Affairs of Mexico.

9. See Kelley, *The Book of Red and Yellow*.

10. Manuel Hernández Juaregui, *Las leyes de reforma y las disposiciones legales in materia de culto religioso y disciplina externa* (Mexico, DF: Talleres Gráficos de la Nación, 1927). Hernández Juaregui presented this speech at an agrarian congress in Mexico City in October 1926.

11. Philip C. Hanna to Secretary of State, Monterey [*sic*], July 11, 1914, Internal Affairs of Mexico.

12. James R. Silliman to Secretary of State, Guadalajara, Jalisco, February 13, 1918, Internal Affairs of Mexico.

13. James R. Silliman to Secretary of State, Guadalajara, Jalisco, August 12, 1918, and Dudley Dwyre to Secretary of State, Guadalajara, Jalisco, April 27, 1926, both in Internal Affairs of Mexico.

14. Oscar C. Harper to Secretary of State, Piedras Negras, Coahuila, June 2, 1927, Internal Affairs of Mexico. Harper does not disclose how he acquired this information from the director of the Mexican immigration service.

15. Hanna to Secretary of State, July 11, 1914.

16. On education, see Hanna to Secretary of State, San Antonio, Texas, March 16, 1917, Internal Affairs of Mexico. Hanna, while U.S. consul of Monterrey, often reported from San Antonio. It is unclear if his presence there was a matter of perceived safety or comfort.

17. John Q. Wood to James R. Sheffield, Veracruz, Veracruz, February 18, 1926, and Dudley G. Dwyre to Secretary of State, Guadalajara, Jalisco, July 28, 1926, Internal Affairs of Mexico.

18. See Mexico Files, Knights of Columbus Supreme Council Archives.

19. John Lind to William Jennings Bryan, March 23, 1914, Mexican Mission Papers of John Lind, Minnesota Historical Society [hereafter Lind Papers]. Lind was a career politician, having served three terms in the House of Representatives and as governor of Minnesota.

20. "Our Problem in Mexico," *Current Opinion* 55, no. 3 (September 1913), 147, Lind Papers.

21. John Lind, "The Mexican People," *The Bellman*, December 5 and 12, 1914, 22–23, 31 (my emphasis), Lind Papers. J. C. Enríquez, to John Lind, New York City, December 19, 1914, Lind Papers.

22. William Jennings Bryan to James P. Maher, Washington DC, January 21, 1915, Internal Affairs of Mexico. Consuls reported on many outrages but often deemed sources unreliable if they were not familiar with the individual or group that reported incidents.

23. Robert Lansing to Reverend T. V. Shannon, Washington DC, October 29, 1915, Internal Affairs of Mexico.

24. Frank B. Kellogg to President, Washington DC, August 26, 1926, Internal Affairs of Mexico.

25. See, for example, Redinger, "'To Arouse and Inform'"; and Redinger, *America Catholics*.

26. See James R. Sheffield to Secretary of State, Mexico City, March 8, 1926, Sheffield, Ambassador Statement for Mexican Foreign office, Mexico City, Sheffield to Secretary of State, Mexico City, March 18, 1926, John Q. Wood to Sheffield, Veracruz, March 18, 1926, and Division of Mexican Affairs Report, Washington DC, March 31, 1926, all in Internal Affairs of Mexico.

27. State Department Memorandum, March 3, 1926, Internal Affairs of Mexico.

28. See Ansell, *Oil Baron of the Southwest*, in particular, as well as Hall, *Oil, Banks, and Politics*. Both report on sizable loans from Doheny and other oilmen to Obregón. They also indicate that early on, oil and banking leaders in the United States learned that to best protect their interests, they should go directly to the Mexican leadership, rather than negotiate through the U.S. government.

29. Woodrow Wilson to James Cardinal Gibbons, Washington DC, August 12, 1914, Internal Affairs of Mexico.

30. Department of State, Division of Mexican Affairs, memorandum, March 3, 1926, Internal Affairs of Mexico.

31. James R. Sheffield to Secretary of State, Mexico City, March 8, 1926.

32. F. M. G. to Secretary of State, Washington DC, May 1, 1926, Sheffield to Secretary of State, Mexico City, June 30, 1926, Robert E. Olds to Ernest Hammond, Washington DC, July 12, 1926, and Robert E. Olds to Bishop William T. Russell, Washington DC, May 28, 1926, all in Internal Affairs of Mexico. Caruana, a native of Malta, had been secretary to Cardinal Dennis Dougherty of Philadelphia, where he became a U.S. citizen. He was later bishop of Puerto Rico and papal nuncio to Cuba. The National Catholic War Council was established by the American hierarchy in 1917 to demonstrate the Catholic commitment to supporting the United States in World War I. In 1919 it was renamed the National Catholic Welfare Council, and in 1922, the National Catholic Welfare Conference. Based in Washington DC, the NCWC coordinated activities among the hierarchy, Catholic organizations, and Catholic publications. For more on the NCWC and Mexico, see Slawson, "The National Catholic Welfare Conference." See also M. Warner, *Changing Witness*.

33. Philip C. Hanna to Secretary of State, San Antonio, Texas, August 14, 1918, Internal Affairs of Mexico.

34. T. J. Walsh to Secretary of State, Baltimore, Maryland, July 29, 1917, Internal Affairs of Mexico.

35. Cardoso de Oliviera to Secretary of State, Mexico City, February 19, 1915, and William Jennings Bryan to Brazilian Minister, Washington DC, February 21, 1915, both in Internal Affairs of Mexico.

36. James R. Silliman to Secretary of State, Mexico City, February 19, 1915, Internal Affairs of Mexico. Silliman was a special representative of the State Department, consul in Mexico City, and later consul in Guadalajara.

37. Juan Raiño y Gayangos to W. J. Bryan, Washington DC, February 21, 1915, Internal Affairs of Mexico.

38. James R. Sheffield to Secretary of State, Mexico City, February 24, 1925, all in Internal Affairs of Mexico.

39. Division of Mexican Affairs, Department of State, Memorandum, March 3, 1926, Internal Affairs of Mexico, emphasis added.

40. Pope Benedict XV to President, Vatican, January 26, 1917. In later years, Pope Pius XI appealed to the U.S. president through the apostolic delegate. Peter Fumasoni-Biondi to Frank B. Kellogg, Washington DC, January 10, 1927, both in Internal Affairs of Mexico.

41. Robert Lansing to Miss M. S. Wilson, Washington DC, February 25, 1915, Internal Affairs of Mexico.

42. Joseph E. Ransdell to Charles Evans Hughes, Washington DC, July 12, 1924, Sister M. Angela to H. F. Arthur Schoenfeld, Puebla, August 3, 1924, Internal Affairs of Mexico.

43. Statement by Catarina Stecker, notarized by Francis D. Roach, to Division of Mexican Affairs, Department of State, Washington DC, February 2, 1916, Internal Affairs of Mexico, and James D. Barry to Secretary of State, Nogales, Arizona, December 10, 1915, in Internal Affairs of Mexico. For the case of a U.S. businessman who was being harassed by "bandits," see Edward H. Mall to Secretary of State, Durango, July 9, 1927, Internal Affairs of Mexico.

44. See Baldwin, *Protestants and the Mexican Revolution*; and Vinz, *Pulpit Politics*, especially chapter 3.

45. Henry P. Fletcher to Secretary of State, Mexico City, March 18, 1917, and Louis B. Fritts to President Coolidge, Hermosillo, August 9, 1923, both in Internal Affairs of Mexico, emphasis added. Fritts wrote to Coolidge only days after the untimely death of Warren Harding, perhaps thinking Coolidge would be more favorable to Catholic concerns. James R. Sheffield to Secretary of State, Mexico City, May 28, 1926, TMG to Secretary of State, March 10, 1926, and J. M. Regier to Department of State, Pandora, Ohio, February 4, 1928, all in Internal Affairs of Mexico.

46. Bishop Miguel de la Mora to Cardinal James Gibbons, San Antonio, Texas, August 14, 1914, Internal Affairs of Mexico.

47. William Jennings Bryan to James Cardinal Gibbons, Washington DC, n.d., Internal Affairs of Mexico.

48. See George T. Summerlin to Secretary of State, Mexico City, November 7, 1922, and January 26, 1923, Bartley F. Yost to Secretary of State, Torreon, July 16, 1926, and James R. Sheffield to Secretary of State, Mexico City, August 2, 1926, Internal Affairs of Mexico.

49. C. Martínez and Pedro Rentería to James R. Sheffield, Mexico City, May 30, 1927, Internal Affairs of Mexico.

50. H. F. A. Schoenfeld to Secretary of State, Mexico City, September 30, 1924, and James R. Sheffield to Secretary of State, Mexico City, February 24, 1925, both in Internal Affairs of Mexico.

51. "Catholics to Approach Congress," *El Universal*, August 30, 1928, Dwight W. Morrow Papers, Amherst College Archives and Special Collections.

52. James R. Sheffield to Secretary of State, Mexico City, June 30, 1926, Internal Affairs of Mexico.

53. Dwight W. Morrow, meeting notes, May 16, 1929, Morrow Papers.

54. James R. Sheffield to Secretary of State, Mexico City, July 22, 1926, Internal Affairs of Mexico.

55. Frank B. Kellogg to President, Washington DC, August 26, 1926, Internal Affairs of Mexico.

56. Arthur Bliss Lane to Mr. Secretary and Mr. Olds, Washington DC, December 12, 1927, Internal Affairs of Mexico.

57. On oil see Ansell, *Oil Baron of the Southwest*; and Hall, *Oil, Banks, and Politics*.

58. Dwight W. Morrow, meeting notes, February 6, 1928, Morrow Papers; "Memorandum shown to the Ambassador by Mr. Miguel Cruchaga and Stated to him to have been prepared for Dr. Walsh, S.J., Dean of the Georgetown School of Foreign Service, and Shown by Dr. Walsh to the Pope in June of 1928," April 1, 1928, Morrow Papers. Many letters (see Internal Affairs of Mexico) and publications called into question the actions of Wilson, in particular. *Mexico: A Weekly to Promote Intelligent Discussion of Mexican Affairs* most often came out in opposition to Wilson's administration. Also see Eisenhower, *Intervention*; Bulnes, *The Whole Truth about Mexico*; and Chamberlain, *Is Mexico Worth Saving*.

59. Oscar E. Duplan, title of article omitted by unnamed translator, *El Universal Gráfico*, August 23, 1928, Morrow Papers.

60. Bishop Vincent Wehrle to Wilson, Bismarck, North Dakota, November 10, 1915, and Charles I. Denechaud to Bryan, Baltimore, September 29, 1914, both in Internal Affairs of Mexico.

61. William T. Russell to Frank B. Kellogg, Charleston, South Carolina, May 18, 1926, Internal Affairs of Mexico.

## 4. An American Catholic Diplomacy

1. Francis C. Kelley, Chicago, to Cardinal George W. Mundelein, Chicago, April 14, 1918, Madaj Collection, ACARC.

2. Francis C. Kelley, Chicago, to Cardinal George W. Mundelein, Chicago, December 18, 1918, Madaj Collection, ACARC. The U.S. Census lists 1,141 Mexicans in Chicago in 1920. This is surely a significant undercount. U.S. Bureau of the Census, *Fifteenth Census of the United States* (Washington DC: Government Printing Office, 1933).

3. New York has always been two dioceses—the Archdiocese of New York and the Diocese of Brooklyn. The Archdiocese of Los Angeles became larger than the Archdiocese of Chicago in the 1980s.

4. Shanabruch, *Chicago's Catholics*, 208–10.

5. See McGreevy, *Parish Boundaries*.

6. Pope Leo XIII, *Testem Benevolentiae Nostrae*.

7. The 1915 revival of the Ku Klux Klan also fanned anti-Catholicism in parts of the United States. See Baker, *Gospel According to the Klan*; and Neal, "Christianizing the Klan."

8. Mundelein speaking at the founding of Catholic Charities of Chicago, April 10, 1917, in *Two Crowded Years*, 146–47.

9. Cardinal John Patrick Cody, archbishop of Chicago from 1965 to 1982, ended the tradition of having Illinois license plate number "1" in 1970, characterizing the practice as inappropriate for someone committed to serving others. Dave McKinney, *Chicago Sun-Times*, July 4, 2012. http://www.suntimes.com/news/watchdogs/13574345–452/illinois-most-covered-license-plate-no-1-could-be-available-again.html.

10. Willard F. Jabusch, "Lord of the Rings," *Commonweal*, September 27, 2002.

11. Corcoran was visiting Mundelein the night he died. Rumors abounded regarding Mundelein's death. Some sources indicated he was homosexual and was murdered by his lover. Others indicated that Hitler ordered his assassination in retaliation for remarks Mundelein made criticizing Nazism and characterizing Hitler as "an Austrian paperhanger—and a poor one at that." Mundelein was berated by Berlin newspapers and praised in the United States. See Mundelein's obituary, "Mundelein Career Began on East Side," *New York Times*, October 3, 1939; *Chicago Magazine*, December 2000; and James Winters deposition, July 1, 1985, *James Winters v. Andrew Greeley*. On Coughlin in contrast to Mundelein, see especially Donald Warren, *Radio Priest: Charles Coughlin, the Father of Hate Radio* (New York: The Free Press, 1996).

12. Shanabruch, *Chicago's Catholics*, 201.

13. The Workers Party later became the Communist Party. Frank Duffy, Indianapolis, to Cardinal George Mundelein, Chicago, April 7, 1926, Madaj Collection, ACARC, 1.

14. "Welcome," *Chicago Tribune*, June 16, 1926. For more on the Eucharistic Congress, see chapter 5.

15. Winthrop Hudson in Edward R. Kantowicz, "Cardinal Mundelein and Chicago," in Skerrett, Kantowicz, and Avella, *Catholicism, Chicago Style*, 78.

16. Redinger, *American Catholics*, 55. Redinger refers specifically to Cardinal William O'Connell of Boston, but the same could be said of the rest of the hierarchy.

17. Gaffey, *Francis Clement Kelley*, 1:233.

18. Most Reverend Francis C. Kelley, Chicago, to Benedict XV, Rome, October 18, 1918, Madaj Collection, ACARC, 1–2.

19. Francis Kelley to Sante Tampieri, September 17, 1912.

20. Gaffey notes that Kelley also went to Rome to assess the status of his own promotion to monsignor. Curiously, Gaffey did not believe Kelley sought such honors for himself: "During his first decade with Extension, he was interested in papal honors for himself, such as a monsignorship; but no evidence has ever suggested that his motive was self-serving" (*Francis Clement Kelley*, 1:126). Gaffey indicates that Kelley's desire for a monsignorship was entirely about helping the Extension Society gain legitimacy in the United States and access in Rome—an extremely naive assessment given Kelley's tendency to overextend his station in the Catholic hierarchy, whether or not the society was at issue. Kelley was clearly disturbed that Alfred E. Burke, president of the Extension Society of Canada, had received a monsignorship. As president of the first Extension Society, Kelley believed he deserved one first. When he did receive his "promotion," it was to a rank lower than Burke's monsignorship. "Instead of elating Kelley and his associates, this news came as a shock to Chicago, where there were plans to postpone the announcement until the memory of Burke's higher dignity had faded." Eventually, Kelley was granted the protonary monsignorship he desired. Gaffey, *Francis Clement Kelley*, 1:128.

21. Kelley served as chaplain to a Michigan volunteer regiment during the Spanish-American War, so he had some previous experience with military chaplaincy.

22. George Mundelein, to Frank Polk, Acting Secretary of State, Washington DC, March 27, 1919. The Society of the Divine Word (Societas Verbi Divini, or S.V.D.), whose North American province was in a Chicago suburb, was founded by a German priest in exile in the Netherlands in 1875 and staffed primarily by German priests. Around the same time, Mundelein chose the S.V.D. missionaries to work with black Catholics in Chicago, despite their specialization in China. See Madaj Collection, ACARC, and Robert M. Myers Archives, Society of the Divine Word, Chicago Province, Techny, Illinois.

23. Gaffey, *Francis Clement Kelley*, 1:273.

24. Francis Clement Kelley to Sir William Tyrell, London, July 13, 1920, Kelley Papers.

25. Kelley to Cardinal Gibbons, September 23, 1920, Kelley Papers.

26. Francis Clement Kelley, Oklahoma City, to Cardinal Cerretti, The Vatican, February 4, 1929, Kelley Papers.

27. Francis Kelley, Oklahoma City, to William D. O'Brien, Chicago, April 9, 1929.

28. Kelley to Cerretti, February 4, 1929, Kelley Papers. In this lengthy report, Kelley used his diaries and memory to reconstruct his role in the negotiations.

29. See Kelley, Oklahoma City, to Hugh C. Boyle, Pittsburgh, May 20 and June 17, 1929, Kelley Papers.

30. Jacobson, *Barbarian Virtues*, 3.

31. Kelley, *The Story of Extension*, 195. Kelley met Carnegie in January 1915 and shared his plan with the industrialist. His correspondence does not detail the plan. Kelley, Chicago, to Andrew Carnegie, Pittsburgh, January 27, 1915, Kelley Papers.

## 5. Crisis in the Catholic Borderlands

1. John Cornyn, "Mexican Secret Police to Watch Pilgrims Here," *Chicago Tribune*, June 18, 1926, 3.

2. John Clayton, "Mexico Plots to Oust Church, Prelate Avers," *Chicago Tribune*, June 20, 1926, 3.

3. On January 11, 1923, Archbishop José Mora y del Río presided over the ceremony where Monsignor Ernesto Filippi, the apostolic delegate to Mexico, laid the cornerstone for the monument. Two days later, Calles ordered Filippi's expulsion for violating the Constitution of 1917.

4. Krauze, *Mexico, Biography of Power*, 405. Like so many descriptions of Mexican revolutionary figures, this one is romanticized. Krauze writes: "To society at large, Plutarco Elías Calles was illegitimate because his father never married, but he was even more so in the eyes of religion. Denying the authority of religion would at least in part be an attempt to negate his own illegitimacy" (406). And later: "He was still—at the age of forty-six—troubled and pursued by the illegitimacy of his birth" (413). Krauze starts his chapter on Calles with a quote from Thomas Mann's *Moses*: "His birth was disorderly, and this perhaps explains his passionate love of order, the inviolable, of what should and should not be done" (405). Describing Calles's life prior to becoming involved in the Revolution, Bailey writes: "The hotel burned down, the farm went into bankruptcy, and the milling business failed. But his talents were not suited to the world of middle-class respectability. His *metier* was revolution" (*¡Viva Cristo Rey!* 48).

5. See Miguel Palomar y Vizcarra Papers, Conflicto Religioso, Subdirección de documentación, INAH.

6. Ricardo T. Villalpando, Aguascalientes, Aguascalientes, to Sr. Presidente, December 20, 1925, and General Teodoro Escalona, Colima, Colima, to Sr. Presidente, May 4, 1925, Colección Obregón-Calles, Archivo General de la Nación.

7. "Internal Report," n.d., section of report dated September 5, 1924, National Catholic Welfare Conference Papers, CUA.

8. Eventually the schismatic church closed because it was not meeting the standards of the 1917 Constitution. For more on the Iglesia Católica Apostólica Mexicana, see K. C. Miller, "Un Iglesia Más Mexicana."

9. Bailey, *¡Viva Cristo Rey!* 55.

10. Conflicto Religioso (INAH) contains correspondence between the Liga and L'Union Mondiale de membres Hon de la LDLR du Mexique, Union Internatio-

nale de tous amis de la ligue pour la defense de la liberté religieuse de Mexique, and Unión Internacional de Todos los Amigos de la Liga Nacional Defensora de la Libertad Religiosa. Later, a likely more militant group formed in Latin America, the Resonancia Mundial del Movimiento Armado Católica de México.

11. See the Palomar y Vizcarra Papers and the Aurelio R. Acevedo Papers, Conflicto Religioso, INAH. The collection includes journal and newspaper articles from national and international sources, as well as correspondence, broadsides, and other materials on religious conflict in Mexico dating from 1904 to 1957. The bulk of the material consists of Palomar y Vizcarra's papers from his work as part of the Liga.

12. Kristina A Boylan, "Mexican Catholic Action (Acción Católica Mexicana)," in *Encyclopedia of Modern Christian Politics*, ed. Roy P. Domenico (Westport CT: Greenwood Press, 2006), 373.

13. See L. Lujual G., Chicago Consul to Secretaría de Relaciones Exteriores, April 28, 1926, SRE.

14. To the Mexican Consul: American, European and Asian sections, May 20, 1926, SRE.

15. Enrique Liekens, El Paso, Texas, to Roberto Garía, C. Consul de México, June 23, 1926, SRE.

16. Cardinal George Mundelein, Chicago, to The Most Reverend George Caruana, June 8, 1926, and Archbishop George Caruana, Washington DC, to His Eminence Cardinal G. W. Mundelein, June 14, 1926, Madaj Collection, ACARC.

17. Joseph Mary Gonzales, Archbishop of Durango, Durango, Mexico, to Most Eminent George Cardinal Mundelein, D.D., May 26, 1926, ACARC. Similar sentiments were expressed by the archbishop of Oaxaca. José (Giuseppe) Ottone Nuñez, Archbishop of Oaxaca, Oaxaca, Mexico, to Very Reverend C. J. Quille, General Secretary of the International Eucharistic Congress, May 29, 1926, ACARC.

18. See Pedro Rosales Manguía, secretary, LDLR, Mexico City, to Father Ricardo B. Anaya, Paris, France, November 18, 1925, and Rosales Manguía, Mexico City, to Gabriel Fernández Somellera, Santander, Spain, November 18, 1925, both in Palomar y Vizcarra Papers, INAH.

19. Edmundo F. Bemonte, executive secretary, LNDR, Mexico City, to *Revista Católica*, El Paso, Texas, May 27, 1925, Palomar y Vizcarra Papers, INAH.

20. Author unkown [likely José Mora y del Rio],Mexico City, To the Catholic Hierarchy in the United States of America, October 8, 1926, and Board of Directors, LNDLR, Mexico City, to María G. Hawks, President, Council of Catholic Women of the United States, Washington, February 1, 1928, Palomar y Vizcarra Papers, INAH.

21. The Liga had the endorsement of the Mexican hierarchy for the boycott. See José Mora y del Río and Pascual Díaz, Mexico City, to Rafael Ceniceros y

Villarreal, Luis G. Bustos, and René Capistrán Garza, Mexico City, July 14, 1926, Palomar y Vizcarra Papers, INAH.

22. Board of Directors, Liga Nacional Defensora de la Libertad Religiosa, Circular 2A, July 14, 1926, Palomar y Vizcarra Papers, INAH, capitalization in the original.

23. Dudley Dwyre, U. S. consul in Guadalajara, reported that the boycott was "90 per cent effective with the department stores and refreshment parlors and a conservative estimate of 80 per cent is given in connection with motion pictures." Dudley Dwyre, Guadalajara, Jalisco, to Secretary of State, August 6, 1926, Internal Affairs of Mexico.

24. Aurelio de los Reyes, "La Tumultuosa Bienvenida a Lindbergh, el niño fidencio y el exito de *Rey de Reyes*, ¿Expresión de la persecución religiosa en México, 1925–1929," in *Los Cristeros* (Mexico City: Centro de Estudios de Historia de México Condumex, 1996), 86. The title translates as "The Tumultuous Welcome of Lindbergh, 'el niño Fidencio' and the success of *King of Kings*, expressions of religious persecution in Mexico, 1925–1929." El niño Fidencio was a faith healer–folk phenomenon in Mexico in the late 1920s and early 1930s. *King of Kings* is a U.S. film on the life of Christ that was released in Mexico in the late 1920s.

25. Ambassador Sheffield, Mexico City, to Secretary of State, August 2, 1926, Internal Affairs of Mexico.

26. Dwight Morrow, "Outline of Statement of Lic. Mestre made in conversation with Ambassador Morrow on October 8, 1928," 3–5, Morrow Papers.

27. Purnell, *Popular Movements*, 88. This project does not explicitly engage the debates on the Cristeros, but there is a well-developed literature on this era. See J. A. Meyer, *The Cristero Rebellion*; Tuck, *The Holy War in Los Altos*; Butler, *Popular Piety*; Gruening, *Mexico and Its Heritage*; Vaughn and Lewis, *The Eagle and the Virgin*; Wright-Rios, *Revolutions in Mexican Catholicism*; and J. A. Meyer, *Las naciones frente al conflicto religioso en México*.

28. Colegio Pontificio Pio Latino Americano, Rome, to Your Eminences, care of Cardinal Dennis Dougherty, Philadelphia, January 17, 1927, Palomar y Vizcarra Papers, INAH.

29. "Glory to Mexico," broadside, 1927, Palomar y Vizcarra Papers.

30. For local Catholic newspapers, see Palomar y Vizcarra Papers, INAH, and Boletín de Guerra, Comité Especial de Información Bélica en México, DF.

31. See Elías, *The Mexican People and the Church*. A copy of this booklet, signed by Elías on February 2, 1927, would indicate it was in use in early 1927. A Spanish version was published in 1926. See also "Both Sides of the Controversy between the Roman Catholic Church Hierarchy and the Mexican Government," originally printed in the *New York World* on February 5, 1928.

32. See Dudley Dwyre, Guadalajara, to Secretary of State, April 27, 1927, Internal Affairs of Mexico.

33. Ambassador Sheffield, Mexico City, to Secretary and Undersecretary of State, April 26, 1927, Internal Affairs of Mexico. Sheffield's report, marked "STRICTLY CONFIDENTIAL," is secondhand and contains inaccurate references to the Catholic Party, which did not exist at this time. He is likely referring to the Liga. Sheffield's confusion bears witness to the considerable chaos in Mexico during these battles and to his failure to understand the divisions within Mexico as a whole.

34. Ambassador Sheffield, Mexico City, to Secretary of State, April 26, 1927. This second letter was in reference to a previous dispatch regarding the arrest and deportation of Mexican priests.

35. Ambassador Sheffield, Mexico City, to Secretary of State, April 26, 1927, Internal Affairs of Mexico. As evidence of the centrality of the religion question in U.S.-Mexican relations, this was the third dispatch Sheffield sent to Washington on April 26, each having some aspect of the religious situation as its subject.

36. Sheffield often blamed rural unrest on the "class" of men involved, regardless of the cause they were attacking or defending. It is likely that the Indians to whom he referred were rural peasants.

37. Because the rebellion was so widespread in both time and geography, accurate counts are impossible. The U.S. War Department estimated that there were less than 10,000 Cristeros as late as September 1927. In October that number swelled to over 10,000, and over 20,000 by December. Numbers tapered off in April 1928, when an estimated 16,000 rebels were active. In May 1929, an estimated 21,000 federal troops battled 10,000 Cristeros. Purnell, *Popular Movements*, 87.

38. Martha Elena Negrete, "Enrique Gorostieta: Un Cristero Agnostico," in *Los Cristeros* (Mexico City: Centro de Estudios de Historia de Mexico Condumex, 1996), 64. *For Greater Glory* (2012), a critically panned and historically flawed film, portrayed Gorostieta as an agnostic with an interest in developing a talented young Cristero into a military leader. A Spanish-language subtitled version, *La Cristiada*, appeared to better reviews in Mexico several months earlier than the U.S. release. Dean Wright, director, *For Greater Glory*, 2012.

39. San Antonio was an important Catholic touchstone for Mexican immigrants. See Matovina, *Guadalupe and Her Faithful*; and K. C. Miller, "Un Iglesia Más Mexicana."

40. F. Arcoacha, "La liga y el gobierno de norteamerica," n.d. Based on the content, it was probably written in late 1928 or early 1929.

41. José Tello, secretary, National League for the Defense of Religious Liberty, to The Honorable Secretary, State Department, Washington DC, April 5, 1929, 3, Palomar y Vizcarra Papers, INAH.

42. Tello to Secretary of State, April 5, 1929, 5.

43. Walter Lippmann, editorial, *New York World*, December 29, 1927.

44. Morrow to Olds, December 9, 1927, Morrow Papers.

45. Morrow's notes from conference with "Mr. A, Mr. B and Mr. C. . . . Mr. Montavon was present," February 6, 1928, Morrow Papers. Montavon was the legal representative of the NCWC.

46. Luella Herr to Richard Herr, February 22, 1928, in Herr, *An American Family*, 226, 227. The book consists of letters from a U.S. family with silver-mining interests living in Mexico to their families in the United States.

47. Quirk, *The Mexican Revolution*, 232.

48. Vasconcelos dubbed himself the "Mexican Ulysses" in his autobiography. Vasconcelos, *A Mexican Ulysses*, 212.

49. José Vasconcelos, "What Is Happening in Mexico?" *Paris-Madrid*, November 10, 1927. *Paris-Madrid* was a Spanish-language newspaper in Paris. This article and its translation was sent to the State Department by Sheldon Whitehouse, Chargé d'Affaires ad interim, Paris. Whitehouse to Secretary of State, Paris, November 23, 1927. Internal Affairs of Mexico.

50. See Vasconcelos, "A Mexican's Point of View," 136.

51. Marantes, *José Vasconcelos*, 154.

52. Wilbur Bates, New York, to Louis Wiley, April 11, 1929, Morrow Papers.

53. General Roberto Cruz quoted in Krauze, *Mexico, Biography of Power*, 430.

54. Liga Nacional Defensora de la Libertad Religiosa, Mexico City, to Honorable Mr. Herbert Hoover, Washington DC, November 15, 1929, Palomar y Vizcarra Papers, INAH.

55. Varios católicos, "En defensa de la nacionalidad," Orizaba, Veracruz, July 1926, Palomar y Vizcarra Papers, capitalization in the original.

56. Calixto Maldonado quoted in Haddox, *Vasconcelos of Mexico*, 8.

57. Krauze, *Mexico, Biography of Power*, 423. Krauze cites a decline of 38 percent in agricultural production between 1926 and 1929.

58. The PNR became the Partido Revolucionario Institucional (PRI), the party that ruled Mexico from 1929 until 2000, when Vicente Fox, a Catholic, was elected president. Many have argued that this was Mexico's first legitimate election.

59. See López Ortega, "Inexactitud de lo afirmado por Jean Meyer."

## 6. Preaching *Mestizaje*

1. "Mexican Strays in California," *Eugenical News*, June 1926, 88.

2. Larson, "Biology," 184. On Mexican immigrants, see Stern, *Eugenic Nation*.

3. Among the titles of the era are *The Super Race*; a 1922 pamphlet *Human Thoroughbreds* (reported on in *Eugenical News*, March 1922, 63); and *The Rising Tide of Color against White Supremacy*.

4. Nearing, *The Super Race*, 31.

5. Cooper and Ryan were both members of the AES Committee on Cooperation with Clergy, which sponsored sermon contests and other projects to help leaders across denominations reach their flocks. A 1931 AES publication, *Organized Eugenics*, which promoted sterilization and birth control, led both priests to leave the AES. See Rosen, *Preaching Eugenics*.

6. Leo Francis Lamb, "The Catholic Church and Eugenics," 1926, John A. Ryan Papers, CUA, in Rosen, *Preaching Eugenics*, 145. Cooper and Kelley were both candidates for the rectorship of Catholic University in 1928, but they do not appear to have corresponded. For more on Cooper's work, see McKeown, "From Pascendi to Primitive Man"; and Brown and McKeown, *The Poor Belong to Us*. On Ryan and sterilization, see S. M. Leon, "'A Human Being." Also see chapter 5 of Rosen, *Preaching Eugenics*.

7. Kelley produced the book with the "documentation and notes" of Eber Cole Byam. Byam spent a great deal of time in Mexico reporting to Kelley regularly on the continued anti-Catholic sentiment of the government and other bodies.

8. This title plays on Christine Rosen's *Preaching Eugenics*.

9. Benn Michaels, *Our America*, 32.

10. Nearing, *The Super Race*, 75.

11. Cogdell, *Eugenic Design*, 4.

12. See *Eugenical News*, January 1924.

13. Lugo, "Border Inspections."

14. Stern, *Eugenic Nation*, 22.

15. The Extension Society protested the National Origins Act for its potential effect on Spanish priests in Puerto Rico. Francis Kelley, "Four but Especially Two; Two but Especially One," *Extension Magazine*, May 1924, 6. The NCWC resisted the Nation Origins Act shortly before the quotas were to go into effect. See William Montavon, "Shall the National Origins Law Be Enforced?" *N.C.W.C. Bulletin*, May 1929, 1–4.

16. "Citizenship of Foreign-Born White Populations," *Eugenical News*, May 1922, 63.

17. "Citizenship of Foreign-Born White Population," 63.

18. *Eugenical News*, May 1922, 63.

19. "Inability to Speak English," *Eugenical News*, August 1922, 94.

20. Thomas R. Garth, "An Investigation of the Intelligence of Mexican and Full and Mixed Blood Indian Children," *Eugenical News*, September 1922, 105.

21. Stern, *Eugenic Nation*, 21.

22. See David Gutierrez, *Walls and Mirrors: Mexican Americans, Mexican Immigrants and the Politics of Ethnicity*, (Berkeley: University of California Press, 1995), 55.

23. Buck v. Bell, U.S. 200, 1927.

24. "Memorandum on Immigration Quotas," *Eugenical News*, March 1927, 27.

25. Kelley and Ryan corresponded regarding Mexico and assorted Extension Society projects, but they do not appear to have engaged on Ryan's eugenic activities or Kelley's version of Mexican history.

26. Flick, *Eugenics*, 27.

27. Edmond Taylor, "Pope Flays Sex Codes of Today as Deadly Sins: Bans Birth Control and Divorce," *Chicago Daily Tribune*, January 9, 1931, 1.

28. Pius XI, *Casti Connubii*, section 96.

29. Pius XI, *Casti Connubii*, section 69.

30. Benito Juárez, speaking of the execution of Maximilian in 1867. There is rich irony in this quote. Juárez was a Zapotec Indian from Oaxaca. This statement demonstrates the power of the myth that Aztecs are *the* ancestors of Mexican people and culture. Juárez quoted in Paul Vanderwood, "Betterment for Whom? The Reform Period: 1855–75," in M. C. Meyer and Beezley, *The Oxford History of Mexico*, 391.

31. Lomnitz, *Deep Mexico, Silent Mexico*, 87.

32. Pope Leo XIII, *Rerum Novarum*, quoted in Blancarte, *Historia de la Iglesia Católica en México*, 44. On papal criticism of capitalism, see Budde, *The Two Churches*; and Novak, *The Catholic Ethic*.

33. For more on the PLM, see Albro, *To Die on Your Feet*, 19; and Albro, *Always a Rebel*.

34. Elizabeth McKillen also writes about the PLM in "Ethnicity, Class, and Wilsonian Internationalism Reconsidered: The Mexican-American and Irish-American Left and U.S. Foreign Relations, 1914–1922." Her subtitle is misleading, though. The Flores Magón brothers' focus never turned away from Mexico, even when they worked with Mexican migrants in the United States. Calling them "Mexican-American" mischaracterizes their activity.

35. Lomnitz-Adler, *Exits from the Labyrinth*, 2. This is Lomnitz-Adler's summation of Manuel Gamio's *indigenismo*.

36. Mendieta, "Modernity's Religion," 123.

37. *México imaginario* literally translates as "imaginary Mexico"; *México profundo* literally translates as "profound Mexico." The spirit of these terms is difficult to translate. *México imaginario* refers to that Mexico which strives to imitate the West, while *México profundo* is an attempt to embrace indigenous cultures, histories, and structures in place of the Western-oriented ones that dominate contemporary Mexico. I use the Spanish terms as a better description of the phenomenon Bonfil Batalla describes and to avoid confusion between Anderson's *Imagined Communities* and the idea of "Imagined Mexico," which I will use to describe nationalist visions of a future Mexico. Translator Philip A. Dennis also has a curious translation of the subtitle of *México profundo*. The literal translation is "A Civilization

Denied," but Dennis chooses "Reclaiming a Civilization," which casts a very different light on *México profundo*. Lomnitz translates *México profundo* as "deep Mexico," which underestimates the powerful phenomenon Bonfil Batalla is trying to capture. Bonfil Batalla, *Mexico Profundo: Una civilización negada*; Bonfil Batalla, *México Profundo: Reclaiming a Civilization*; Lomnitz, *Deep Mexico, Silent Mexico*.

38. Lomnitz, *Deep Mexico, Silent Mexico*, xxi.

39. Balderrama and Rodríguez, *Decade of Betrayal*, 203. Also see Gamio, *Mexican Immigration to the United States*.

40. Quoted in Lomnitz-Adler, *Exits from the Labyrinth*, 2.

41. For other analyses of Mexican Revolutionary ideologies, see Lomnitz-Adler, *Exits from the Labyrinth*; Lomnitz, *Deep Mexico, Silent Mexico*; Fuentes, *A New Time for Mexico*; Britton, *Revolution and Ideology*; and Knight, "Racism, Revolution, and *Indigenismo*: Mexico, 1910–1940." See also Gamio, *Forjando patria*; Vasconcelos and Gamio, *Aspects of Mexican Civilization*; and Bonfil Batalla, *México Profundo*.

42. The prominence and length of Gamio's career, his activity in both the United States and Mexico, and his involvement in government projects have made him a frequent subject for study. See, for examples, Walsh, "Eugenic Acculturation."

43. Gamio, *Forjando patria*, 10–11. Gamio is trying to define citizenry in this text. His use of "forging" is meant quite literally. His metaphors for Mexican race, culture, and society portray bronze meeting iron to create a new amalgamation.

44. B. Anderson, *Imagined Communties*. See also Noble, *Death of a Nation*, chapter 7.

45. Gamio, *Forjando patria*, 211–12.

46. Chatterjee, *The Nation and Its Fragments*. While Chatterjee is analyzing postcolonial India, his framework has relevance for revolutionary Mexico. Many of the structures he describes as part of the colonial picture in India are similar to those of Mexico during the Porfiriato. In reference to independence and nationalism in India, he discusses the material and spiritual elements of colonial societies. "The material is the domain of the 'outside,' of the economy and of statecraft, of science and technology; a domain where the West has proved its superiority and the East has succumbed." In contrast, the spiritual is "an 'inner' domain bearing the 'essential' marks of cultural identity." Chatterjee identifies this dichotomy as the foundation of Asian and African anticolonial nationalisms.

47. Gamio, "Indian Basis of Mexican Civilization," 109–10. This is the text of a lecture Gamio presented at the University of Chicago in 1926. José Vasconcelos was the other lecturer. Their two lectures make up *Aspects of Mexican Civilization*.

48. Paraphrasing Noble, in reference to literary critic Paul Jay. Noble, *Death of a Nation*, 231.

49. Gamio, "Indian Basis of Mexican Civilization," 121–22.

50. See Hart, *Revolutionary Mexico*, chapter 5.

51. Chatterjee's pressing question is "Whose imagined community?" He sees Benedict Anderson's framework as limiting Asian and African movements to imitating Western notions of nationalism—perhaps the same trap into which Gamio fell. "History, it would seem, has decreed that we in the postcolonial world shall be perpetual consumers of modernity. Europe and the Americas, the only true subjects of history, have thought out on our behalf the only script of colonial enlightenment and exploitation, but also that of our anticolonial resistance and postcolonial misery. Even our imaginations must remain forever colonized." Chatterjee, *The Nation and Its Fragments*, 8.

52. On Tepoztlán, see Redfield, *Tepoztlán*; and Lewis, *Tepoztlán*. On collaboration between U.S. and Mexican anthropologists, see Delpar, *The Enormous Vogue*, chapter 3.

53. Gamio, *Forjando patria*, 37. See also Tenorio-Trillo, "Stereophonic Scientific Modernisms."

54. Gamio, "Indian Basis of Mexican Civilization," 126.

55. On colonization programs, see and Balderrama and Rodríguez, *Decade of Betrayal*.

56. Gamio, *Forjando patria*, 324, emphases in original.

57. Gamio, *Forjando patria*, 5.

58. Gamio, *Forjando patria*, 4.

59. Gamio, "Indian Basis of Mexican Civilization," 111.

60. Gamio, *Forjando patria*, 162–63.

61. Gamio, *Forjando patria*, 162.

62. Gamio, *Forjando patria*, 163.

63. In Mexico, Catholicism has served a role similar to caste in India. Chatterjee's description of the debate regarding caste seems helpful here. On one hand, the nationalist left saw caste as a result of precapitalist social formations that, if suppressed, would also eliminate caste. On the other hand, caste was seen as a defining feature of Indian society. This group saw the caste system as the route India took to achieve social order, a requirement for any harmonious society. In both of these cases, however, modernization was seen as central to India's future nationalism. "Both, however, accept the premise of modernity, the former espousing it to condemn caste as an oppressive and antiquated institution inconsistent with a modern society, the latter asserting caste in its ideal form is not oppressive and not inconsistent with the aspirations of individuality within the harmony of a unified social order." The same could be said of Catholicism in Mexico. Chatterjee, *The Nation and Its Fragments*, 174–75.

64. See Quirk, *The Mexican Revolution*, chapter 2.

65. "Guía teórico-práctica del Partido Católico Nacional," *Restauración Social*, December 15, 1911.

66. *La Nación*, September 16, 1912.

67. "Sección Editorial: Los liberales son los conservativos," *La Nación*, September 21, 1912.

68. "A los Católicos Mejicanos," *La Nación*, March 23, 1913.

69. The challenges to certification were reported in *La Nación*. Robert Quirk reported that thirty members were elected. Quirk, *The Mexican Revolution*, 32.

70. *La Nación*, April 16, 1913.

71. See Quirk, *The Mexican Revolution*, chapter 2.

72. "Convención PCN," *La Nación*, September 25, 1913.

73. *La Nación*, September 30, 1913.

74. "Sección Editorial: El Remedio de Nuestros Males," *La Nación*, January 25, 1911.

75. "El Remedio de Nuestros Males."

76. *La Nación*, September 18, 1912.

77. "Sección Editorial: El P. Católico y Sus Obras," *La Nación*, January 3, 1913. "Editorial Section: The Catholic Party and Its Work." *Verdadero fantasma* means "true phantasm."

78. Baldwin, *Protestants and the Mexican Revolution*.

79. Lomnitz, *Deep Mexico, Silent Mexico*, 31.

80. Saldaña-Portillo, "Reading a Silence."

81. "Effective suffrage, no reelection" dates to the mid-nineteenth century. "Land and liberty" was coined by the followers of Emiliano Zapata. "Justice and charity" was the Catholic slogan of the 1910s. *Indigenismo* is what the notions expressed in *Forjando patria* came to be called. Today, *indigenismo* encompasses a broad range of ideas that reflect on Mexico's and/or Latin America's indigenous past, though not all use this past in the same way. For a fine history of *indigenismo*, particularly the work of Gamio's Instituto Indigenista Interamericano, see the "Review of Developments Pertaining to the Promotion and Protection of Human Rights and Fundamental Freedoms of Indigenous Populations, including Economic and Social Relations between Indigenous Peoples and States," issued by the Commission on Human Rights, United Nations, May 12, 1992.

82. See Vasconcelos, *La raza cósmica*. This essay was originally published in 1925.

83. Vasconcelos, *La raza cósmica*, 26–27 (English), 66–67 (Spanish). Vasconcelos uses "el cruce de sangre," which Jaén translates as "interbreeding." This is a fairly crude interpretation. I would translate it as "mixing of blood."

84. Vasconcelos, "Prologue to the 1948 Edition," *La raza cósmica*, 5.

85. On white superiority, see Vasconcelos, *La raza cósmica*, 25.

86. Vasconcelos, *La raza cósmica*, 11.

87. Vasconcelos again expressed the very spiritual nature of his views. While he did have significant insights into racial issues in the United States, his comments on other races and cultures were often troubling, such as his belief that the Chinese "under the saintly guidance of Confucian morality multiply like mice." Vasconcelos, *La raza cósmica*, 18–19.

88. Vasconcelos, *La raza cósmica* 20, 25. On white superiority, see Vasconcelos, 25.

89. Flandrau, *Viva Mexico*, 53. This travel narrative was written by a U.S. citizen traveling in Mexico in the 1940s.

90. Francis Clement Kelley, "Where the Gates of Hell Are Open," *Extension Magazine*, November 1914, 4.

91. See Sánchez, *Telling Identities*, for discussion of Bancroft's deeds and misdeeds where the Californio *testimonios* are concerned. As Holly Beachley Brear shows, the history of U.S.-Mexican contact is particularly contested in Texas. Brear documents the ongoing battle for control of the Alamo as a cultural and historic symbol. Beachley Brear, *Inherit the Alamo*.

92. "Isolated frontier," of course, was a bit inaccurate. Bolton, "The Epic of Greater America," in *Wider Horizons*, 31.

93. Bolton to Roscoe Hill, August 6, 1919, quoted in Magnaghi, *Herbert E. Bolton*, 55. Also see Bannon, *Bolton and the Spanish Borderlands*.

94. This quote is from a 1915 proposal to Samuel Gompers, president of the American Federation of Labor (AFL), from John Murray, socialist journalist, and Santiago Iglesias, AFL organizer in Puerto Rico. Murray and Iglesias envisioned an organization to counteract the Pan-American Financial Congress, since it had no labor representation. Levenstein, *Labor Organizations*, 24.

95. See Kelley, *Blood-Drenched Altars*, chapter 4. The United States, on the other hand, brutalized "its" Indians. Interestingly enough, in these early stages the United States is villain to Spain's hero. Presumably, the Protestant influence in the United States makes its motives suspect at this time.

96. Kelley, *Blood-Drenched Altars*, 355.

97. Ann Stoler explores racial mixing in the context of the Dutch presence in Java. "In a context in which 'mixed-blood' children of European fathers and Asian mothers occupied a thick corridor between colonizer and colonized, race could never be a matter of physiology alone. Competency in Dutch customs, a sense of 'belonging' in a Dutch cultural milieu, a 'distance' and disaffiliation with things Javanese . . . made up the ethnography of race." Stoler, "Racial Histories," 197.

98. Fields, "Ideology and Race in American History," 149.

99. Young, *Colonial Desire*, 19.

100. John Lind, "The Mexican People," presented at the Chicago Industrial Club, December 5 and 12, 1914, and printed in *The Bellman*, December 1914, 16.

101. Kelley, *Blood-Drenched Altars*, 149, emphasis in original.

102. Kelley, *Blood-Drenched Altars*, 280–281.

103. Kelley, *Blood-Drenched Altars*, 281.

104. Kelley, *Blood-Drenched Altars*, 286. Kelley, a generally outspoken historian, provides particularly pointed commentary where protestants are concerned. See also Kelley, *The Story of Extension*, 1922.

105. Kelley, *The Story of Extension*, 180. There also was a 1919 visit to Mexico by a Monsignor Burke, a British priest based in New York. Burke was called into service while Kelley was in Rome. His trip was financed by the Archdiocese of Chicago. There seems to have been some conflict within the church regarding the results of Burke's visit, including reports to President Wilson. Emmanuel Ledvina, Chicago, to Archbishop George William Mundelein, Chicago, March 21, 1919, and A. E. Burke to President Wilson, March 4, 1919, Madaj Collection, ACARC.

106. Kelley, *The Story of Extension*, 182.

107. Arturo M. Elías, New York, to general public, United States, August 13, 1926, Madaj Collection, ACARC, 2–3.

108. Kelley, *The Bishop Jots It Down*, 183.

109. Fabian here writes of Iberian missions to convert and civilize indigenous populations, but the sentiment seems the same. Fabian, *Time and the Other*, 26.

110. Kelley, *The Story of Extension*, 180. Kelley also refers to one of the San Antonio priests as "the little man from Texas."

111. Kelley, *The Story of Extension*, 183.

112. Kelley, *The Bishop Jots It Down*, 198.

113. Fabian, *Time and the Other*, 143–44.

### Conclusion

1. Gaffey, *Francis Clement Kelley*, 2:97.

2. For more on Montezuma Seminary, see R. P. Pablo López de Lara, *Historia del Seminario de Montezuma: Sus precedentes, fundación y consolidación* (Mexico DF: Editorial Jus, 1962); Martínez, "'From the Halls of Montezuma'"; and Medina Ascencio, *Historia del Seminario de Montezuma*.

3. Quinn, *Montezuma*. Gaffey claimed a 1937 publication date, but 1938 seems more likely, as the first class did not graduate until 1938 and the publication reports that thirty-one students had been ordained and had returned to Mexico. See Quinn, *Montezuma*, 23.

4. Cañizares Esguerra, *Puritan Conquistadors*, 31.

5. Solomon Rahaim, "The Problem of the Spanish-Americans in the United States," n.d., Catholic Church Extension Society Papers, LUC, 5. This report was sent to the Archdiocese of Chicago Chancery Office, postmarked March 2, 1943.

6. Francis Kelley to Bishop Joseph Henry Schlarman, April 20, 1943, Catholic Church Extension Society Papers, LUC.

7. "Minutes, Montezuma, New Mexico," March 9, 1955, Catholic Church Extension Society Papers, LUC. A Jesuit, López de Lara was appointed rector of Montezuma Seminary by the Mexican hierarchy.

8. "Minutes, Montezuma, New Mexico," March 9, 1955.

# Bibliography

### Archives

Amherst College Archives and Special Collections, Amherst, Massachusetts
Archdiocese of Chicago Joseph Cardinal Bernardin Archives and Records Center, Chicago, Illinois
Archdiocese of Los Angeles Historical Apostolate, Mission Hills, California
Archdiocese of Oklahoma City, Oklahoma City, Oklahoma
Archivo General de la Nación, Mexico City
Catholic University of America, Washington DC, Archives and Manuscript Collections
Centro de Estudios de Historia de México, Condumex, Mexico City
Instituto Nacional de Anthropolgía e Historia, Mexico City, Subdirección de Documentación
Knights of Columbus Supreme Council Archives, New Haven, Connecticut
Loyola University of Chicago, Archives and Special Collections, Chicago, Illinois
Minnesota Historical Society, St. Paul, Minnesota
National Archives and Records Administration, Washington DC
Secretaría de Relaciones Exteriores, Mexico City, Archivo Genaro Estrada
Society for the Divine Word, Chicago Province Archives, Techny, Illinois
Universidad Nacional Autónoma de México, Mexico City

### Published Sources

*XXVIII International Eucharistic Congress.* Chicago: Manz Corporation, 1926.
Abrams, Elliott, ed. *The Influence of Faith: Religious Groups and U.S. Foreign Policy.* Lanham MD: Rowman and Littlefield, 2001.
Acuña, Rodolfo F. *Corridors of Migration: The Odyssey of Mexican Laborers, 1600–1933.* Tucson: University of Arizona Press, 2007.
Adelman, Jeremy, and Stephen Aron. "From Borderlands to Borders: Empires, Nation-States, and the Peoples in Between in North American History." *American Historical Review* 104, no. 3 (June 1999): 814–41.

Aguilar Camín, Héctor, and Lorenzo Meyer. *In the Shadow of the Mexican Revolution: Contemporary Mexican History, 1910–1989*. Trans. Luis Alberto Fierro. Austin: University of Texas Press, 1993.

Aguilar Rivera, José Antonio. *The Shadow of Ulysses: Public Intellectual Exchange across the U.S.-Mexico Border*. Lanham MD: Lexington Books, 2000.

Aguirre Cristiani, María Gabriela. *¿Una Historia Compartida? Revolución Mexicana y Catolicismo Social, 1913–1924*. Mexico City: Universidad Autónoma Metropolitana, 2008.

Albro, Ward S. *Always a Rebel: Ricardo Flores Magón and the Mexican Revolution*. Fort Worth: Texas Christian University Press, 1992.

———. *To Die on Your Feet: The Life, Times and Writings of Práxedis Guerrero*. Fort Worth: Texas Christian University Press, 1996.

Alexander, Charles C. *The Ku Klux Klan in the Southwest*. Lexington: University of Kentucky Press, 1966.

Anderson, Benedict. *Imagined Communities: Reflections on the Origin and Spread of Nationalism*. London: Verso, 1983.

Anderson, Warwick. *Colonial Pathologies: American Tropical Medicine, Race, and Hygiene in the Philippines*. Durham: Duke University Press, 2006.

Andrews, Gregg. *Shoulder to Shoulder? The American Federation of Labor, the United States, and the Mexican Revolution, 1910–1924*. Berkeley: University of California Press, 1991.

Ansell, Martin R. *Oil Baron of the Southwest: Edward L. Doheny and the Development of the Petroleum Industry in California and Mexico*. Columbus: Ohio State University Press, 1998.

Anzaldúa, Gloria. *Borderlands/La Frontera: The New Mestiza*. San Francisco: Spinsters/Aunt Lute, 1987.

Bacevich, Andrew J. "Tragedy Renewed: William Appleman Williams." *World Affairs Journal* (Winter 2009). http://www.worldaffairsjournal.org/article/tragedy-renewed-william-appleman-williams.

Bailey, David C. *¡Viva Cristo Rey! The Cristero Rebellion and the Church-State Conflict in Mexico*. Austin: University of Texas Press, 1974.

Baker, Kelley J. *Gospel According to the Klan: The KKK's Appeal to Protestant America, 1915–1930*. Lawrence: University Press of Kansas, 2011.

Balderrama, Francisco E., and Raymond Rodríguez. *Decade of Betrayal: Mexican Repatriation in the 1930s*. Albuquerque: University of New Mexico Press, 1995.

Baldwin, Deborah J. *Protestants and the Mexican Revolution: Missionaries, Ministers, and Social Change*. Urbana: University of Illinois Press, 1990.

Baldoz, Rick. *The Third Asiatic Invasion: Empire and Migration in Filipino America, 1898–1946*. New York: New York University Press, 2011.

Bannon, John Francis, ed. *Bolton and the Spanish Borderlands.* Norman: University of Oklahoma Press, 1964.

Barg, Paul A. *Missionaries, Chinese, and Diplomats: The American Protestant Missionary Movement in China, 1890–1952.* Princeton: Princeton University Press, 1958.

Barker, Eugene C. *A History of Texas and Texans.* Chicago: American Historical Society, 1916.

Barquín y Ruíz, Andrés, and Miguel Palomar y Vizcarra. "La influencia de los Estados Unidos sobre Mexico en materia religiosa." In *El caso ejemplar Mexicano, Folleto IV.* Mexico City: Editorial "Rex-Mex," 1941.

Beachley Brear, Holly. *Inherit the Alamo: Myth and Ritual at an American Shrine.* Austin: University of Texas Press, 1995.

Beals, Carleton. "The Mexican Church Goes on Strike." *The Nation,* August 8, 1926, 145–47.

———. "The Mexican Church on Trial." *Survey Graphic,* October 1, 1926, 12–15, 47–49.

Becker, Marjorie. *Setting the Virgin on Fire: Lázaro Cárdenas, Michoacán Peasants and the Redemption of the Mexican Revolution.* Berkeley: University of California Press, 1995.

Bell, Sidney. *Righteous Conquest: Woodrow Wilson and the Evolution of New Diplomacy.* Port Washington NY: National University Publications, 1972.

Benbow, Mark. *Leading Them to the Promised Land: Woodrow Wilson, Covenant Theology, and the Mexican Revolution, 1913–1915.* Kent OH: Kent State University Press, 2010.

Bender, Thomas, ed. *Rethinking American History in a Global Age.* Berkeley: University of California Press, 2002.

Benjamin, Thomas. *La Revolución: Mexico's Great Revolution as Memory, Myth, and History.* Austin: University of Texas Press, 2000.

Bennison, Sarah. "Americanizing the West: Protestant and Catholic Missionary Education on the Rosebud Reservation, 1870–1920." *Teachers College Record* 113, no. 3 (March 2011): 431–62.

Benn Michaels, Walter. *Our America: Nativism, Modernism and Pluralism.* Durham: Duke University Press, 1995.

Beveridge, Albert J. *The Meaning of the Times and Other Speeches.* Indianapolis: Bobbs-Merrill, 1908.

Black, Edwin. *War against the Weak: Eugenics and America's Campaign to Create a Master Race.* New York: Four Walls Eight Windows, 2003.

Blancarte, Roberto J., ed. *El pensamiento social de los católicos mexicanos.* Mexico City: Fondo Cultural Económica, 1996.

———. *Historia de la Iglesia Católica en México.* Mexico City: Fondo Cultural Económica, 1992.

Blum, Edward J. *Reforging the White Republic: Race, Religion, and American Nationalism*. Baton Rouge: Louisiana State University Press, 2005.

Bokovoy, Matt. *The San Diego World's Fairs and Southwestern Memory, 1880–1940*. Albuquerque: University of New Mexico Press, 2005.

Bolton, Herbert E. "The Mission as a Frontier Institution in the Spanish-American Colonies." *American Historical Review* 23, no. 1 (1917): 42–61.

———. *The Spanish Borderlands: A Chronicle of Old Florida and the Southwest*. New Haven: Yale University Press, 1929.

———. *Wider Horizons of American History*. Notre Dame: University of Notre Dame Press, 1967.

Bonfil Batalla, Guillermo. *México Profundo: Una civilización negada*. Mexico City: Conaculta, 2001.

———. *México Profundo: Reclaiming a Civilization*. Trans. Philip A. Dennis. Austin: University of Texas Press, 1996.

Boucher, Arline, and John Tehan. *Prince of Democracy: James Cardinal Gibbons*. Garden City NY: Hanover House, 1962.

Bourne, Randolph. "Trans-National America." *Atlantic Monthly*, July 1916, 86–97.

Brack, Gene M. *Mexico Views Manifest Destiny, 1821–1846: An Essay on the Origins of the Mexican War*. Albuquerque: University of New Mexico Press, 1975.

Brands, H. W. *What America Owes the World: The Struggle for the Soul of Foreign Policy*. Cambridge: Cambridge University Press, 1998.

Breslin, Thomas. *China, American Catholicism, and the Missionary*. University Park: Pennsylvania State University Press, 1980.

Britton, John A. *Revolution and Ideology: Images of the Mexican Revolution in the United States*. Lexington: University Press of Kentucky, 1995.

Brown, Dorothy M., and Elizabeth McKeown. *The Poor Belong to Us: Catholic Charities and American Welfare*. Cambridge: Harvard University Press, 1997.

Budde, Michael L. *The Two Churches: Catholicism and Capitalism in the World System*. Durham: Duke University Press, 1992.

Bulnes, Francisco. *The Whole Truth about Mexico: President Wilson's Responsibility*. New York: M. Bulnes, 1916.

Butler, Matthew. *Popular Piety and Political Identity in Mexico's Cristero Rebellion, Michoacán, 1927–1929*. Oxford: British Academy, 2004.

Byam, Eber Cole. "Religious Conditions in Mexico." *Studies: An Irish Quarterly Review* 12, no. 47 (September 1923): 425–42.

Byrkit, James W., ed. *Charles Lummis: Letters from the Southwest: September 20, 1884–March 14, 1885*. Tucson: University of Arizona Press, 1989

Calvert, Peter. *The Mexican Revolution, 1910–1914: The Diplomacy of Anglo-American Conflict*. Cambridge: Cambridge University Press, 1968.

Camp, Roderic Ai. *Crossing Swords: Politics and Religion in Mexico.* New York: Oxford University Press, 1997.

Cañizares Esguerra, Jorge. *How to Write the History of the New World: Histories, Epistemologies, and Identities in the Eighteenth-Century Atlantic World.* Stanford: Stanford University Press, 2001.

———. *Puritan Conquistadors: Iberianizing the Atlantic, 1550–1700.* Stanford: Stanford University Press, 2006.

Capistrán Garza, René. *La Iglesia y la Revolución Mexicana: Prontuario de ideas políticas.* Mexico City: 1964.

Carrera, Magali M. *Imagining Identity in New Spain: Race, Lineage and the Colonial Body in Portraiture and Casta Paintings.* Austin: University of Texas Press, 2003.

Carroll, Michael P. *American Catholics in the Protestant Imagination: Rethinking the Academic Study of Religion.* Baltimore: Johns Hopkins University Press, 2007.

———. *The Penitente Brotherhood: Patriarcy and Hispano-Catholicism in New Mexico.* Baltimore: Johns Hopkins University Press, 2002.

Castañeda, Jorge G. *Perpetuating Power: How Mexican Presidents Were Chosen.* New York: The New Press, 2000.

*The Catholic Encyclopedia.* New York: Encyclopedia Press, 1922.

*The Catholic Encyclopedia and Its Makers.* New York: Encyclopedia Press, 1917.

Chakrabarty, Dipesh. "Postcoloniality and the Artifice of History: Who speaks for 'Indian' Pasts?" *Representations* 37 (Winter 1992): 1–26.

———. *Provincializing Europe: Postcolonial Thought and Historical Difference.* Princeton: Princeton University Press, 2000.

Chamberlain, George Agnew. *Is Mexico Worth Saving.* Indianapolis: Bobbs-Merrill, 1920.

Chatterjee, Partha. *The Nation and Its Fragments: Colonial and Postcolonial Histories.* Princeton: Princeton University Press, 1992.

Cheng, Lucie, and Edna Bonacich, eds. *Labor Immigration under Capitalism: Asian Workers in the United States before World War II.* Berkeley: University of California Press, 1984.

Chesnut, R. Andrew. *Devoted to Death: Santa Muerte, the Skeleton Saint.* Oxford: Oxford University Press, 2012.

Clymer, Kenton J. *Protestant Missionaries in the Philippines, 1898–1916.* Urbana: University of Illinois Press, 1986.

Coerver, Don M., and Linda B. Hall. *Tangled Destinies: Latin America and the United States.* Albuquerque: University of New Mexico Press, 1999.

Cogdell, Christina. *Eugenic Design: Streamlining America in the 1930s.* Philadelphia: University of Pennsylvania Press, 2004.

Costeloe, Michael P. "Prescott's *History of the Conquest* and Calderón de Barca's *Life in Mexico*: Mexican Reaction, 1843–1844." *The Americas* 47, no. 3 (January 1991): 337–48.

Cronon, William, George Miles, and Jay Gitlin, eds. *Under an Open Sky: Rethinking America's Western Past.* New York: Norton, 1992.

Cummings, Kathleen Sprows. *New Women of the Old Faith: Gender And American Catholicism in the Progressive Era.* Chapel Hill: University of North Carolina Press, 2009.

D'Agostino, Peter R. *Rome in America: Transnational Catholic Ideology from the Risorgimento to Fascism.* Chapel Hill: University of North Carolina, 2004.

Deloria, Philip J. *Indians in Unexpected Places.* Lawrence: University of Kansas Press, 2004.

Delpar, Helen. *The Enormous Vogue of Things Mexico: Cultural Relations between the United States and Mexico, 1920–1935.* Tuscaloosa: University of Alabama Press, 1992.

Deverell, William. *Whitewashed Adobe: The Rise of Los Angeles and the Remaking of Its Mexican Past.* Berkeley: University of California Press, 2004.

Díaz-Stevens, Ana María. *Oxcart Catholicism on Fifth Avenue: The Impact of the Puerto Rican Migration upon the Archdiocese of New York.* Notre Dame: University of Notre Dame Press, 1993.

Dolan, Jay P. *The American Catholic Experience: A History from Colonial Times to the Present.* Garden City NY: Doubleday, 1985.

——. *The Immigrant Church: New York's Irish and German Catholics, 1815–1865.* Notre Dame: University of Notre Dame Press, 1975.

Dolan, Jay P., and Gilberto M. Hinojosa, eds. *Mexican Americans and the Catholic Church, 1910–1965.* Notre Dame: University of Notre Dame Press, 1994.

Dries, Angelyn. *The Missionary Movement in American Catholic History.* Maryknoll NY: Orbis Books, 1998.

Dye, Ryan D. "Irish-American Ambivalence toward the Spanish-American War." *New Hibernia Review* 11, no. 3 (Autumn 2007): 98–113.

Eisenhower, John S. D. *Intervention! The United States and the Mexican Revolution, 1913–1917.* New York: Norton, 1993.

Elías, Arturo M. *The Mexican People and the Church.* New York: Arturo M. Elías, n.d.

——. *El pueblo mexicano y La Iglesia.* New York: F. Mayans, 1926.

Elizondo, Virgilio. *The Future Is Mestizo: Life Where Cultures Meet.* Boulder: University Press of Colorado, 2000.

——. *Galilean Journey: The Mexican-American Promise.* Maryknoll NY: Orbis Books, 1990.

————. *Guadalupe: Mother of the New Creation*. Maryknoll NY: Orbis Books, 1999.

Espinosa, Gastón, and Mario T. García, eds. *Mexican American Religions: Spirituality, Activism and Culture*. Durham: Duke University Press, 2008.

*The Eucharistic Congress as Reported in the "Chicago Tribune."* Chicago: Chicago Tribune Company, 1926.

Fabian, Johannes. *Time and the Other: How Anthropology Makes Its Object*. New York: Columbia University Press, 1983.

Fairbank, John K. "Assignment for the '70s." *American Historical Review* 74, no. 3 (February 1969): 861–79.

Fields, Barbara. "Ideology and Race in American History." In *Region, Race and Reconstruction: Essays in Honor of C. Vann Woodward*, ed. J. Morgan Kousser and James M. McPherson, 143–77. New York: Oxford University Press, 1982.

"The Figure of Columbus." *Atlantic Monthly*, March 1892, 409–12.

*The First American Catholic Missionary Congress*. Chicago: J. S. Hyland, 1909.

Fisher, James T. *Communion of Immigrants: A History of Catholics in America*. Oxford: Oxford University Press, 2008.

Flandrau, Charles Macomb. *Viva Mexico!* Mexico City: The Mexico Press, 1950.

Flick, Lawrence F. *Eugenics*. Philadelphia: John Joseph Movey, 1913.

Foreman, John, *The Philippine Islands: A Political, Geographical, Ethnographical, Social and Commercial History of the Philippine Archipelago, Embracing the Whole Period of Spanish Rule with and Account of the Succeeding American Insular Government*. Shanghai: Kelley and Walsh, 1906.

Frahm, Sally. "The Cross and the Compass: Manifest Destiny, Religious Aspects of the Mexican-American War." *Journal of Popular Culture* 35, no. 2 (Fall 2001): 83–99.

Franchot, Jenny. *Roads to Rome: The Antebellum Protestant Encounter with Catholicism*. Berkeley: University of California Press, 1994.

Frank, Patrick. *Posada's Broadsheets: Mexican Popular Imagery, 1890–1910*. Albuquerque: University of New Mexico Press, 1998.

Fuentes, Carlos. *A New Time for Mexico*. Berkeley: University of California Press, 1996.

Fuller, John Douglas Pitts. *The Movement for the Acquisition of All Mexico, 1846–48*. New York: Da Capo Press, 1935.

Fulton, Justin D. *Washington in the Lap of Rome*. Boston: W. Kellaway, 1888.

Gaffey, James P. *Francis Clement Kelley and the American Catholic Dream*. 2 vols. Bensenville IL: Heritage Foundation, 1980.

Gamio, Manuel. *Forjando patria (pro-nacionalismo)*. Mexico City: Librería de Porrúa Hermanos, 1916.

————. *Mexican Immigration to the United States: A Study of Migration and Adjustment*. Chicago: University of Chicago Press, 1930.

García, Mario T. *Católicos: Resistance and Affirmation in Chicano Catholic History*. Austin: University of Texas Press, 2008.

Gibbons, James. *The Faith of Our Fathers: Being a Plain Exposition and Vindication of the Church Founded by Our Lord Jesus Christ*. Baltimore: John Murphy, 1917.

Gómez-Quiñones, Juan. *Porfirio Díaz, los intelectuales, y la Revolución*. Mexico: Ediciones el Caballito, n.d.

Gould, Eliga H. "Entangled Histories, Entangled Worlds: The English-Speaking Atlantic as a Spanish Periphery." *American Historical Review* 112, no. 3 (June 2007): 764–86.

Gould, Lewis L. *The Spanish-American War and President McKinley*. Lawrence: University Press of Kansas, 1980.

Graf, Mercedes. "Band of Angels: Sister Nurses in the Spanish American War." *Prologue* 34, no. 3 (Fall 2002): 196–209.

Greenberg, Amy S. *A Wicked War: Polk, Clay, Lincoln and the 1846 U.S. Invasion of Mexico*. New York: Random House, 2012.

Griffin, Eric. "From Ethos to Ethnos: Hispanizing 'the Spaniard' in the Old World and New." *New Centennial Review* 2, no. 1 (Spring 2002): 69–116.

Gruening, Ernest. *Mexico and Its Heritage*. 1928. New York: Greenwood Press, 1968.

Gruzinski, Serge. *The Mestizo Mind: The Intellectual Dynamics of Colonization and Globalization*. Trans. Deke Dusinberre. New York: Routledge, 2002.

Guarneri, Carl, and David Alvarez, eds. *Religion and Society in the American West: Historical Essays*. Lanham MD: University Press of America, 1987.

Hackett, Charles W. "Mexican Church and State End Three-Year Conflict." *Current History* 30 (August 1929): 918–20.

Haddox, John H. *Vasconcelos of Mexico: Phiflosopher and Prophet*. Austin: University of Texas Press, 1967.

Hall, Linda B. *Álvaro Obregón: Power and Revolution in Mexico, 1911–1920*. College Station: Texas A&M Press, 1981.

———. *Oil, Banks, and Politics: The United States and Postrevolutionary Mexico, 1917–1924*. Austin: University of Texas Press, 1995.

Hanke, Lewis. "A Modest Proposal for a Moratorium on Grand Generalizations: Some Thoughts on the Black Legend." *Hispanics American Historical Review* 50, no. 1 (February 1971): 112–27.

Hart, John Mason. *Empire and Revolution: The Americans in Mexico since the Civil War*. Berkeley: University of California Press, 2002.

———. *Revolutionary Mexico: The Coming and Process of the Mexican Revolution*. Berkeley: University of California Press, 1997.

Hayashi, Brian. *"For the Sake of Our Japanese Brethren": Assimilation, Nationalism and Protestantism among the Japanese of Los Angeles, 1895–1942*. Stanford: Stanford University Press, 1995.

Hayes, Joy Elizabeth. *Radio Nation: Communication, Popular Culture, and Nationalism in Mexico, 1920–1950.* Tucson: University of Arizona Press, 2000.

Hernández Jauregui, Manuel. *Las leyes de reforma y las disposiciones legales en materia de culto religioso y disciplina externa.* Mexico City: Talleres Gráficos de la Nación, 1927.

Herr, Robert Woodmansee, in collaboration with Richard Herr. *An American Family in the Mexican Revolution.* Wilmington DE: Scholarly Resources, 1999.

Higham, John. *Strangers in the Land: Patterns of American Nativism, 1860–1925.* New Brunswick: Rutgers University Press, 1994.

Hill, Patricia R. *The World Their Household: The American Woman's Foreign Mission Movement and Cultural Transformation, 1870–1920.* Ann Arbor: University of Michigan Press, 1985.

Hofstadter, Richard. "Manifest Destiny and the Philippines." In *America in Crisis: Fourteen Crucial Episodes in American History,* ed. Daniel Aaron, 109–32. New York: Knopf, 1952.

Hoganson, Kristin L. *Fighting for American Manhood: How Gender Politics Provoked the Spanish-American and Philippine-American Wars.* New Haven: Yale University Press, 1998.

Hondagneu-Sotelo, Pierrette. *Gendered Transitions: Mexican Experiences of Immigration.* Berkeley: University of California Press, 1994.

Horsman, Reginald. *Race and Manifest Destiny: The Origins of American Racial Anglo-Saxonism.* Cambridge: Harvard University Press, 1981.

Hurley, Vic. *Jungle Patrol: The Story of the Philippine Constabulary, 1901–1936.* Salem OR: Cerberus Corp, 2011.

Hutchison, William R. *Errand to the World: American Protestant Thought and Foreign Missions.* Chicago: University of Chicago Press, 1987.

Isasi-Díaz, Ada María, and Fernando F. Segovia, eds. *Hispanic/Latino Theology: Challenge and Promise.* Minneapolis: Fortress Press, 1996.

Isasi-Díaz, Ada María, and Yolanda Tarango. *Hispanic Women: Prophetic Voice in the Church.* San Francisco: Harper and Row, 1998.

Jacobs, Michael. "Co-Opting Christian Chorales: Songs of the Ku Klux Klan." *American Music* 28, no. 3 (Fall 2010): 368–77.

Jacobson, Matthew Frye. *Barbarian Virtues: The United States Encounters Foreign Peoples at Home and Abroad, 1876–1917.* New York: Hill and Wang, 2000.

———. *Special Sorrows: The Diasporic Imagination of Irish, Polish and Jewish Immigrations in the United States.* Cambridge: Harvard University Press, 1995.

Joseph, Gilbert M., Catherine C. LeGrand, and Ricardo D. Salvatore, eds. *Close Encounters with Empire: Writing the Cultural History of U.S.-Latin American Relations.* Durham: Duke University Press, 1998.

Joseph, Gilbert M., and Daniel Nugent, eds. *Everyday Forms of State Formation: Revolution and the Negotiation of Rule in Modern Mexico*. Durham: Duke University Press, 1994.

Kagan, Richard, L. "Prescott's Paradigm: American Historical Scholarship and the Decline of Spain." *American Historical Review* 101, no. 2 (April 1996): 425–35.

———. *Spain in America: The Origins of Hispanism in the United States*. Urbana: University of Illinois Press, 2002.

———. "The Spanish Craze in the United States: Cultural Entitlement and the Appropriation of Spain's Cultural Patrimony, ca. 1890-ca. 1930." *Revista Complutense de Historia de América* 36 (2010): 37–58.

Kaplan, Amy, and Donald E. Pease, eds. *Cultures of United States Imperialism*. Durham: Duke University Press, 1993.

Kaplan, Edward S. *U.S. Imperialism in Latin America: Bryan's Challenges and Contributions, 1900–1920*. Westport CT: Greenwood Press, 1998.

Katz, Friedrich. *The Life and Times of Pancho Villa*. Stanford: Stanford University Press, 1998.

Kauffman, Christopher J. *Faith and Fraternalism: The History of The Knights of Columbus, 1992–1982*. New York: Harper and Row, 1982.

———. *Patriotism and Fraternalism in the Knights of Columbus: A History of the Fourth Degree*. New York: Crossroad, 2001.

Keen, Benjamin. "The Black Legend Revisited: Assumptions and Realities." *Hispanic American Historical Review* 49, no. 4 (November 1969): 703–9.

———. "The White Legend Revisited: A Reply to Professor Hanke's 'Modest Proposal.'" *Hispanic American Historical Review* 51, no. 2 (May 1971): 336–55.

Kelley, Francis Clement. *The Bishop Jots It Down: An Autobiographical Strain on Memories*. New York: Harper and Brothers, 1930.

———. *Blood-Drenched Altars: Mexican Study and Comment*. Milwaukee: Bruce, 1935.

———. *The Book of Red and Yellow: Being a Story of Blood and a Yellow Streak*. Chicago: Catholic Church Extension Society of the United States of America, 1915.

———. "The Church Side of the Conflict." *Survey Graphic* 57, no. 1 (1 October 1926): 16–19.

———. *The Story of Extension*. Chicago: Extension Press, 1922.

Kidd, Colin. *The Forging of Races: Race and Scripture in the Protestant Atlantic World, 1600–2000*. Cambridge: Cambridge University Press, 2006.

Knight, Alan. "Racism, Revolution, and Indigenismo: Mexico, 1910–1940." In *The Idea of Race in Latin America, 1870–1940*, ed. Richard Graham, 71–113. Austin: University of Texas Press, 1990.

Kramer, Paul. *The Blood of Government: Race, Empire, the United States, and the Philippines.* Chapel Hill: University of North Carolina Press, 2006.

———. "Empires, Exceptions, and Anglo-Saxons: Race and Rule between the British and United States Empires, 1880–1910." *Journal of American History* 88, no. 4 (March 2002): 1315–53.

———. "Making Concessions: Race and Empire Revisited at the Philippine Exposition, St. Louis, 1901–1905." *Radical History Review* 73 (1999): 74–114.

———. "Power and Connection: Imperial Histories of the United States in the World." Review essay. *American Historical Review* 16, no. 4 (December 2011): 1348–91.

———. "Race, Empire, and Transnational History." In *Colonial Crucible: Empire in the Making of the Modern American State*, ed. Alfred W. McCoy and Francisco A. Scarano, 199–209. Madison: University of Wisconsin Press, 2009.

———. "Race-Making and Colonial Violence in the U.S. Empire: The Philippine-American War as Race War." *Diplomatic History* 30, no. 2 (April 2006): 169–210.

Krauze, Enrique. *Mexico, Biography of Power: A History of Modern Mexico, 1810–1996.* Trans. Hank Heifetz. New York: HarperCollins, 1995.

Kropp, Phoebe S. *California Vieja: Culture and Memory in a Modern American Place.* Berkeley: University of California Press, 2006.

Laracy, Hugh. "Maine, Massachusetts, and the Marists: American Catholic Missionaries in the South Pacific." *Catholic Historical Review* 85, no. 4 (October 1999): 566–90.

Larson, Edward J. "Biology and the Emergence of the Anglo-American Eugenics Movement." In *Biology and Ideology from Descartes to Dawkins*, ed. Denis R. Alexander and Ronald L. Numbers, 165–91. Chicago: University of Chicago Press, 2010.

*Latino Studies Journal.* Special issue: "Latinos and the Sacred." 5, no. 3 (September 1994).

Latané, John Holladay. "The Effects of the Panama Canal on Our Relations with Latin America." *Annals of the American Academy of Political and Social Science* 54 (July 1914): 84–91.

Lavie, Smadar, and Ted Swedenburg, eds. *Displacement, Diaspora, and Geographies of Identity.* Durham: Duke University Press, 1996.

Lea, Henry Charles. "The Decadence of Spain." *Atlantic Monthly*, July 1898, 36–46.

LeFeber, Walter. *The New Empire: An Interpretation of American Expansion, 1860–1898.* 35th anniversary ed. Ithaca: Cornell University Press, 1998.

Leo XIII. *Rerum Novarum.* May 15, 1891.

———. *Testem Benevolentiae Nostrae.* January 22, 1899.

Leon, Luis. *La Llorona's Children: Religion, Life and Death in the U.S.-Mexican Borderlands.* Berkeley: University of California Press, 2004.

Leon, Sharon Mara. "Beyond Birth Control: Catholic Responses to the Eugenics Movement in the United States, 1900–1950." PhD diss., University of Minnesota, 2004.

———. "'A Human Being, and Not a Mere Social Factor': Catholic Strategies for Dealing with Sterilization Statutes in the 1920s." *Church History* 73, no. 2 (June 2004): 383–411.

LeRoy, James A. "Our Spanish Inheritance in the Philippines." *Atlantic Monthly*, March 1905, 340–46.

———. *Philippine Life in Town and Country.* New York: Putnam, 1907.

———. "Race Prejudice in the Philippines." *Atlantic Monthly*, July 1902, 110–12.

Levenstein, Harvey A. *Labor Organizations in the United States and Mexico: A History of Their Relations.* Westport CT: Greenwood, 1971.

Levin, Gordon, Jr. *Woodrow Wilson and World Politics: America's Response to War and Revolution.* New York: Oxford University Press, 1968.

Lewis, Oscar. *Tepoztlán: Village in Mexico.* New York: Holt, Rinehart and Winston, 1960.

Limerick, Patricia Nelson. "Going West and Ending Up Global." *Western Historical Quarterly* 32, no. 1 (Spring 2001): 4–23.

———. *The Legacy of Conquest: The Unbroken Past of the American West.* New York: Norton, 1987.

Limón, José E. *American Encounters: Greater Mexico, the United States, and the Erotics of Culture.* Boston: Beacon Press, 1998.

Link, Arthur. *The Higher Realism of Woodrow Wilson.* Nashville: Vanderbilt University Press, 1971.

———. *Wilson.* 5 vols. Princeton: Princeton University Press, 1947–65.

———. *Woodrow Wilson: A Brief Biography.* Cleveland: World Publishing, 1963.

———. *Woodrow Wilson and the Progressive Era, 1910–1917.* New York: Harper and Row, 1954.

———. "Woodrow Wilson: Presbyterian in Government." In *Calvinism and the Political Order*, ed. George L. Hunt and John T. McNeill, 157–74. Philadelphia: Westminster, 1965.

Lomnitz, Claudio. *Deep Mexico, Silent Mexico: An Anthropology of Nationalism.* Minneapolis: University of Minnesota Press, 2001.

Lomnitz-Adler, Claudio. *Exits from the Labyrinth: Culture and Ideology in the Mexican National Space.* Berkeley: University of California Press, 1992.

López Ortega, José Antonio. "Inexactitud de lo afirmado por Jean Meyer en su obra 'La Cristiada' de que el Santo Padre Pio XI no sufrió engaño en los arreglos de la cuestión religiosa en México, celebrados el 21 de junio de 1929." Mexico City: self-published, 1976.

Lowe, Lisa, and David Lloyd, eds. *The Politics of Culture in the Shadow of Capital*. Durham: Duke University Press, 1997.

Lucassen, Jan, and Leo Lucassen, eds. *Migration, Migration History, History: Old Paradigms and New Perspectives*. Bern: Peter Lang, 1997.

Luce, Henry R. "The American Century." *Diplomatic History* 23, no. 2 (Spring 1999): 159–71.

Lugo, Alejandro. *Fragmented Lives, Assembled Parts: Culture, Capitalism and Conquest at the U.S.-Mexico Border*. Austin: University of Texas Press, 2008.

———. "Theorizing Border Inspections." *Cultural Dynamics* 12, no. 3 (2000): 353–73.

Lummis, Charles F. *Some Strange Corners of Our Country: The Wonderland of the Southwest*. New York: Century Co., 1903.

———. *A Tramp across the Continent*. New York: Scribner, 1913.

Lummis Fiske, Turbesé, and Keith Lummis. *Charles F. Lummis: The Man and His West*. Norman: University of Oklahoma Press, 1975.

MacKenzie, Kenneth M. *The Robe and the Sword: The Methodist Church and the Rise of American Imperialism*. Washington DC: Public Affairs Press, 1961.

Magee, Malcolm D. *What the World Should Be: Woodrow Wilson and the Crafting of Faith-Based Foreign Policy*. Waco: Baylor University Press, 2008.

Magnaghi, Russel M. *Herbert E. Bolton and the Historiography of the Americas*. Westport CT: Greenwood Press, 1998.

Malone, Michael P., ed. *Historians and the American West*. Lincoln: University of Nebraska Press, 1983.

Maloney, Dierdre M. *American Catholic Lay Groups and Transatlantic Social Reform in the Progressive Era*. Chapel Hill: University of North Carolina Press, 2002.

Marantes, Luis A. *José Vasconcelos and the Writing of the Mexican Revolution*. New York: Twayne, 2000.

Markoe, Ralston J. *Impressions of a Layman*. St. Paul MN: Willwersheid and Raith, 1909.

Marlett, Jeffrey D. *Saving the Heartland: Catholic Missionaries in Rural America, 1920–1960*. DeKalb: Northern Illinois University Press, 2002.

Martínez, Anne M. "'From the Halls of Montezuma': Seminary in Exile of Pan-American Project?" *U.S. Catholic Historian* 20, no. 3 (Fall 2002): 35–51.

Marty, Martin E. *Modern American Religion*. Vol. 1, *The Irony of It All, 1893–1919*. Chicago: University of Chicago Press, 1986.

———. *Modern American Religion*. Vol. 2, *The Noise of Conflict, 1919–1941*. Chicago: University of Chicago Press, 1991.

———. *Righteous Empire: The Protestant Experience in America*. New York: Dial, 1970.

Matovina, Timothy, ed. *Beyond Borders: Writings of Virgilio Elizondo and Friends*. Maryknoll NY: Orbis Books, 2000.

———. *Guadalupe and Her Faithful: Latino Catholics in San Antonio, from Colonial Origins to the Present*. Baltimore: Johns Hopkins University Press, 2005.

———. *Latino Catholicism: Transformation in America's Largest Church*. Princeton: Princeton University Press, 2012.

———. "Remapping American Catholicism." *U.S. Catholic Historian* 28, no. 4 (Fall 2010): 31–72.

Matovina, Timothy, and Gerald E. Poyo. *¡Presente! U.S. Latino Catholics from Colonial Origins to the Present*. Maryknoll NY: Orbis Books, 2000.

Matovina, Timothy, and Gary Riebe-Estrella. *Horizons of the Sacred: Mexican Traditions in U.S. Catholicism*. Ithaca: Cornell University Press, 2002.

McBrien. Richard P., gen. ed. *The HarperCollins Encyclopedia of Catholicism*. San Francisco: Harper San Francisco, 1987.

McCartney, Laton. *The Teapot Dome Scandal: How Big Oil Bought the Harding White House and Tried to Steal the Country*. New York: Random House, 2008.

McCoy, Alfred W. *Policing America's Empire: The United States, the Philippines and the Rise of the Surveillance State*. Madison: University of Wisconsin Press, 2009.

McCoy, Alfred W., and Francisco A. Scarano, eds. *Colonial Crucible: Empire in the Making of the Modern American States*. Madison: University of Wisconsin Press, 2009.

McEniry, Blanche Marie. "American Catholics in the War with Mexico." PhD diss., Catholic University of America, 1937.

McGreevy, John T. *Catholicism and American Freedom: A History*. New York: Norton, 2003.

———. *Parish Boundaries: The Catholic Encounter with Race in the Twentieth-Century Urban North*. Chicago: University of Chicago Press, 1996.

McKeown, Elizabeth. "From Pascendi to Primitive Man: The Apologetics and Anthropology of John Montgomery Cooper." *U.S. Catholic Historian* 13, no. 2 (Spring 1995): 1–21.

McKillen, Elizabeth. "Ethnicity, Class, and Wilsonian Internationalism Reconsidered: The Mexican-American and Irish-American Left and U.S. Foreign Relations, 1914–1922." *Diplomatic History* 25, no. 4 (2001): 553–87.

McLean, Robert N. *The Northern Mexican*. New York: Home Missions Council, 1930.

McNally, Michael J. *Catholicism in South Florida, 1868–1968*. Gainesville: University Presses of Florida, 1982.

McWilliams, Carey. *North from Mexico: The Spanish-Speaking People of the United States*. Westport CT: Greenwood Press, 1968.

Medina, Lara. *Las Hermanas: Chicana/Latina Religious-Political Activism in the U.S. Catholic Church*. Philadelphia: Temple University Press, 2004.

Medina Ascencio, Luis. *Historia del Seminario de Montezuma: Sus precedentes, fundación, y consolidación*. Mexico City: Editorial Jus, 1962.

Mendieta, Eduardo. "Modernity's Religion: Habermas and the Linguistification of the Sacred." In *Perspectives on Habermas*, ed. Lewis Edwin Hahn, 123–38. Peru IL: Open Court, 2000.

Merk, Frederick. *Manifest Destiny and Mission in American History: A Reinterpretation*. New York: Vintage Books, 1963.

Meyer, Jean A. *The Cristero Rebellion: The Mexican People between Church and State, 1926–1929*. Cambridge: Cambridge University Press, 2008.

———. *La Cristiada*. Mexico City: Siglo XXI, 2000–2007.

———, ed. *Las naciones frente al conflict religioso en México, 1926–1929*. Mexico City: Tusquets Editores, 2010.

Meyer, Michael C., and William H. Beezley, eds. *The Oxford History of Mexico*. Oxford: Oxford University Press, 2000.

Meyer, Michael C., William L. Sherman, and Susan M. Deeds, eds. *The Course of Mexican History*. 6th ed. New York: Oxford University Press, 1999.

Meyers, William K. *Forge or Progress, Crucible of Revolt: The Origins of the Mexican Revolution in La Comarca Lagunera, 1880–1911*. Albuquerque: University of New Mexico Press, 1994.

Michaelsen, Robert S. "Red Man's Religion/White Man's Religious History." *Journal of the American Academy of Religion* 51, no. 4 (December 1983): 667–84.

Michaelson, Scott, and David E. Johnson, eds. *Border Theory: The Limits of Cultural Politics*. Minneapolis: University of Minnesota Press, 1997.

Miller, Kristin Cheasty. "Un Iglesia Más Mexicana: Catholics, Schismatics, and the Mexican Revolution in Texas, 1927–1932." *U.S. Catholic Historian* 26, no. 4 (Fall 2008): 45–70.

Miller, Perry. *Errand into the Wilderness*. Cambridge: Belknap Press, 1956.

Miller, Randall, and Thomas Marzik, eds. *Immigrants and Religion in Urban America*. Philadelphia: Temple University Press, 1977.

Miller, Robert Moats. "A Note on the Relationship between the Protestant Churches and the Revived Ku Klux Klan." *Journal of Southern History* 22, no. 3 (August 1956): 355–68.

Miller, Robert Ryal. *Shamrock and Sword: The Saint Patrick's Battalion in the U.S.-Mexican War*. Norman: University of Oklahoma Press, 1989.

Miller, Stuart Creighton. *Benevolent Assimilation: The American Conquest of the Philippines, 1899–1903*. New Haven:Yale University Press, 1984.

Moloney, Deirdre M. *American Catholic Lay Groups and Transatlantic Social Reform in the Progressive Era*. Chapel Hill: University of North Carolina Press, 2002.

Mundelein, George. *Two Crowded Years: Being Selected Addresses, Pastorals and Lectures Issued During the First Twenty-Four Months of the Episcopate of the Most Reverend George William Mundelein, D.D., as Archbishop of Chicago*. Chicago: Extension Press, 1918.

*N. W. Ayer and Son's American Newspaper Annual and Directory*. Philadelphia: N. W. Ayer and Son, 1910.

Nabhan-Warren, Kristy. *The Virgin of El Barrio: Marian Apparitions, Catholic Evangelizing, and Mexican American Activism*. New York: New York University Press, 2005.

Nations, Gilbert O. *Constitution or Pope? Why Alien Roman Catholics Can Not Be Legally Naturalized*. Cincinnati: Standard Publishing Company, 1915.

——. *Papal Sovereignty: The Government Within Our Government*. Cincinnati: Standard Publishing Company, 1917.

Neal, Lynn S. "Christianizing the Klan: Alma White, Branford Clarke, and the Art of Religious Intolerance." *Church History* 78, no. 2 (June 2009): 350–78.

Nearing, Scott. *The Super Race: An American Problem*. New York: B. W. Huebsch, 1912.

Noble, David W. *Death of a Nation: American Culture and the End of Exceptionalism*. Minneapolis: University of Minnesota Press, 2002.

——. *The End of American History: Democracy, Capitalism, and the Metaphor of Two Worlds in Anglo-American Historical Writing, 1880–1980*. Minneapolis: University of Minnesota Press, 1985.

Nordstrom, Justin. *Danger on the Doorstep: Anti-Catholicism and American Print Culture in the Progressive Era*. Notre Dame: University of Notre Dame Press, 2006.

Norton, William Bernard. *Religion Today! Reprinting a Series of Religious Editorials by Prominent Churchmen, Which Have Appeared in the "Chicago Tribune."* Chicago: Chicago Tribune Company, [1926].

Novak, Michael. *The Catholic Ethic and the Spirit of Capitalism*. New York: The Free Press, 1993.

Nugent, Daniel. *Rural Revolt in Mexico: U.S. Intervention and the Domain of Subaltern Politics*. Durham: Duke University Press, 1998.

Nugent, Walter. *Habits of Empire: A History of American Expansion*. New York: Knopf, 2008.

O'Brien, John A. *The White Harvest: A Symposium on Methods of Convert Making*. New York: Longmans, Green and Co., 1927.

*Official Report of the Second American Catholic Missionary Congress*. Chicago: J. S. Hyland, 1914.

Oktavec, Eileen. *Answered Prayers: Miracles and Milagros along the Border.* Tucson: University of Arizona Press, 1995.

O'Toole, James. *The Faithful: A History of Catholics in America.* Cambridge: Harvard University Press, 2008.

Paredes, Américo. *Folklore and Culture on the Texas-Mexican Border.* Ed. Richard Bauman. Austin: University of Texas Press, 1993.

————. *A Texas-Mexican Cancionero: Folksongs of the Lower Border.* Austin: University of Texas Press, 1976.

————. *With His Pistol in His Hand: A Border Ballad and Its Hero.* Austin: University of Texas Press, 1958.

Parmar, Inderjeet. *Foundations of the American Century: The Ford, Carnegie, and Rockefeller Foundations in the Rise of American Power.* New York: Columbia University Press, 2012.

Pascoe, Peggy. *Relations of Rescue: The Search for Female Moral Authority in the American West, 1874–1939.* New York: Oxford University Press, 1990.

Pike, Frederick B. *Hispanismo, 1898–1936: Spanish Conservatives and Liberals and Their Relations with Spanish America.* Notre Dame: University of Notre Dame Press, 1971.

Pinheiro, John C. "'Extending the Light and Blessings of Our Purer Faith': Anti-Catholic Sentiment among American Soldiers in the U.S.-Mexican War." *Journal of Popular Culture* 35, no. 2 (Fall 2001): 129–52.

Pius XI. *Casti Connubii*, December 31, 1930.

————. *Iniquis Afflictisque*, November 18, 1926.

Plummer, Brenda Gayle. *Rising Wind: Black Americans and U.S. Foreign Affairs, 1935–1960.* Chapel Hill: University of North Carolina Press, 1996.

Pollard, Edward B. *The Rights of the Unborn Race.* Philadelphia: American Baptist Publication Society, 1914.

Powell, Philip Wayne. *Tree of Hate: Propaganda and Prejudices Affecting United States Relations with the Hispanic World.* Albuquerque: University of New Mexico Press, 2008.

Purnell, Jennie. *Popular Movements and State Formation in Revolutionary Mexico: The Agraristas and Cristeros of Michoacán.* Durham: Duke University Press, 1999.

Quinn, Joseph J. *Montezuma: The American Douai.* The Committee of Bishops on the Mexican Seminary, n.d.

Quirk, Robert E. *The Mexican Revolution and the Catholic Church, 1910–1929.* Bloomington: Indiana University Press, 1973.

Rafael, Vicente. *Contracting Colonialism: Translation and Christian Conversion in Tagalog Society under Early Spanish Rule.* Durham: Duke University Press, 2005.

Redfield, Robert. *Tepoztlán, a Mexican Village: A Study of Folk Life*. Chicago: University of Chicago Press, 1930.

Redinger, Matthew A. *American Catholics and the Mexican Reovlution, 1924–1936*. Notre Dame: University of Notre Dame Press, 2005.

———. "'To Arouse and Inform': American Catholic Attempts to Influence United States–Mexican Relations, 1920–1937." PhD diss., University of Washington, 1993.

Reher, Margaret Mary. *Catholic Intellectual Life in America: A Historical Study of Persons and Movements*. New York: Macmillan, 1989.

Rivera, Luis N. *A Violent Evangelism: The Political and Religious Conquest of the Americas*. Louisville: Westminster/John Knox Press, 1992.

Robert, Dana L. "The Influence of American Missionary Women on the World Back Home." *Religion and American Culture* 12, no. 1 (Winter 2002): 59–90.

Roberts, Dorothy E. *Killing the Black Body: Race, Reproduction and the Meaning of Liberty*. New York: Pantheon Books, 1997.

Robinson, William J. *Practical Eugenics: Four Means of Improving the Human Race*. New York: The Critic and Guide Company, 1912.

Rodríguez, Cristóbal. *La Iglesia y La Rebelión Cristera en México, 1926–1929*. Juárez: Editorial La Voz de Juárez, 1960.

Rodriguez, Jeanette. *Our Lady of Guadalupe: Faith and Empowerment among Mexican-American Women*. Austin: University of Texas Press, 1994.

Roosevelt, Theodore. "State of the Union." December 3, 1901. http://www.let.rug .nl/usa/presidents/theodore-roosevelt/state-of-the-union-1901.php.

Rosaldo, Renato. "Imperialist Nostalgia." *Representations*: Special Issue, Memory and Counter-Memory, no. 26 (Spring 1989): 107–22.

Rosen, Christine. *Preaching Eugenics: Religious Leaders and the American Eugenics Movement*. Oxford: Oxford University Press, 2004.

Ruiz, Ramón Eduardo. *From Out of the Shadows: Mexican Women in Twentieth-Century America*. New York: Oxford University Press, 1998.

Rushdie, Salman. *Step across This Line: Collected Nonfiction, 1992–2002*. New York: Modern Library. 2002.

Said, Edward. *Orientalism*. New York: Random House, 1978.

Saldaña-Portillo, María Josefina. "Reading a Silence: The 'Indian' in the Era of Zapatismo." *Nepantla: Views from the South* 3, no. 2 (2002): 287–314.

Saldívar, José David. "Americo Paredes and Decolonization." In *Cultures of United States Imperialism*, ed. Amy Kaplan and Donale E. Pease, 292–311. Durham: Duke University Press, 1993.

———. *Border Matters: Remapping American Cultural Studies*. Berkeley: University of California Press, 1997.

———. *The Dialectics of Our America: Genealogy, Cultural Critique and Literary History*. Durham: Duke University Press, 1991.

Saldívar, Ramon. *The Borderlands of Culture: Américo Paredes and the Transnational Imaginary*. Durham: Duke University Press, 2006.

Sánchez, Rosaura. *Telling Identities: The Californio Testimonios*. Minneapolis: University of Minnesota Press, 1995.

Sánchez-Walsh, Arlene. *Latino Pentecostal Identity: Evangelical Faith, Self and Society*. New York: Columbia University Press, 2003.

Schmidt-Nowara, and John M. Nieto-Phillips, eds. *Interpreting Spanish Colonialism: Empires, Nations and Legends*. Albuquerque: University of New Mexico Press, 2005.

Schoonover, Thomas. *Dollars over Dominion: The Triumph of liberalism in Mexican–United States Relations, 1861–1867*. Baton Rouge: Louisiana State University Press, 1978.

Scott, James Brown, ed. *President Wilson's Foreign Policy: Messages, Addresses, Papers*. New York: Oxford University Press, 1918.

Selden, Steven. "Transforming Better Babies into Fitter Families: Archival Sources and the History of the Eugenics Movement, 1908–30." *Proceedings of the American Philosophical Society* 149, no. 2 (June 2005): 199–225.

Shanabruch, Charles. *Chicago's Catholics: The Evolution of an American Identity*. Notre Dame: University of Notre Dame Press, 1981.

Shea, John G. *History of the Catholic Missions among the Indian Tribes of the United States, 1529–1854*. New York: Edward Dunigan, 1855.

Sheehan, Michael J. *Four Hundred Years of Faith: Seeds of Struggle, Harvest of Faith*. Santa Fe: Archdiocese of Santa Fe, 1998.

Skerrett, Ellen, Edward R. Kantowicz, and Steven M. Avella. *Catholicism, Chicago Style*. Chicago: Loyola University Press, 1993.

Slawson, Douglas J. "The National Catholic Welfare Conference and the Church-State Conflict in Mexico, 1925–1929." *The Americas* 47, no. 1 (July 1990): 55–93.

Solomon, Deborah. "Novel Politics: Questions for Carlos Fuentes." *New York Times Magazine*, April 30, 2006.

Stern, Alexandra Minna. *Eugenic Nation: Faults and Frontiers of Better Breeding in Modern America*. Berkeley: University of California Press, 2005.

———. "Eugenics beyond Borders: Science and Medicalization in Mexico and the U.S. West, 1900–1950." PhD diss., University of Chicago, December 1999.

———. "Making Better Babies: Public Health and Race Betterment in Indiana, 1920–1935." *American Journal of Public Health* 92, no. 5 (May 2002): 742–52.

Stoler, Ann Laura. "Racial Histories and Their Regimes of Truth." *Political Power and Social Theory* 11 (1997): 183–255.

Strong, Josiah. *Our Country: Its Possible Future and Its Present Crisis*. New York: American Home Missionary Society, 1885.

Streeby, Shelley. *American Sensations: Class, Empire, and the Production of Popular Culture*. Berkeley: University of California Press, 2002.

Stout, Harry S., and D. G. Hart, eds. *New Directions in American Religious History*. New York: Oxford University Press, 1997.

Szasz, Ferenc M. *Religion in the Modern American West*. Tucson: University of Arizona Press, 2000.

Szasz, Ferenc M., and Richard W. Etulain, eds. *Religion in Modern New Mexico*. Albuquerque: University of New Mexico Press, 1997.

Taylor, Wilma Rugh. *Gospel Tracks through Texas: The Mission of Chapel Car Good Will*. College Station: Texas A&M University Press, 2005.

Tenorio-Trillo, Mauricio. *Mexico at the World's Fairs: Crafting a Modern Nation*. Berkeley: University of California Press, 1996.

————. "Stereophonic Scientific Modernisms: Social Science between Mexico and the United States, 1880s-1930s." *Journal of American History* 86, no. 3 (December 1999): 156–87.

Thelen, David. "The Nation and Beyond: Transnational Perspectives on United States History." *Journal of American History* 83, no. 3 (December 1999): 965–75.

Treviño, Roberto R. *The Church in the Barrio: Mexican American Ethno-Catholicism in Houston*. Chapel Hill: University of North Carolina Press, 2006.

Truett, Samuel, and Elliott Young, eds. *Continental Crossroads: Remapping U.S.-Mexico Borderlands History*. Durham: Duke University Press.

Tuck, Jim. *The Holy War in Los Altos: A Regional Analysis of Mexico's Cristero Rebellion*. Tucson: University of Arizona Press, 1982.

Tweed, Thomas A. *America's Church: The National Shrine and Catholic Presence in the Nation's Capital*. Oxford: Oxford University Press, 2011.

————. *Crossing and Dwelling: A Theory of Religion*. Cambridge: Harvard University Press, 2006.

————. *Our Lady of the Exile: Diasporic Religion at a Cuban Catholic Shrine in Miami*. New York: Oxford University Press, 1997.

————, ed. *Retelling U.S. Religious History*. Berkeley: University of California Press, 1997.

Valdés, Dennis Nodín. *Al Norte: Agricultural Workers in the Great Lakes Region, 1917–1970*. Austin: University of Texas Press, 1991.

Vasconcelos, José. "A Mexican's Point of View." In *American Policies Abroad: Mexico*, ed. J. Fred Rippy, José Vasconcelos, and Guy Stevens, 103–43. Chicago: University of Chicago Press, 1928.

————. *A Mexican Ulysses: An Autobiography*. Trans. and abridged W. Rex Crawford. Westport CT: Greenwood Press, 1963.

———. *La raza cósmica*. Trans. Didier T. Jaén. Baltimore: Johns Hopkins University Press, 1979.

Vasconcelos, José, and Manuel Gamio. *Aspects of Mexican Civilization: Lectures on the Harris Foundation*. Chicago: University of Chicago Press, 1926.

Vaughn, Mark Kay, and Stephen E. Lewis, eds. *The Eagle and the Virgin: Nation and Cultural Revolution in Mexico, 1920–1940*. Durham: Duke University Press, 2006.

Velasco, Jesus. "Reading Mexico: Understanding the United States: American Transnational Intellectuals in the 1920s and 1990s." *Journal of American History* 86, no. 2 (September 1999): 641–67.

Vila, Pablo. *Crossing Borders, Reinforcing Borders: Social Categories, Metaphors, and Narrative Identities on the U.S.-Mexico Frontier*. Austin: University of Texas Press, 2000.

Vinz, Warren L. *Pulpit Politics: Faces of American Protestant Nationalism in the Twentieth Century*. Albany: State University of New York Press, 1997.

Von Eschen, Penny M. *Race against Empire: Black Americans and Anticolonialism, 1937–1957*. Ithaca: Cornell University Press, 1997.

Wallis, George W. "Chronopolitics: The Impact of Time Perspectives on the Dynamics of Change." *Social Forces* 49, no. 1 (September 1970): 102–8.

Walsh, Casey. "Eugenic Acculuration: Manuel Gamio, Migration Studies, and the Anthropology of Development in Mexico, 1910–1940. " *Latin American Perspectives* 31, no. 5 (September 2004): 118–45.

Warner, Michael. *Changing Witness: Catholic Bishops and Public Policy, 1917–1994*. Grand Rapids MI: Eerdmans, 1995.

Warner, R. Stephen, and Judith G. Wittner. *Gatherings in Diaspora: Religious Communities and the New Immigration*. Philadelphia: Temple University Press, 1998.

Weinberg, Albert K. *Manifest Destiny: A Study of Nationalist Expansionism in American History*. Baltimore: Johns Hopkins University Press, 1935.

Wenger, Tisa. *We Have a Religion: The 1920s Pueblo Indian Dance Controversy and American Religious Freedom*. Chapel Hill: University of North Carolina Press, 2009.

Weston, Rubin Francis. *Racism in U.S. Imperialism: The Influence of Racial Assumptions on American Foreign Policy, 1893–1946*. Columbia: University of South Carolina Press, 1972.

White, Richard. "The American West and American Empire." In *Manifest Destinies and Indigenous Peoples*, ed. David Maybury-Lewis, Theodore Macdonald, and Biorn Maybury-Lewis, 203–24. Cambridge: Harvard University Press, 2009.

———. *The Middle Ground: Indians, Empires, and Republics in the Great Lakes Region, 1650–1815*. Cambridge. Cambridge University Press.

Wilkie, James W. "The Meaning of the Cristero Religious War against the Mexican Revolution." *Journal of Church and State* 8 (1964): 214–33.

Williams, William Appleman. *The Tragedy of American Diplomacy.* New York: Dell, 1962.

Willis, Henry Parker. *Our Philippine Problem: A Study of American Colonial Policy.* New York: Henry Holt, 1905.

Wilson, Chris. *The Myth of Santa Fe: Creating a Modern Regional Tradition.* Albuquerque: University of New Mexico Press, 1997.

Wilson, Kathleen. *The Island Race: Englishness, Empire, and Gender in the Eighteenth Century.* London: Routledge, 2003.

Wilson, Woodrow. *A History of the American People.* 5 vols. New York: Harper and Brothers, 1901.

Womack, John, Jr. *Zapata and the Mexican Revolution.* New York: Vintage Books, 1968.

Woods, James M. *A History of the Catholic Church in the American South, 1513– 1900.* Gainesville: University Press of Florida, 2011.

Wooten, Dudley G. *Mexico for the Mexicans.* Mahwah NJ: Paulist Press, 1915.

Wright-Rios, Edward. *Revolutions in Mexican Catholicism: Reform and Revelation in Oaxaca, 1887–1934.* Durham: Duke University Press, 2009.

Yazbeck Haddad, Yvonne, Jane I. Smith, and John L. Esposito, eds. *Religion and Immigration: Christian, Jewish, and Muslim Experiences in the United States.* Walnut Creek CA: AltaMira Press, 2003.

Yohn, Susan M. *A Contest of Faiths: Missionary Women and Pluralism in the American Southwest.* Ithaca: Cornell University Press, 1995.

Young, Robert J. C. *Colonial Desire: Hybridity in Theory, Culture, and Race.* London: Routledge, 1995.

# Index

Page numbers in *italics* indicate illustrations.

Cristo Rey of Cubilete, 165
CROM (Confederación Regional de
  Obreros Mexicanos), 146
Curley, Michael, 216–17

de Anta, E., 54
Deloria, Philip, 43, 46
Denechaud, Charles, 123–24
devotionalism, 13
Díaz, Pascual, 156
Díaz, Porfirio, 18, 153, 173, 186–87, 192, 211
Divine Word foreign missionaries, 136
Dobie, Frank J., 204–5
Dombrowski, M. A., 57
Dougherty, Dennis, 83–84, 157
Drexel, Katharine, 47
Drossaerts, Arthur J., 58, 101, 161, 216–
  17, 236n57
Duffy, Frank, 131–32
Dwyer, Isidore, 63–64, 67–68
Dwyre, Dudley, 103, 105

effective suffrage, 195, 199, 258n81
El Grito de Dolores, 208
Elías, Arturo M., 158, 167, 211, 251n31
Escalona, Teodoro, 146
Eskimos, 46, 59
Estvelt, Rev., 67
Eugenical News, 176, 180–81
eugenics, 176–84, 254n5, 254n6
Extension Magazine, 45; and American
  Indians, 43–47; and American West,
  10–15; and America's Spanish past,
  25; and Catholic missions, 71–98;
  and centralized reporting on U.S.
  Catholic missions, 38; circulation of,
  94, 241n49; content of, 39–42; early
  volumes of, 2; evangelizing the South,
  48–53; founding and purpose of, 33–
  39, 227n25; as fundraising tool, 10, 14–
  15, 25, 33, 38–39, 47–50, 59, 66–68, 109;
  Kelley's voice in, 7; and mestizaje, 204;
  and Mexican immigrant Catholics,
  53–64; overview, 25–26; regaining

Catholic title to the West, 65–69;
  rescue narratives in, 40, 44; and U.S.
  Catholic influence and intervention in
  Mexico, 109
extension priests, 61, 231n3
Extension Society, 37; church building
  by, 38–39; current status of, 222;
  founding and purpose of, 1, 33–39, 133–
  34; and global racial politics, 13; and
  Mexican immigrant Catholics, 53–
  64; and missionary work, 73–74, 75–
  77, 80, 226n22; mission of, 14–16;
  national and international reach of,
  133–34; regaining Catholic title to the
  West, 64–70; special collections for, 38,
  136; and U.S. Catholic influence and
  intervention in Mexico, 109

Fabian, Johannes, 213, 225n13, 260n109
Fairbank, John, 12, 75
Fields, Barbara, 207
Filippi, Ernesto, 145
Finegan, Philip, 80–81
Finneman, William, 81
Flandrau, Charles Macomb, 203
Flick, Lawrence, 183
Flores Magón, Enrique, 186, 188, 255n34
Flores Magón, Jesús, 186, 188
Flores Magón, Ricardo, 186, 188, 255n34
Foreman, John, 83–84
Forjando patria pro-nacionalismo (Gamio),
  189, 192
France and French influence, 17, 23,
  48–53
Francis (pope, Jorge Mario Bergoglio),
  222
Friends of the League for the Defense of
  Religious Freedom in Mexico, 147
Fritts, Louis, 117, 245n45
Frontier Thesis, 11, 74

Gaffey, James, 133
Gamio, Manuel, 179, 188–94, 197, 199,
  201, 256n43, 257n51